# The Warcraft Civilization

# The Warcraft Civilization

## Social Science in a Virtual World

**William Sims Bainbridge**

**The MIT Press**
**Cambridge, Massachusetts**
**London, England**

For information about special quantity discounts, please e-mail special_sales@mitpress.mit.edu.

This book was set in Stone Sans and Stone Serif by Toppan Best-set Premedia Limited.
Printed and bound in the United States of America.

Library of Congress Cataloging-in-Publication Data

Bainbridge, William Sims.
The warcraft civilization : social science in a virtual world / William
Sims Bainbridge.
   p. cm.
Includes bibliographical references and index.
ISBN 978-0-262-01370-3 (hardcover : alk. paper)
1. Computer games—Social aspects. 2. World of Warcraft. 3. Shared virtual environments.
4. Virtual reality—Social aspects. 5. Online identities—Social aspects. I. Title.
GV1469.27.B32   2010
794.8—dc22

2009021236

10 9 8 7 6 5 4 3 2

# Contents

# 1  Entrance

I am Incognita, one of the Undead. I entered World of Warcraft, also called Azeroth, in the Shadow Grave crypt, deep beneath the ground near Deathknell. I understood that the time was midnight on the sixth of March 2007, but I knew little of my previous existence. Unlike a newborn child, I could talk, reason, read, and take complex actions, although there was much I needed to learn. I had some knowledge but few memories. My skills were terribly underdeveloped. It is said that Humans wonder what will happen after they die, but we Undead wonder what happened before we died.

The first thing I saw was the trash-strewn floor of the crypt, lifeless gray like the walls. Then the flickering light revealed two tiers of niches where disordered bones indicated that Human bodies had once lain. Each niche was decorated by a grim, carved skull, shaped from the same gray stone as everything else within my field of view. In one niche, a stout, oddly shaped candle kept vigil over a mound of dirt hinting at the flesh that once covered the bones. A torch on the wall behind me mirrored another across the shallow pit, lighting a stone staircase. I ascended, turned left at the landing where more carven skulls supported shallow arches, and ascended again past cobwebs and the dust of ages. The third flight of stairs brought me to the surface of my new world. Gross stone columns, with the same skull motif, framed the exit from the crypt into a desolate graveyard.

Waiting for me was the undertaker, who spoke: "About time you woke up. We were ready to toss you into the fire with the others, but it looks like you made it. I am Mordo, the caretaker of the crypt of Deathknell. And you are the Lich King's slave no more." Somehow I found myself thinking like an anthropologist, or perhaps a linguist. *Mordo*, I hypothesized, came from the Latin word for "dead," *mors* in the nominative or *mortis* in the genitive, related to *morbidus* meaning "deceased." I looked at his bared teeth and wondered if the word *mordere*, meaning "to bite," was a better derivation. Death bites, does it not? The German word for "murder" is *Mord*. Who was this Lich King, of whom Mordo spoke? A *lich-gate* is the place in a churchyard where the corpse waits for burial, and *litchfield* is an old word for "cemetery." Perhaps the Lich King was the king of corpses, cognate with the German word for "corpse," *Leiche*, Norwegian *lik*, and Dutch *lijk*.

Mordo told me to speak with Shadow Priest Sarvis, who could be found at the bottom of the hill, in a decayed chapel. When I entered the building, I saw no religious symbols, and the boarded windows admitted no daylight. Sarvis said to me, "No other race on Azeroth has suffered as much as our people, priest. To laugh in the face of death has become second nature for all of us." Then I realized that I, like Sarvis, was a member of the priestly class, although an untrained one. I noticed he was wearing red and lavender robes and holding in his right hand a staff topped with a symbol at the top vaguely reminiscent of a cross, but with four rods forming a diamond shape around a red gem. As I was admiring his finery, Sarvis explained that our new leader was Lady Sylvanas, who had liberated us from the Lich King. "The Dark Lady guides us in our war against the hated Scourge and the holdouts of humanity who dog our every step."

I then received my first combat task, exterminating the Mindless Ones, eight one-armed Wretched Zombies and eight Mindless Zombies, whose brains had been pierced by arrows. This was a sad task, because they were Undead like me, but lacking full consciousness. When I returned to the blasted chapel to report my success, Sarvis gave me a Hallowed Scroll written by Dark Cleric Duesten, the local priest trainer, telling me, "feel blessed that your spirit was not released to the Nether," and suggesting I learn to deal with the fact that "the people you once knew, perhaps even cared for, are no longer!" When I presented it to Duesten, he commented, "The Holy Light no longer concerns you, the spirits of your forefathers are fairy tales, and creatures from the Nether don't want you . . . There is only one thing you must know: we have survived through will alone. It is faith in ourselves that separates us from others, and with our powers, we will cause great change in all of Azeroth."

More grim tasks were given to me: collecting magically useful organs from animals such as bats and wolves, and exterminating more of my brothers and sisters who had failed to make the complete return to consciousness after death. I looted valuable items, which I exchanged for money, and I began to gird myself with worn pieces of armor taken from those I killed. I learned with mixed pleasure and revulsion that we Undead can gain sustenance by eating the corpses of those we slew. As I interacted with the other Undead in the ruined village, they gave me advice: "Embrace the shadows." "Trust no one." "Beware the living." Novice Elreth bestowed a blessing, "Dark Lady watch over you!" Executor Arren asked the chilling question, "What would you ask of Death?" (See figure 1.1.)

The nature of my opponents changed fundamentally when Executor Arren assigned me the mission of killing twelve converts and initiates of the Scarlet Crusade. These were healthy, young Humans who, unlike me, had never died. They stood straight, whereas I hunched over, and they seemed filled with health. Given these contrasts, it was easy to hate them. Then I intercepted a map carried by the Red Messenger, showing where they had infiltrated our territory with agents. Arren ordered me to leave Deathknell and take the map swiftly to Executor Zygand, in Brill, our main Tirisfal settlement. Here I learned more about the huge conflict in which we Undead found ourselves, hunted as traitors by

**Figure 1.1**
Incognita, an Undead priest, at the church in Deathknell, between Shadow Priest Sarvis and Novice Elreth.

the forces of the Lich King, and invaded by Humans, who resented that we had seized Tirisfal from them just a few years before.

Repeatedly, I encountered the religious fanatics of the Scarlet Crusade. Sometimes, as we fought, they would shout at me, but I could not understand their words. On four occasions, I had the presence of mind to write down what they said: *"Bur wirsh ras wirsh va ras faergas Sturume ko majis ras landowar skilde." "Ras Vassild Lithtos eynes majis ras valesh ash garde noth dana novas eynes." "Ras garde hamerung nud nud valesh noth Hir bur dana bor." "Ergin lo ti danieb nud bur Ras Lithtos eynes vassild nud nud wirsh ras firalaine wirsh."* At first, I thought they might be speaking Swedish, or some northern Indo-European tongue. But now, I am not so sure. It perplexes me that I cannot speak with the Humans, even though I myself seem to be the reincarnation of one of them. At the time, a general truce existed between our people and the Humans, but rogue groups like the Scarlet Crusade refused to recognize it. I wondered what drove them to annihilate us, and wished I could speak with them about the growing tragedy we shared.

In some of my Tirisfal assignments, I assisted Apothecary Johann, who was trying to develop new biological weapons to use against our enemies. I learned that the original Plague of Undeath had been used by the Lich King in his invasion of Human territory, and I guessed my own metamorphosis had been caused by it. Having declared independence from the Lich King's Scourge, we Forsaken needed our own bioweapon technology, both to counterattack against the Scourge and perhaps to defend ourselves if the Humans attacked in force. Johann had me collect the blood of darkhounds, vile murloc scales, and night web spider venom. Once he had brewed his new plague, we tested it on a captured Dwarf.

The scope of my labors expanded again when Magistrate Sevren sent me to Bethor Iceshard, a high-ranking mage in Undercity, the capital of the Forsaken Undead, hidden beneath the ruins of Lordaeron. I understand that *Lordaeron* means something like "the land of the peaceful people," or "the place of peace for people," combining three words from three different languages. But the Scourge killed the people in the Third War, and we built our metropolis in the sewers beneath it. The access elevators, ironically enough, operate from the crypt of King Terenas Menethil II, who had led the Alliance against the Horde in the Second War. As I stepped hesitantly into the elevator, on my first journey to the Undercity, I was filled with trepidation, but was curious to learn more about my place as a priest of the Forsaken, a member of the Horde, and a citizen of a vast and disintegrating world.

**The Game**

Incognita is a character in World of Warcraft (WoW), the most popular massively multiplayer online role-playing game (MMORPG), created by Blizzard Entertainment. By December 2008, WoW had eleven million players in North America, Europe, and Asia. It is a fantasy game, because it concerns an imaginary world where magic exists and historical events have taken a unique course. In this, for example, it is different from realistic online battle games set in World War II or some comparable historical context. WoW is similar in many respects to *EverQuest*, Sony's fantasy MMORPG. Indeed, it is solidly rooted in a rich tradition of fantasy stories and games, distinctive chiefly for its quality and massive size. Thus, WoW cannot be said to be terribly innovative, but from the social-scientific point of view, this is a good thing.

World of Warcraft not only represents but also includes within itself a great culture, on the surface as modern as the Internet itself, but reaching down to the very origins of European civilization. It is so complex, and offers players so much scope for action, that it transcends the game category to become a virtual world. As the editors of a special WoW issue of the journal *Games and Culture* write, "The World of Warcraft is a complex world indeed, an extraordinary mixture of art and design, technologies, economics, the social and the cultural. It is a game, a virtual world, and an online community."[1] As such, it is a laboratory where the social and behavioral sciences can thrive and contribute to information science and technology by supporting innovations in human-centered computing.

Note the themes in Incognita's brief narrative. She is lost and seeking to discover who she is and what she must do within a mysterious environment. Some would say this is the fundamental human condition, merely exaggerated in her case. She lacks understanding and skills, so she must learn. She will do so in a world gripped by conflict, where the group she belongs to seeks to define her identity in terms of competition against other groups. Her identity is also defined by religion, as a member of one sect in conflict with another. She struggles to think social-scientifically about her environment, and this brief narrative highlights linguistics, because language is both a marker of group boundaries and a barrier to communication. She also reasons historically, laboring to understand the present as a consequence of past events. Technology is crucially important, in this case, biotechnology devoted to the development of weapons of mass destruction. The vignette ends as she is about to enter an underground city created by her faction in the ruins of a defeated civilization, symbolizing both the possibility of rebirth and the ever-present danger of annihilation. This is an allegory of the real world in which we find ourselves today.

World of Warcraft is usually called a *game*, but this word has multiple and ambiguous meanings. An example is the classic 1924 short story "The Most Dangerous Game," by Richard Connell, which has been adapted many times for movies, radio drama, and television.[2] A big-game hunter, Sanger Rainsford, washes ashore on a remote island ruled by General Zaroff, who also has an addiction to hunting. Zaroff confesses that he had become bored with hunting the ordinary and not very intelligent animals such as cape buffalo and tigers, and wanted a prey he could match wits with. So he set up the island as a hunting preserve for humans, where he chased and killed lost sailors lured there by false navigation beacons. Rainsford becomes Zaroff's latest prey: the hunter becomes the hunted. Only by outwitting Zaroff can Rainsford avoid becoming another stuffed head on the trophy wall. Thus, the word *game* in the title has two meanings: the prey in a hunt, and the play in a strategy contest.

In terms of sales over the years, *The Sims* is the most popular computer game, and yet by many definitions it is not a game at all. I feel a special connection to the Sims, not only because my middle name literally is Sims, or because people mistakenly think "Sims" is a computer moniker I adopted to express my interest in virtual worlds. Rather, I am interested because I have programmed artificial intelligence computer simulations of human interaction for a quarter century, and my daughters used to be avid players of *The Sims*. It simulates the everyday activities of virtual people, called "Sims," in complex but rather ordinary environments, starting with a home where the player can set up furniture and appliances like those in real American suburbs. There is, however, no real winning and losing. The originator, Will Wright, prefers to call it a "software toy."

World of Warcraft has the essential quality that people generally associate with games: competition. Players must struggle against adversity to increase many point scores, of which the most crucial is experience, which takes them up a graded series of levels. Attaining a high level is a source of pride. Leveling up faster than somebody else makes a player feel superior. Both blind chance and clever tactics are important in determining the outcome of many brief battles, and battles chain together into quests.[3] However, there is no ultimate victory. Thus, WoW is a virtual world that includes thousands of games, rather than simply being a game itself. As Cory Ondrejka has said, "No other medium provides such breadth and depth of experience, intermingling the social while encouraging exploration and discovery."[4]

If "game" is a complex concept, "role-playing" is even more so, and the combination of the two adds further complexities.[5] In the real world, we constantly play roles, some, such as "customer" and "teacher," that follow well-developed scripts provided by the culture, and others that we largely invent ourselves. Every mentally normal person is able to pretend to be someone else, as well as to play roles while being himself or herself. Perhaps there are three dimensions to role-playing. First is the *competence* a person needs to play a given role, and roles differ in the demands they make on players. I can do a pretty good imitation of a priest, although I have never taken holy orders, but I am quite incompetent in impersonating a ballet dancer. Second is the degree to which the role is pre-scripted rather than creatively *improvised*. An actor playing Romeo in the balcony scene when he courts Juliet must say certain exact words and is not free to improvise as the same actor must when he courts the actress offstage. The third dimension is *genuineness*, the extent to which the person's thoughts and intentions match those apparently associated with the role. The actor playing Romeo is genuine, because we all know the drama is fiction, but a question often arises about the sincerity of used-car salesmen, even though it is safe to assume they really do have cars to sell.

We explore the concept of role-playing more deeply in the chapter on identity, but for now it is enough to say that the player must take on the perspective of the character he or she is playing, with some degree of competence, improvisation, and genuineness. All these are matters of degree, and Blizzard Entertainment takes explicit notice of this fact. In a sense, World of Warcraft is not one virtual world but hundreds of them, called *realms*. Technically, a realm is a separate computer or Internet server maintaining one instance of the world. In computer lingo, this is also called a *shard* of the world. Players can interact only with players who are in the same realm, and each character is restricted to a single realm. A player can enter multiple realms, one at a time, but needs a different character for each, with the very rare exception of a player paying to move a character from one realm to another. Each realm develops its own qualities, reflecting the players who enter it, and a few have been officially set aside as "role-playing realms" by Blizzard:

If you enjoy role-playing (RP) and would like to imagine that you are an inhabitant of a fantasy-based world, then a role-playing realm may be for you. Players who choose to play on an RP realm should abide by the Role-Playing realm policies and remain in-character at all times. Role-Playing realms give players the chance to develop characters with a backstory who do not simply progress from quest to quest, but instead assist or hamper the efforts of others for reasons of their own.[6]

Given that role-playing has many dimensions in online role-playing games, it is worth noting a very different technical definition of *role-playing game*, or RPG. This does not concern the relation between the player and a character in the game but the mechanics of combat inside the game. Consider the difference between two classic Nintendo games for single players, *Super Mario World* and *Super Mario RPG*. In *Super Mario World*, a mustached Italian plumber needs to explore and fight his way through a number of levels, which are separate environments, more like the geographic zones of WoW than the experience levels. Along the way, he encounters many enemies. If one bumps into him from the side, Mario dies. If he hops on its head, the enemy dies. Sometimes Mario can get a *power-up*, which means he does not die the first time he is touched but the second time. However, interaction between Mario and an enemy is very simple.

In *Super Mario RPG*, interactions between Mario and his enemies are far more complex. Much of the time, Mario is wandering around the landscape, picking up resources, and finding his way toward goals, just as in his traditional Nintendo games. But when he encounters an enemy, the play switches to combat mode. Mario and the enemy take a series of turns. On each turn, one strikes the other or casts a spell. The amount of damage done by this attack depends on a hidden mathematical algorithm that can combine numbers representing several things: Mario's strength, the enemy's strength, the particular attack used, the defendant's armor, and a random number. Characters have a number, or a variable, called *hit points* or *health*, which is reduced after each hit by the number of points of damage that resulted from the algorithm. The damage numbers are typically displayed on the screen in RPGs, and the character's health may be represented by a number on the screen or a bar graph. When the health reaches zero, the character dies. When either Mario or his enemy is killed, the game exits combat mode.

Hit points are a very old concept. Electronic RPGs are very much influenced by the 1974 tabletop card game *Dungeons and Dragons*, which used hit points, but there is a much earlier example. In the early 1950s, my sister and I played a card game simply called *War*. We sat on the floor, shuffled a deck of cards, and dealt them all out so each of us had twenty-six, or sometimes we used two or more decks for a really long game. In each round of the game, each of us would place three cards facedown in a line, then one card face up. Whoever placed the higher card face up, took all those on the floor. If the two cards were the same value, we put three more cards facedown, and another face up, again winner taking all. When one player had all the cards, the game was won. Notice that the number of cards I held were comparable to hit points, and when I had very few, I got concerned that I would lose. This was a pure game of chance, and we were not allowed to look at the cards in our own hands and make a strategy about how to play them.

In complex modern RPGs, the player does have choices during a combat, including running away, and there may not be explicit turn taking. But the basic principle is the same, a series of exchanges causing damage that is the result of a number of factors including random numbers. Modern RPGs enhance the player's experience by giving great freedom between combat episodes. Richard Rouse calls the outdated approach to electronic games "linear," because it allowed only one route from start to finish. In contrast, World of Warcraft is highly nonlinear:

In terms of gaming, this means that the player is not locked into achieving different goals in a specific order or in achieving all of the goals she is presented with. Instead, the player is able to move through the game in a variety of paths and can be successful in a variety of ways. Non-linearity leaves the player with more choice to play the game her own way.[7]

The greater the nonlinearity, and the greater the choices in general, the more the game becomes a world. Consider the evolution of Mario's environment. *Super Mario Bros.* was released in 1985, when the video game industry was in a slump, and it was instrumental in launching the genre toward its current high popularity. Mario has a single goal, to rescue Princess Toadstool. To do this, he needs to fight his way through a number of distinct levels, essentially running linearly from left to right, with many jumps and climbs providing the semblance of a second dimension. At the end of each level, he is ported to the next level, in a set order. *Super Mario World*, issued five years later, takes this approach to its logical extreme, a huge number of levels, most of which however are entirely linear. There are a few major choices, some hidden areas, a map through which the player may revisit old levels, and the possibility of finishing the game without accessing every last one of them. However, this is not yet a virtual world, despite the name. One reason is simply the limitations of the game console, the Super Nintendo, although a few games such as *Star Fox* went some distance in the direction of the third dimension, by means of additional computing power in the game cartridge.

*Super Mario 64*, released in 1996 for the more capable Nintendo 64 system, offered three dimensions of movement and gave the player many choices. Because it is non-linear, it encourages the player to explore the world, thus gratifying a wider range of human emotions than a game that consists of one predetermined jump or combat after another. The game is won by collecting stars, but Mario can rescue Princess Peach without finding all of them. Thus, there can be two different definitions of winning: rescuing the princess or getting all the stars. *Super Mario 64* is very nearly a virtual world. Most crucially, it lacks other people, because it is a one-player game. Also, it is a game rather than a world, precisely because it has an ending. A player can win games inside a virtual world, but cannot really win the entire world itself. Finally, an electronic environment is not fully a world unless it gives people the freedom to create things of their own design.

World of Warcraft is far more than a game. It contains in excess of five thousand completable quests, each of which might be considered a game, but WoW cannot be completed as a whole.[8] The nearest thing to an end goal, when it was released in 2004, was the highest experience level achievable, which was sixty. In 2007, the top experience level was increased to seventy, and in November 2008, the top level rose again to eighty. But even at the top level, there are many challenges still to meet, in the form of dungeons or instances, battlegrounds, and the collection of valuable virtual items to strengthen one's character in duels or to give one's character martial beauty.

There are many opportunities to interact with other people. No information system yet built could handle ten million people at once, and too many people competing to kill the same boss enemy would spoil one another's enjoyment of triumph. The North American region has nearly 250 separate, parallel realms (or computer servers), and each one can handle a maximum of 4,000 players simultaneously. A character is limited to one realm, but each player may have characters in multiple realms, or multiple characters in the same realm. A player cannot run more than one player at a given time, however, without purchasing a separate account for each character, and using multiple computers. Despite such limitations, social life in WoW is exceedingly diverse, and 4,000 characters are quite enough for a complex social structure.

The main area of limitation is the creation of virtual objects. A number of professions that players may choose for their characters involve assembling complex objects from multiple parts, but one cannot invent an object and construct it entirely from scratch. This contrasts with the popular nongame virtual world *Second Life*, in which one may use a graphics program to create a physical object, upload images to cover its surface, then write a script program to make it do things.[9]

There are two reasons WoW is limited in this way. First, all the graphic images reside on the user's computer, rather than being downloaded laboriously from the server as in *Second Life*. This means that the graphics are much smoother in WoW, allowing a character to run from one environment into another without pausing for the graphics files to download. A consequence of this design choice is that you cannot create your own graphics, because they would not be available to all the other players. Second, because WoW is still promoted as a game, the designers need to be very careful to prevent computer-savvy players from gaining an advantage over others with less programming expertise. If I could create any object I want, I could forge a sword that kills any enemy in a single blow. However, as we see in later chapters, the social software included in the WoW user interface gives players wide scope for creating social groups, notably guilds, with user-defined membership ranks, evocative names, role-playing styles, goals, and memberships. Thus, the opportunities for creativity are significant without being infinite.

WoW retains many features of a game while being more than a game. It is worth noting also that many social scientists view the real world in gaming terms. The influential 1944 book *Theory of Games and Economic Behavior*, by John von Neumann and Oskar Morgenstern, launched game theory as a branch of economics, social exchange theory, and an analysis of society more broadly.[10] However, this was far from the first influential classic that considered society in terms of games. *Homo Ludens*, written in 1938 by Johan Huizinga, argued that humans by their very nature play games, and that cultural innovations generally arise in play.[11] Indeed, we should consider how World of Warcraft is also something between a game and a world, namely, a civilization. Every major civilization is an integration of multiple societies and cultures, and thus it presents huge challenges for social science.

### Social Science in a Virtual World

Contemporary social sciences are fragmented, undecided about fundamental issues of theory and methods, and rather low in social status. Superficially, the computer and information sciences appear to enjoy demonstrable success and high social status. Beneath the surface, however, these apparently separate fields have much in common. Most important, they have much to contribute to each other.

Arguably, sociology was the most computational of all the sciences a century ago, but ironically, it has been left out of some of the most sociological developments in recent computer science. The roots of computational sociology were firmly planted by Herman Hollerith's work to analyze the data from the 1900 census of the United States.[12] To analyze social data, Hollerith developed the entire system of punched cards, complex programming of counting machines, and automatic tabulation that dominated information processing for three quarters of a century. Most sociologists still think of computing in terms of rectangular data sets in which columns represent variables, and rows represent cases, and they have been slow over the past quarter of a century to adopt new methodological perspectives.

At the same time, an increasing number of scientists with training in such fields as physics or who otherwise have little connection to sociology have been encroaching upon "our" territory, because they are able to handle computers creatively and have become interested in social issues. For example, to a classically trained sociologist who happens also to program computer simulations, it is alarming that the leading textbook *Simulation for the Social Scientist*, by Nigel Gilbert and Klaus Troitzsch, fails to cite more than a handful of computer simulation studies published in standard social science journals.[13] Many such articles exist, but the broader simulation community ignores them. However, despite numerous examples of good social computer simulation research, it remains a peripheral method, largely exiled to the outer reaches of social science publications.

A quarter century ago I was exploring multiagent systems, in some ways reminiscent of the programming that controls the herds of beasts in World of Warcraft, to explore the way religious faith spreads through a human community by social influence and communication. In 1987, I was able to publish a set of neural network and multiagent simulations, but only disguised as educational software.[14] With great difficulty, I was much later able to get a couple articles based on the research into marginal sociology journals, and only in 2006 could I publish a scholarly book reporting that work in expanded form, even including a table I generated way back in 1984.[15] The gap between the social and computer sciences is so vast that few people on either side see any reason to take account of those on the other, let alone collaborate with them.

My perspective is quite different: social science is an information science, and information science is a social science. Both are radical movements aiming to transform society, as well as being sciences. Humanly meaningful data—whether we call it *information* or *knowledge*—can be articulated only within an appropriate culture. Like other cultural products, therefore, information is a socially constructed phenomenon.[16] Properly understood, twenty-first century sociology needs to draw heavily upon computer science as a means for developing theory as well as for tools of data analysis. Most important, only by combining can they achieve their revolutionary potential.

In the early 1980s, the National Science Foundation considered creating a new Directorate for Social, Behavioral, and Information Sciences, but then bowed to disciplinary chauvinism and established first the Directorate for Computer and Information Science and Engineering (CISE), and then the Directorate for Social, Behavioral and Economic Sciences (SBE).[17] Following the principle of "back to the future," I suggest that it is high time to merge social and information sciences. Having worked for years in both SBE and CISE, I believe I have a clear perspective on how their fields relate. In the cover article of the July 27, 2007, issue of the journal *Science*, I explained how virtual worlds like World of Warcraft could be laboratories for uniting these fields.[18]

Many scientists and scholars are already conducting research about virtual worlds, and they are beginning to use them as environments to ask general social-scientific questions. Economist Edward Castronova argues that an increasing fraction of human life, economy, and culture will take place in these novel environments, so they need to be studied as important phenomena in their own right.[19] In a study of social and economic coordination, Castronova has shown that it can be fruitful to compare results from research in different virtual worlds, just as is true for nations on Earth.[20] There is some evidence that they serve as hatcheries for new cultural movements—for example, facilitating the consolidation of post-Christian religious ideologies[21]—and are substituting for disintegrating social institutions in the real world.[22]

It is especially important to study virtual worlds now because the current period of transformation may not last much longer and because it may be impossible to reconstruct its key processes and phenomena entirely from historical records that are naturally preserved. Practically all of the classic one-player electronic games can still be played, either because computer emulators of the old systems have been created, or because the games have been ported over to new systems. But the same is unlikely to be true for today's virtual worlds because they depend on the extensive social infrastructure of the companies that support them and on the current population of people who inhabit them.

Virtual worlds are good environments in which to explore wider issues related to emerging technologies, such as intellectual property rights and the sociotechnical implications of online misbehavior.[23] Research concerning the cultural boundaries of virtual worlds includes studies of the following issues: the extent to which gender-specific behavioral norms transfer to these nontraditional environments;[24] comparisons with role-playing games that are not electronic, such as *Dungeons and Dragons*;[25] the human impacts of alternative architectural philosophies;[26] the social processes through which cooperation emerges;[27] the possibility of addiction to virtual worlds;[28] and the different meanings that participants attach to virtual life and death.[29] There has even been research on how World of Warcraft and other virtual worlds can illuminate social factors implicated in the spread of disease epidemics.[30] To date, much of the research has followed the twin qualitative paradigms of anthropological ethnography and sociological participant observation,[31] but quantitative approaches using rigorous statistical and computational techniques show very great promise.

WoW is a very conducive environment for quantitative research because it encourages individuals to write "mod" or "add-on" programs, and scientists can use some existing software as research tools or write their own. These range all the way from very simple sequences of character behaviors constructed using macros built in to the WoW user interface, to long programs written in the Lua language. For example, one widely used program called Auctioneer analyzes prices on the WoW virtual item auction system, and CensusPlus tallies all the players currently online by several characteristics. With census data on more than 200,000 WoW characters, a team centered at the Palo Alto Research Center analyzed the factors associated with the upward status mobility of individuals and the dynamics of social groups.[32]

This book uses qualitative rather than quantitative methods, and I save my more technical studies for journals that regularly publish statistical research. I hesitate to say that this book is more oriented toward theory, because the very word *theory* conjures up images of dry abstractions, as if hundreds of pages of desert lay ahead rather than the lush jungles that WoW has actually prepared for us. On one level, this book analyzes World of Warcraft from multiple standpoints of the history of social thought. By doing so, it suggests a second level, on which information-science design of virtual worlds must take account of the nature of human beings and the societies they construct. And on a third level, the book seeks insights about life in the so-called real world.

Why would WoW be an especially good place to look for insights about Western civilization? One reason is that it bridges past and future, rooted in a major Western cultural tradition, yet aiming toward the virtual worlds we can create in times to come. WoW is tremendously eclectic. Consider the ten races. Orcs are derived most directly from J. R. R. Tolkien's *The Lord of the Rings* tetralogy, and Tolkien was a leading scholar of historical linguistics who based his fantasies on the legends of Britain.[33] Tolkien told us that Elves were especially tall, as the Night Elves in WoW are, but shorter ones are found in *Grimm's Fairy Tales*, along with very short Dwarves including seven who lived with Snow White.[34] The brothers Grimm, Jacob and Wilhelm, were scholars who collected folk stories as later anthropologists would, and who contributed substantially to the advancement of linguistics. Gnomes were made familiar to modern audiences in the Oz books of L. Frank Baum, which also pioneered the mixture of fantasy adventure and cultural parody we find in WoW.[35] The mountain king in *Peer Gynt*, a drama by Henrik Ibsen with music by Edvard Grieg, is a troll. WoW's Tauren are minotaurs, familiar to us from the ancient Greek myth of Theseus, Daedalus, and Icarus. The Undead are reminiscent of zombies, but they especially resonate in popular movies about semidead humans, notably George Romero's *Night of the Living Dead* (1968) and the three movies based on a science fiction novel by Richard Matheson: *The Last Man on Earth* (1964), *The Omega Man* (1971), and *I Am Legend* (2007).[36]

Dwarves also feature in Richard Wagner's titanic cycle of four grand operas, *Der Ring des Nibelungen*. For Wagner, *Nibelung* essentially means *Dwarf*, and the magical ring was forged by Dwarves from pure gold. Based on Norse or Germanic mythology, but also modeled after ancient Greek dramatic cycles, *The Ring* cast long shadows over the political and cultural future of Europe. One can still debate whether Wagner was at all responsible for the rise of the Nazis, long after his death, or whether his popularity was merely exploited by them. We could also debate the extent to which *The Ring* influenced Tolkien's rather different ring tetralogy, the music in *Star Wars*, and World of Warcraft. Remarkably, in 1849, Wagner prophesied that the future of art would go in a direction that today looks rather like WoW.

In 1848, a wave of largely unsuccessful revolutions swept Europe, and Wagner was rather unsuccessfully involved in a radical movement in Germany. As soon as he had settled in exile in Switzerland, he began writing *The Ring* and developing an aesthetic justification he called *The Art-Work of the Future*.[37] This little book really presents two ideas: the concept of a total work of art, and the notion that great artists could speak with the voice of the people.

A total work of art, or *Gesamtkunstwerk* in German, is an artwork that combines multiple different arts. Wagner wrote both the poetry and the music for *The Ring*. He also felt a *Gesamtkunstwerk* would combine the visual arts of painting and dance, although the sets in traditional presentations of *The Ring* look like uninspired landscape pictures, and the singers on stage hardly move at all. One innovation that tied together Wagner's poetry and music was the leitmotif, a melody that represented a specific character or concept. All these principles apply to World of Warcraft, as they do to *Star Wars*. Each of the main cities or geographic areas in WoW has its own leitmotif, particular music that plays when a character arrives there. Although it is hard to find much dancing, the characters all move, often in ways that are both subtle and pronounced. One can invest marvelous hours documenting the particular spasms with which each kind of enemy dies, for example. The varied environments of nature and architecture are often quite beautiful and express the particular nature of events that take place in them. Weaving everything together are the threads of a tapestry of myths, as complex as any in the ancient sagas.

A *Gesamtkunstwerk* derives its strength from the *Volk*, according to Wagner, the common people conceptualized as an ethnic or cultural group. The Nazi era and World War II largely discredited this part of his thesis, but at the time Wagner wrote, the distinction between right-wing populism and left-wing populism was not yet clear. Wagner assumed that the common folk shared a traditional culture, and that great artists could refine it to produce the greatest works of art. This is what the builders of World of Warcraft have done. Drawing upon deep popular traditions of fantasy and science fiction, they have created a virtual world that attracts millions of ordinary folk, while at the same time posing a radical critique of the dominant culture of their society. Note that *Der Ring des Nibelungen* and World of Warcraft are saturated with supernatural phenomena but have absolutely nothing to do with Christianity. The political systems in them are feudal, with occasional hints that capitalism is wicked or distorted, and the dominant elite acts largely from selfish motives. Without granting Wagner's ideology any special privileges, I must note that World of Warcraft is the most perfect fulfillment to date of his vision of a total work of art, combining many artforms while expressing popular criticism of the existing society.

As Georg Simmel pointed out a century ago, strangers can often see a society more clearly than its members.[38] By visiting the very strange world of WoW and making sense of what we find there, we are able to look at our own world with fresh eyes. Indeed, WoW is in great measure an allegory, so its exaggerations can call our attention to facts we tend to miss as we go about our habitual activities in the real world. Because it is a complex, functioning civilization, WoW takes account of human nature and the implicit laws of human interaction. Following Simmel, my prime research method has been to send several virtual explorers into the world of WoW, then to dialogue with them about the meaning of what they discovered and what it says about our own civilization.

## Research Methods

I studied World of Warcraft through ethnographic participant observation for two years, from January 2007 through December 2008, totaling more than 2,300 hours in this virtual world.[39] My goal was to explore the entire territory, which covers a subjective area of hundreds of square miles of diverse terrain, and to observe social relations among players of all visible kinds. Socially and culturally, this world is extremely complex. A series of disruptive wars and religious schisms has produced many fault lines along which conflict rages. The characters operated by players are divided into two hostile factions, the Horde and the Alliance, who have a somewhat shaky truce between them. The world also overflows with dozens and dozens of groups of non-player characters, or NPCs, only some of whom belong to the factions. Characters take on quests, either for their factions or for other individual or grouped NPCs, that send them gallivanting out into the virtual world to hunt enemies and gather resources. All this takes place in a complex, interwoven set of mythic cultures and the society created by the players, as they cooperate in short-term raiding parties and long-term guilds.

When I began this study by entering my first character into Elwynn Forest, World of Warcraft boasted 8,000,000 subscribers, but the number had reached about 11,000,000 before my data collection was done. A major upgrade, The Burning Crusade, was released in January 2007, and 2,400,000 copies were sold the first day. The second major upgrade, Wrath of the Lich King, came in November 2008, and 2,800,000 copies were sold the first day. Although quite affordable by individual players, in the aggregate, serious money is involved.

I did not interact with all the other players by any means, because I worked in only 6 of the roughly 250 North American realms (computer servers or *shards*). Two were so-called normal servers: Shandris was low in population and Hydraxis was high. Three were role-playing servers: Earthen Ring, Scarlet Crusade, and Sentinels. The sixth, Emerald Dream, was not only a role-playing server but also a player-versus-player (PvP) server, which meant that combat between the Horde and the Alliance was encouraged. On regular servers, whether role-playing or not, both players usually must agree before a member of the Horde can fight a member of the Alliance. On PvP servers, outside one's own starter zones, one is always open to being attacked.

On each server, I had at least one Horde and one Alliance character, and I initially placed four additional Alliance characters on Shandris so I could study the details of interaction between members of the same faction. To make it possible to run two characters at once, I had two World of Warcraft accounts and sometimes used two computers, side by side. My initial seventeen characters covered all ten *races*. The five races of the Alliance are Human, Night Elf, Dwarf, Gnome, and Draenei. The five races of the Horde are Orc, Troll, Tauren, Undead, and Blood Elf. The characters covered all nine *classes*: priest, shaman, mage, druid, warlock, rogue, paladin, hunter, and warrior. To explore the diversity of supernatural cultures, I ran seven priests, two shamans, and two druids, but initially just one of each of the other classes except for two rogues to explore "deviant" behavior. At least one character practiced each of the following professions: mining, herbalism, alchemy, enchanting, skinning, leatherworking, tailoring, blacksmithing, engineering, jewelcrafting, fishing, cooking, and first aid.

In late March 2008, I decided to stage a scientific conference inside World of Warcraft. The suggestion came from John Bohannon, who creates the Gonzo Scientist feature of the journal *Science*, published by the American Association for the Advancement of Science, who had been inspired by the cover article about virtual worlds that I had published in *Science* the previous July. To help with the preparations and the aftermath, I created three new characters, moved one of my best-established characters across servers, and did the same with a nonentity character I had started merely as a tool for running census analysis software. The conference produced new knowledge, some of which I have incorporated in this book, and brought my total number of characters to twenty-one (see figure 1.2). When the Lich King expansion came in November 2008, I added one more character, a death knight.[40]

Because World of Warcraft is a role-playing game, it seemed appropriate to use role-playing in the research. Early in my career, before ethical issues had been raised about role-play research in the real world, I had in fact infiltrated a number of radical groups in order to study them, pretending to be a real member. My most extensive research in this vein consisted of two full years inside a more-or-less Satanic cult, called the Process Church of the Final Judgement, and six months inside Scientology, but I had also done this with Transcendental Meditation, the Hare Krishna movement, and the John Birch Society.[41] The Process, in particular, was immensely theatrical and reminds me of the Scarlet Crusade sect in WoW. I viewed my WoW characters almost as real people—my research assistants or native informants—who helped me do my ethnographic research. I found this was the easiest way to think and talk about them, although each of them developed a distinctive personality in my mind. I felt very differently about them, and experienced different moods through them. As I explain more fully in chapter 7, "Identity," they were largely me, but also beings somewhat different from me. I found them very effective role-playing tools for carrying out participant observation.[42]

I ran two of the priests, Maxrohn, a Human, and Catullus, a Blood Elf, all the way up to level 70, the highest possible experience level during the main period of my research. Then, when the Lich King expansion came, I ran one of them up to level 80. Three other characters reached level 30: Lunette, a Night Elf priest; Minotaurus, a

**Figure 1.2**
Scientists and scholars meeting in the Undercity sewer, for the May 2008 academic conference.

Tauren shaman; and Etacarinae, a Draenei shaman. Sixteen characters reached level 20: Papadoc, a Troll priest; Incognita, an Undead priest; Price, an Undead warlock; Zodia, a Draenei priest; Lusea, a Dwarf priest; Adalgisa, a Tauren druid; Vadvaro, a Human rogue; Marcya, a Troll rogue; Aristotle, a Human mage; Ozma, a Human mage; Alberich, a Dwarf hunter; Stephie, a Gnome warlock; Folwell, a Night Elf druid; Llana, a Blood Elf paladin; Sciencemag, a Blood Elf hunter; and Tarkas, an Orc warrior. As a death knight, Annihila, an Undead, started already at level 55, and was still inching her way up the ladder toward 80 when this book went to press.

This range of races and levels allowed me to experience each of the sixty-two major zones of this virtual world with the proper level and faction. There are eight widely separated starter zones suitable for characters around levels 1 through 10. The Dwarves and Gnomes begin in the same place as each other, as the Orcs and Trolls do in another location, but each of the other races has a distinctive origin. Beginning characters or players are called *newbies* or *noobs*, and the first two areas they experience are *newbie zones* especially designed to be less difficult and to contain quests that must be described as training exercises.

My main tool of data collection was saving about 22,000 images off the computer screen, what are commonly called *screen shots*. Initially, the WoW software system saved the images as very large uncompressed files in the .tga, or Targa, format, but thankfully I was soon able to switch to the more conventional and much more efficient .jpg, or JPEG, format. For this project, I did not take advantage of the "/chatlog" method of recording text from the interplayer communication system, because I found that saving the whole screen provided the context for the words, as well as recording all kinds of nonverbal information. The automatic name of each file was the exact time and date the screen was copied, so I did not attempt to give them descriptive names. Rather, I saved the screen shots into folders for each of the characters, then later arranged them by topic, and put them in "used" subfolders after writing out what was useful for this book.

The virtual world itself was by no means the only source of data. I also collected and read all serious publications about World of Warcraft I could find, including novels, graphic novels (manga), instruction manuals, scientific journal articles, and conference papers. Huge troves of rather reliable information are available on the web, notably vast databases like wowwiki.com, wowhead.com, thottbot.com, and wow. allakhazam.com. Excellent maps of the virtual world are available at mapwow.com. As my higher-level characters joined major guilds in WoW, I gained access to their own websites. The authoritative World of Warcraft website includes much official lore, a vast array of forums where players discuss the game and its mythology, and an astonishing database called the Armory with detailed information about every guild and every one of the millions of characters that had reached level 10.[43] As a computer programmer interested in artificial intelligence and multiagent systems, I also paid close attention to WoW's simulated animals and people.

## Nonplayer Characters

Many of the "people" and other creatures in WoW are not operated by players, but are nonplayer characters, or NPCs. Another word for *NPC* often used in the electronic game community is *mob*, short for *mobile*. Given its origins, this word should properly be pronounced *mobe*, but players tend to pronounce it *mob*. Some of the WoW NPCs don't move very much—the vendors and guards from which a character may buy things or get information—but most of them walk around a set territory, then react violently either when an enemy character comes within their *aggro* range, or when attacked.

An insignificant but fairly common category of mobs are the many *critters* found outdoors, like rabbits, squirrels, snakes, and the like. These are very weak, will not attack, and cannot even defend themselves. Far more important are the *beasts*, all of whom will at least defend themselves, and many of whom will attack if one comes too near. While some of these are fanciful, many are familiar, such as boars, wolves, big cats, owls, and vultures. A character possessing the skinning skill can take hide from many of these beasts, generally the mammals, after they have been killed and their corpses looted of any items they may be carrying. *Humanoids* are intelligent—possessing culture, religion, and often speech—and they cannot be skinned. They include NPCs representing all ten races that players may use as characters, plus several others. Two nonplayer races that logically could be used as player characters in future versions of WoW are Goblins and Furbolgs, both of which have extensive settlements and interact in complex ways with players.

These categories are rather separate. The distinction between beasts and humanoids is very clear inside WoW, and hunters have a mapping tool that allows them to see the locations of all nearby beasts or humanoids, but not both simultaneously. The distinction between player character and NPC is also clear. True, fighting one may not seem very different from fighting the other, but the consequences are different. For example, one may earn honor from killing a character, but not from killing an NPC guard. When a player's character is killed, it reappears at a nearby graveyard and can *resurrect* (or *rez*). It may then seek vengeance against the killer. A few minutes after a beast or humanoid NPC dies, another takes its place, not resurrecting but *spawning*. The logic would seem to be that this is a new tiger or guard, who has merely been born at the same place as the old one. However, the word *spawn* is used even for NPCs that have individual names, such as the boss NPCs, whose killing is the goal of many quests. Notably, a spawned NPC has no memory of the prior death, whereas a rezzed character starts out with greatly diminished health and other damage, as well as the player's own memory of the defeat.

NPCs may be described as artificial intelligences or AIs, but they are really rather stupid. The realism of these artificial characters is enhanced by their physical movements and occasional speech, which are based on motion capture and voice recordings of real people. Look closely at a guard standing in one spot, and you will see that he appears to be breathing. Vendors and trainers often speak prerecorded messages, typically gesturing as they do so. What they say is appropriate to their role. In the Cathedral of Light, Priestess Josetta gave Maxrohn two salutations based on their shared faith: "Light be with you!" "Light bless you!" When Maxrohn visited the Elven zone of Moonglade during the 2007 lunar festival, trader Lorelae Wintersons gave him two salutations from her very different religion: "May the stars guide you!" "Goddess watch over you!" Members of the Horde who visited the throne room in Undercity may hear Sylvanas, the Dark Lady banshee who rules the Undead, spit out the words, "What are we if not slaves to this torment?"

When battling an NPC, a player often hears the opponent shout or grunt, suggesting it feels emotions. A very simple programming trick, undoubtedly involving a random number and triggered when the opponent's health drops below a set level, allows many enemies to simulate either rage or fear when the fight is going badly for them. When Stonescythe Alphas have nearly lost their lives, they enter a condition of "desperate rage," during which the damage caused by each of their blows is increased by twenty points, and their attack speed increases 10 percent. Other enemies run away, as if they were afraid. However, they always return to the battle, often after having snared some allies to help them. For example, when battling a murloc on a beach, it may run away, go sideways a distance, then return. If it happens to come near enough to another murloc, that second enemy will come along and give the player a rather rough time.

In general, only very simple programming is required to get very complex behavior from swarms of enemies. Typically, territory is divided into a number of neighborhoods, each with its own mixture of mobs. Some may stand still unless approached, while others will patrol a small territory at random, and others will patrol a wider territory or walk along a set route. This is quite enough to challenge the analytical abilities of all but the most experienced players. The big danger, of course, is that one will get deep into a battle with one enemy, suffering depleted health, when another will wander along at random and enter the fight. Experienced players learn to psych out the NPCs, mentally modeling the complex patterns created by the interactions of their individually simple programming.

It is easy to program NPCs to walk in a particular direction until reaching the limit of their territory, then turn at random and walk back across the territory. Only a couple of trivially simple program lines are required to give it a set probability of pausing at any point, after which it may turn and resume walking. At each step, the program can check how near the NPC is to enemies in the vicinity and attack one if the distance is less than the set aggro range, what ethologists studying real animals call *reaction distance*.

Such simple programming principles can give NPCs the illusion of free will.[44] Both Dorana and Korelor are Alliance NPCs that patrol the road near Sentinel Hill. Aristotle followed them both one day, noticing how they occasionally ran off the path to attack a buzzard or other NPC enemy. On the east-west Duskwood road, north of Yorgen Farmstead, a young black ravager wolf can occasionally be seen killing a rat. At several locations, it is easy for the player to engage an enemy and then *kite* it—make it chase after you—into friendly NPCs who will attack it, thereby saving you. One good place is at Southshore, where a murloc just west of the dock can be kited to where Human NPCs are waiting.

An especially impressive example is the attack on Stillpine hold, experienced by both of my Draenei characters, Zodia and Etacarinae. The high chief of the Stillpine

Furbolgs assigns a mission to determine what corruption could have caused the wildkin to occupy this system of caverns. After a series of adventures, the character reports back to the chief, who sends about a dozen of his raiders into the caverns to kill the wildkin. Etacarinae went in with them and participated in the battle that raged. The Furbolgs enter single file, but spread out when they encounter wildkin, and many separate combats ensue. If a Furbolg kills a wildkin, it may rush to the nearest other wildkin, apparently to help its fellows. When Etacarinae helped kill a wildkin, the Furbolgs fighting it quickly attacked another.

Increasingly, WoW has included puppet-show dramas in which NPCs act out complex actions, either entirely or only partially prescribed. Edward Castronova was especially impressed when he saw the NPC Miss Danna, a school mistress, leading her seven students on a tour of Stormwind City in a prerelease version of World of Warcraft.[45] Lunette encountered Miss Danna and her students on her one visit to the city. They walked along as a group, with the children milling around, sometimes skipping (see figure 1.3). One of the boys fretfully asked if they had to walk any farther. Miss

**Figure 1.3**
Miss Danna, leading her seven students on a tour of Stormwind City.

Danna said, "Here we have the Cathedral of Light, the center of spiritual enlighten-ment here in Stormwind." Another boy asked whether this was the place the paladins train. She replied, "Yes, that is true. Paladins and priests alike train their skills and research great truths behind the walls of the Cathedral." The first boy complained that his feet hurt. When Lunette entered the cathedral, a functionary standing just inside recognized her class and exclaimed, "Greetings, priest!"

A piece of street theater is enacted occasionally in the bazaar of Silvermoon City, when two rebel ideologues, Priest Ennas and Lyria Skystrider, harangue their fellow Blood Elves like soapboxers in London's Hyde Park. Ennas decries the excessive use of magic that ruins the environment and threatens the very destruction of the Blood Elves if pursued without limit. Skystrider decries the unholy alliances with Orcs and the Undead, trusting previous enemies who could betray them at any moment. Members of their skeptical audience praise the wonders magical technology has pro-vided, but Ennas reminds them of the cost and says, "We have all been blinded." When another member of the audience asks if they are being called traitors, Ennas answers, "The magisters are the traitors! They have sealed our doom." At this point, one of the ruling magisters arrives and casts a spell on the two rebels, transforming them into loyalists who parrot the magisters' party line.

Some innovative computer scientists have been developing technologies to give NPCs more complex and realistic behavior, based on such approaches as machine learning. For example, my colleague Mary Lou Maher and her student Kathryn Merrick have designed NPCs that evolve, adapt, and exhibit curiosity toward new experi-ences.[46] However, in many contexts human players may find dumb NPCs more man-ageable, especially in cases when they face a whole swarm of them and their interactions create nearly unmanageable complexity. Fellow human players can provide much of the behavioral richness desired in social interaction, so the need for sophisticated NPCs may primarily be limited to single-player games and educational virtual worlds in which the NPCs teach humans. An exception would be NPCs that play key roles in the legends and mythology of the virtual world.

Thrall, leader of the Orcs, is a perfect example. Members of the Horde can meet him in the throne room at Orgrimmar, where he originates a few quests. He stands up, speaks with dramatic gestures, and gives a few quests, yet one wishes for more. Thrall is a complex and prominent character in the WoW mythos, featuring in two of the novels. In *Cycle of Hatred*, by Keith R. A. DeCandido, Thrall restrains the Orcs from breaking their truce with the Alliance, even after apparent provocations, because he possesses a measure of trust for Lady Jaina Proudmoore, who rules the nearby Human city of Theramore.[47] Thrall is loyal to his own people, the Orcs, but he is able to see things from the perspective of other groups and to imagine a higher level of loyalty, to principles that might unite all intelligent beings.

Christie Golden's novel *Lord of the Clans* is what literary critics call a *bildungsroman*.[48] This German word refers to a novel that chronicles the psychological and moral development of the protagonist, who in this case is Thrall. Orphaned in infancy when his noble parents were assassinated, Thrall is raised by the master of Durnholde Keep, Aedalas Blackmoore, who is the Human administrator of the system of internment camps that held Orc prisoners after the Second War. This was no act of mercy on Blackmoore's part, but his scheme to create a superior gladiator by training Thrall in all the skills of combat. By the very act of naming him Thrall, Blackmoore sought to brand him forever his slave. But during his upbringing, Thrall learned mercy and honor from the sergeant who tutored him, and kindness from Taretha, daughter of the servant ordered to house him. Eventually, after Thrall has become the most formidable warrior in the service of Blackmoore, Taretha helps him escape. In a series of raids, he liberates many of his people and establishes the core of the eventual Horde. When his forces surround Durnholde, and he honorably requests the release of the remaining Orcs, Blackmoore answers him by delivering the severed head of Taretha.

Thrall does display a measure of autonomy in some high-level quests, such as one in the Caverns of Time that depicts his escape from Durnholde Keep. After a team of players releases him from a prison cell, he runs upstairs, dresses in battle armor, then attacks one after another of the Humans barring his way. Just after he has passed through the main gate, he is confronted by a mounted officer. After defeating this enemy, Thrall mounts the man's horse and rides it to nearby Tarren Mill, where he searches both the church and the inn, seeking Taretha (see figure 1.4). Although thoroughly scripted, the action permits much variation, depending on how the battle goes between the rescuers and the captors. The player may never be under the illusion that Thrall is a real person, yet the richness of the story and the complexity of the events provide a credible vision of reality.

## Epilogue: A Warrior's Mission

Tarkas, an Orc warrior, is a member of the Horde, like Incognita. Indeed, the Horde was originally an amalgamation of Orc clans who invaded the world in the First War, whereas the Forsaken broke away from the Scourge and joined the Horde only near the end of the Third War. The high point of his life was when he met Thrall, the Horde leader, who sent him on a mission to infiltrate the Burning Blade sect of the Shadow Council, a secret society whose devious plots had provoked the First War. Thrall succeeded in becoming a spy within the Burning Blade, then carried out quests in Ragefire Chasm, both directly on Thrall's order, and as a covert Thrall operative within the sect.[49] To complete his complex missions in this monster-infested underground dungeon, he of necessity participated in three

**Figure 1.4**
Taretha and Thrall, meeting for the last time, at Tarren Mill.

separate five-person incursions, thus cooperating with a dozen other members of the Horde. After completing every last one of the assigned tasks with honor, he reported back to Thrall, and then disappeared. If Tarkas is under deep cover on a new series of dangerous, secret missions for Thrall, we may or may not ever see him again. Thinking that he would still be in the twenties levels, we are keeping an eye on Fray Island, a special training base for level-30 warriors off the east coast of the Barrens, in case he goes there for a fighting challenge called the Affray. We feel sure he would greet us with the Orc shout of victory: "Lok'tar!"

## 2  Heritage

I am Maxrohn, a Human priest, and this is the story of my personal expedition from Stormwind City through Stranglethorn to the piratical southern port of Booty Bay. My journey had several purposes. Most important for Stormwind, I was on an extended, multistage quest to find a missing diplomat. The most recent of a long series of informants, Mikhail, the bartender in the inn at the port town of Menethil, had told me to voyage to far distant Theramore and seek information from Commander Samaul. Coincidentally, but far less significantly, Vincent Hyal in Menethil had asked me to take a message to his brother in Theramore. Rather than sail directly from Menethil, I decided to take a far more difficult route. From Booty Bay, I could take a ship for Ratchet on the continent of Kalimdor, and from there, hike south along the coast to my destination. One personal motive was the adventure that the tropical jungle of Stranglethorn would afford, and another was the opportunity for collecting new kinds of herbs. My skilled occupations are herbalism and alchemy, and exotic plants can be ingredients for the useful potions I was learning to brew.

On a far more subtle level, I hoped that my journey would deepen my understanding of the history of the conflicts that grip our world. I was then struggling to understand how a priest can fulfill the cardinal virtue of compassion, when nearly everyone seems bent on murder, theft, and betrayal. Some inspiration had come from visiting two Dwarven archaeological sites, Ironband's small excavation south of Loch Modan, and Whelgar's larger dig in the hills overlooking the Wetlands. The technically oriented Dwarves were seeking lost technology that might be useful in today's conflicts, whereas I sought wisdom that might explain and thus help reverse the horrible trend toward violence that I see in the world. Walking the long road from Stormwind to Booty Bay lets one observe with one's own eyes the decline of human civilization, the encroachments by criminals and beasts, and the confrontation between the Alliance and the Horde. But the final leg of the trek, through Stranglethorn Vale, would be exceedingly dangerous, and could not be attempted until I had mastered about half the levels of worldly experience.

As soon as I reached level 35, which occurred while I was battling members of the Syndicate in Sofera's Naze in the Alterac Hills, I returned to Stormwind to prepare for my journey. This great city is the one remaining metropolis for humankind, since we were expelled from the capital, Lordaeron, five years ago. Its spotlessly clean streets, imposing walls, and pleasant shops divided by canals into several districts gives hope that civilization can rise again. To orient my mind to the past, I visited the Keep and the Royal Library that lies within, reading such books as *The Kaldorei and the Well of Eternity*, *The New Horde*, and *Aegwynn and the Dragon Hunt*. After resting and meditating upon the deep histories of the many peoples of Azeroth, I was ready for the last logistical preparations.

I needed to lighten the load I would carry and make room for new herbs, quest items, and other valuables I hoped to find along the way. John Burnside in the counting house of the Trade District provided a storage box for me, and I unloaded many of my herbs and potions. I had too many, so I put the overflow in an herb bag that I had bought earlier, and left it with him also. My next stop was the alchemy shop in the Mage Quarter, a parklike area with lawns instead of roads. There, Eldraeith, the Elvish herbalism supplier, greeted me: "Made by the finest craftsmen in all of Teldrassil, carried by hand from Kalimdor to Azeroth as a sign of the growing alliance between the people of the Great Tree and the humans of this land. If there is anything you require, you have but to ask." I purchased a new herb-carrying bag and thanked her. As I departed, she exclaimed in the Elvish manner, "May the stars guide you!"

Before embarking on my long journey, I entered the Cathedral of Light. Having gained levels since my last visit, I was allowed to train with Brother Joshua for several more magic spells. I was especially excited to learn the Levitate spell, which would allow me to float in the air a few feet off the ground, fall more gently from any height, and cross water without swimming. That cost me one gold coin and eight silver. Then I upgraded three Holy spells (Heal, Desperate Prayer, and Resurrection) and two Shadow Magic spells (Mind Blast and Shadow Word: Pain) for a combined cost of four gold coins, thirty-seven silver, and forty copper. Those were all very valuable spells, and I had relied heavily on weaker versions for some time. In Stranglethorn, I knew I would face very great dangers, and would need every supernatural resource I could use. When I departed, Joshua wished me, "Safe travel!"

Immediately outside the gates of Stormwind lie the relatively peaceful farms and woodlands of Elwynn Forest. When I reached Goldshire, the prosperous town that dominates the region, I took a short detour to Northshire Abbey, where I had first trained for the priesthood, to see if the library held any rare historical books. Indeed, I found a copy of *Civil War in the Plaguelands*, describing the conflict that led to the independence of the Forsaken Undead under the leadership of the banshee, Sylvanas Windrunner, and how Prince Arthas was only barely able to save his liege the Lich King in his war against the Naga and the Blood Elves (see figure 2.1).

I then turned southwest and entered the agricultural territory of Westfall, where many of the farms had just been abandoned to the growing chaos of bandits and beasts that

**Figure 2.1**
Incognita, lying in a trance on the floor of the throne room in the ruins of Lordaeron, meditating between the royal emblem and the huge blood stain that marked the assassination of King Terenas by his son Arthas, who then became the Lich King.

was encroaching upon civilization. Immediately as I crossed the border, I met a pathetic family of refugees named Furlbrow, who begged help collecting the last of their belongings and feeding their elderly horse. I continued down the western road until I reached the town of Moonbrook, which had been taken over by bandits of the Defias Brotherhood. Prior to the First War, the vast underground mines here were the greatest source of gold in the world, so I suppose I should not have been surprised that they would attract vast numbers of thieves and cutthroats. The Defias were much weaker than I, only levels 13 through 15, so it was easy to kill them even two at a time. After taking out my anger on the bandits, I turned east and crossed the bridge into Duskwood.

I had no time for the long eastward hike to Darkshire, a fair-size Human settlement, not to mention Lakeshire that lay beyond it in the Redridge Mountains. The residents of Westfall, Darkshire, and Lakeshire were constantly complaining that Stormwind failed to send forces to protect them, and begging for my help. But my goal lay to the south.

My route took me right past Raven Hill Cemetery, a large and gloomy space dominated by the Lich King's Scourge, so I entered it in search of a rare herb called *grave moss*. A deep, blue mist had rolled in, making it very hard to avoid the Undead creatures that menaced on every side: bone chewers, carrion recluses, flesh eaters, rotted ones, skeletal fiends, and skeletal raiders. I found six samples of grave moss, then returned to the main eastbound road, on which I soon reached the fork that would take me quickly south to Stranglethorn.

Shortly after entering the jungle, I met Hemet Nesingwary Jr., who was leading an expedition to collect samples of wildlife. He said, "Jolly nice to make your acquaintance, Maxrohn. Haven't seen a priest around these parts for some time." His assistant, Barnil Stonepot, then asked me to retrieve lost pages of the manuscript of a historical novel, *The Green Hills of Stranglethorn*, by Nesingwary's father (see figure 2.2). Two other members of the Nesingwary expedition, Ajeck Rouack and S. J. Erlgadin, put me to work collecting

**Figure 2.2**
Hemet Nesingwary Sr. (Ernest Hemingway), big-game hunter and author, with trophy animal heads, at his base camp in Sholazar Basin, Northrend.

specimens of animals, which I thought would be compatible with seeking tropical herbs for my alchemy experiments.

My hope to accomplish something of historical significance received a boost when Brother Nimetz, in a group of pro-Stormwind rebels, asked me to find four ancient Troll tablets that would reveal something important about their ancient legends and the depraved magic based on them today. He told me to seek one in the ruins of Bal'lal, two in the ruins of Zul'Kunda, and the fourth in the Vile Reef, which I knew was near Booty Bay. Given its tortured past, Stranglethorn contains the ruins of many once flourishing towns and stately temples: Aboraz, Bal'lal, Balia'mah, Kal'ai, Jubuwal, Mizjah, Tkashi, Ziata'jai, Zul'Kunda, Zul'Mamwe, and Zuuldaia. It would be an archaeologist's paradise, were it not for the archaic Trolls who seek to kill any who would intrude upon this wreckage of their previous home.

Initially, the Trolls presented an impenetrable barrier to collecting the four ancient tablets. At Bal'lal, for example, I could stand on a hill and see the tablet inside a stone enclosure, but fully six Trolls were guarding it. At level 35, I was confident I could vanquish any one of them, but a pair could kill me easily. The problem was that they were standing close together, so if I attacked one, then two or three would respond. I needed either to gain several levels or to get help. My guild was busy in other regions, so I resolved to settle in Stranglethorn for a while, until I was able to complete the quest for the four tablets.

The rebels enlisted me in their struggle against a renegade officer named Colonel Kurzen, who had set himself up with a private army as a lord of the jungle (see figure 2.3). Nimetz felt that Kurzen might be the victim of Troll magic, and hoped the ancient tablets would provide a clue, perhaps even the details of the spells that had been used. But before I could find these ancient writings, his comrade Lieutenant Doren asked me to kill ten of Kurzen's commandos and six of his magic-wielding headshrinkers. Doren warned, "I know many of Kurzen's troops personally, and I know they are skilled, loyal, and cruel." Then Doren assigned me to enter Kurzen's headquarters deep inside a cavern called the Stockpile, kill ten of his lieutenants, and bring him the colonel's head. I found that this quest was far too difficult for one person, so I teamed up with an Elf named Tallann, who was a hunter and assisted by a trained tiger. We fought valiantly and killed the required six elite followers of Kurzen, plus his four subchiefs, but we were unable to reach Kurzen himself and were forced to retreat.

After this chastening experience, my enthusiasm for the war against Kurzen began to wane. I was invited to join groups that were going after his head, but I did not take advantage of these opportunities. I brooded constantly about the meaning of it all. Eventually I found all four tablets for Nimetz, killing many Trolls in the process. They contained no magic spells that could explain Kurzen's odd behavior. One appeared to be a curse, but it focused narrowly on defending the tomb of the Troll emperor. Two were legends, so

**Figure 2.3**
Colonel Kurzen (based on Kurtz from Joseph Conrad's *Heart of Darkness*) in his Stranglethorn Vale cavern hideout.

fragmentary it was impossible to make sense of them. The other was a poem beginning as follows:

A Moon over the Vale shines
Casting its glow upon the jungle
Where proud Warriors heed the call
To defend our Nation and sacred grounds.

Almost as if my mind could not cope with deep philosophical questions, such as the connection between Kurzen and the Trolls, I found myself concentrating on simple matters. My herb collecting had hit an immediate snag when I entered Stranglethorn, because my skill rating was only 180, and the place was thick with Khadgar's whisker, which requires 185. A special effort dodging tigers and panthers, while taking any herb I could find, increased my skill step-by-step until a goldthorn took me to 185 and gave me the ability to add new species to my collection. After a week, my skill had zoomed up to 225. That qualified me for promotion to the next grade of herbalist. I had started as an apprentice, become a journeyman, and entered Stranglethorn as an expert. Above that were only two more levels, artisan and master. I had been given the name of Flora Silverwind, an herbalism trainer in Booty Bay, and to learn from her I finally trekked to that southernmost town.

Booty Bay is run by Blackwater Raiders, sometimes dubbed *pirates*, in collaboration with the Steamwheedle Cartel, a group of Goblin capitalists. I took on various odd jobs for them, wanting to reach level 40 before setting sail for Ratchet. One especially unpleasant Goblin, named Kebok, hired me to obtain eighteen Troll tusks, which he planned to sell as the more valuable tiger fangs. At this point, I had killed so many Trolls that another dozen or so did not seem an ethical problem, but I was offended when Kebok complained I had not done a good enough job cleaning the gore off their tusks. In a mood more of exhaustion than triumph, I reached my leveling goal and walked to the end of the dock to await the next ship. What had I learned about the history of Azeroth and our chances for the future? Perhaps a long sea voyage would give me a chance to meditate on such questions.

## Three Different Pasts

The heritage of World of Warcraft can be charted on at least three distinct planes. First, there is the history within the story, what is widely called the *backstory*, the action that has already taken place before the curtain on the drama rises. Second, there is the literary and cultural heritage, such as the games and works of literature that probably served as influences and definitely were precursors.[1] Some of these are mentioned in chapter 1, and others are mentioned throughout this book. Third, there is the history of the real world in which both the other heritages were created, including everything from the fall of the Roman Empire to the rise of social science.

Maxrohn tells us a little of the history of his own people, the Humans living in Azeroth. In chapter 1, we hear a little more from Incognita. A decade ago, several Human kingdoms flourished, with major cities like Lordaeron and Stormwind. Then, bioweapons released in the Third War depopulated Lordaeron and the territory to the east, now called the Plaguelands. Stormwind appears to be a brilliant center of culture, but it is losing control over the surrounding districts, and the likely future is a reign of complete chaos.

We would like to sympathize with the Humans, but the conflict between the so-called rebels and Colonel Kurzen's army is the result of failed imperialism in which Stormwind sought to seize the wealth of the Stranglethorn jungle. Kurzen was a Human commander, who ceased responding to orders as Stormwind's control over the intervening districts weakened. Then a small group of men broke away from his army in loyalty to Stormwind. At this point, neither force serves any purpose in defending Human civilization but rather seeks to dominate a small colonial empire. This history not only erodes optimism but also commitment, and Maxrohn could be forgiven for wondering whether any of the contending forces have justice on their side, versus all being bandits of one sort or another.[2]

Many hints suggest the virtual world's artistic heritage. "Hemet Nesingwary" is an anagram of the name of the macho American writer and hunting enthusiast Ernest Hemingway. *The Green Hills of Stranglethorn* is a parody of Hemingway's book *The Green Hills of Africa*. The names of two of his companions, Ajeck Rouack and S. J. Erlgadin, are anagrams of two other authors, Jack Kerouac and J. D. Salinger. No one has been able to figure out what "Barnil Stonepot" is the anagram of, and there is always the possibility it is one of Blizzard's tricks on players, not being the anagram of anything. Many months later, Maxrohn would meet Hemet Nesingwary, Sr., in Nagrand, a very high level zone in Outland, where the senior Nesingwary is still hunting bigger and bigger game. More recently, he has appeared in Sholazar Basin on the newly accessible continent of Northrend, leading a large group of animal hunters. Hemingway was something of an enigma, blood-thirsty yet in many respects left-wing, and both Kerouac and Salinger could be described as alienated.

Colonel Kurzen is based on the character Colonel Kurtz, played by Marlon Brando, in *Apocalypse Now*. That movie critiqued American colonialism in Vietnam and was based on Joseph Conrad's novella *Heart of Darkness*, critiquing European colonialism in Africa, in which the character was called simply Kurtz. Maxrohn remarked upon the Dwarves' fascination with archaeology, which digs beneath the surface to uncover truths about our own origins. The metaphor suggests that digging beneath the surface of Azeroth reveals important truths about America.

The notion that other worlds might contain civilizations that had fallen from their height was proclaimed a century ago by American astronomer Percival Lowell, who claimed he saw straight lines on the surface of Mars and believed they were canals dug millennia ago by a now dying civilization.[3] The first significant American science fiction writer, Edgar Rice Burroughs, based his Barsoom novels on Lowell's notions, beginning with *A Princess of Mars*, written in 1911.[4] His novels established a genre that includes *Flash Gordon* and *Star Wars*, and set high standards for invented cultures. Burroughs imagined that the planet Mars was home to several humanoid races of different colors and species, struggling to hold their territories in competition with one another in the aftermath of the decline of a great civilization. This is exactly the premise of World of Warcraft, in which Azeroth is often described as a planet. One difference, however, is that the fictional Martian environment is dying of natural causes, chiefly the gradual loss of atmosphere into outer space, offset at great effort by technology including atmosphere-generating factories. In contrast, the damage to many zones in WoW is caused by technology and economic exploitation. Remarkably, one of the Barsoom books, *Chessmen of Mars*, actually includes the rules of a playable game representing a battle between two of the Martian races, foreshadowing WoW's competition between the Horde and the Alliance.

A very large number of WoW quests concern environmental pollution and resource degradation, expressing the values of the environmentalist movement. In Felwood, bears have become so corrupted that their hide sloughs off in great patches. Agents of the Emerald Circle of the Night Elves enlist members of the Alliance to document the environmental catastrophe, seek its origins, and undertake remedial action. For example, Arathandris Silversky told Maxrohn that four different plants important in the ecosystem appeared to have been corrupted: songflowers, windblossoms, whipper roots, and night dragons. As an herbalist, Maxrohn possessed the skill set to help her substantially in her work. It turned out that a group of Jadefire satyrs, themselves corrupted Elves, plus a cult of Jadefire Orcs were intentionally spreading the corruption from a moonwell filled with green slime. Maxrohn agreed to kill thirty of the satyrs, including their leader, Xavathras, plus numerous cultists around the Shrine of the Deceiver, a front organization of the Shadow Council that had been responsible for the First War. Some of the waters of Felwood are infested by "toxic horrors," which are corrupted water elementals.

Several of my characters were disgusted by the environmental degradation in the Windshear Crag area of Stonetalon. There, a team from the Venture Company was clear-cutting all the trees, leaving a valley of mud and stumps. Some of them even had the job title "deforester," underscoring the worldwide problem of deforestation. WoW's solution for deforestation is to chop down the deforesters. Along Blackwolf River, Lunette attacked loggers, supervisors, a robot deforester named XT:9, and an immense robotlike vehicle with a circular saw in one hand and the strength to rip an entire tree up with the other. In Zangarmarsh, a littoral region of Outland where lush plant growth abounds, a Night Elf expedition examines the mysterious decline of many wetland species and discovers that something is draining away the water. Lau-ranna Thar'well sends adventurers in search of unidentified plant parts so she can assess the damage, and Ysiel Windsinger sends them to seek the cause of the water depletion, which threatens the ecosystem. The term *water crisis* refers to the depletion of water resources in arid lands, such as the state of California where Blizzard Enter-tainment created World of Warcraft. Both Maxrohn and Catullus sabotaged some of the pumps by which selfish Naga were draining the wetlands of Zangarmarsh. Whether in its depiction of environmental destruction or societal disintegration, World of Warcraft warns that our own world is in danger of catastrophic collapse.

## Decline and Fall

To seek the truth about a society, one may search in many sources including political rhetoric and social science. One may well doubt the words of most politicians, but the most thoughtful of them draw upon their extensive experience in the public sphere to understand their society and not merely to flatter their constituents. Among the most remarkable passages of American political literature, both inspiring and challenging, is this paragraph that Abraham Lincoln spoke to the Wisconsin State Agricultural Society in 1859:

> It is said an Eastern monarch once charged his wise men to invent him a sentence to be ever in view, and which should be true and appropriate in all times and situations. They presented him the words, "And this, too, shall pass away." How much it expresses! How chastening in the hour of pride! How consoling in the depths of affliction! "And this, too, shall pass away." And yet, let us hope, it is not quite true. Let us hope, rather, that by the best cultivation of the physical world beneath and around us, and the intellectual and moral world within us, we shall secure an individual, social, and political prosperity and happiness, whose course shall be onward and upward, and which, while the earth endures, shall not pass away.[5]

For more than fifteen hundred years, literate members of Western civilization have been aware that the fall of the Roman Empire casts a shadow across the future of their own society.[6] It is often said that the remarkable thing about the fall of Rome was how long it took to happen, five centuries from the assassination of Julius Caesar. Yet, as World of Warcraft explicitly reminds us, modern weapons of mass destruction threaten a much more rapid collapse of civilization, if ever they were released.

World War I, coming at a time when social science was in a period of rapid development, naturally stimulated new ideas about the decline and fall of a civilization. Among the most influential ideas is in Oswald Spengler's book *The Decline of the West*. It postulates that every great civilization is based on a core idea, and dies when the potential of that idea has been exhausted.[7] Interestingly, the key idea which Spengler felt defined Western civilization is *boundless space*, and today one could speculate that the Apollo voyages to the Moon were the high point, after which the decline fully set in.[8] Conservative thinkers have repeatedly returned to Spengler's thesis, notably James Burnham in his 1964 book, *Suicide of the West*, and Patrick Buchanan in his 2002 book, *The Death of the West*.[9] They might well quote the sign at the entrance to Deadman's Crossing in World of Warcraft, which in turn quotes Dante's *Inferno*: "Abandon hope, all ye who enter here."

To my mind, the most interesting theory of the fall of civilizations is a more sophisticated development of Spengler's ideas, propounded by the founder of the sociology department at Harvard University, Pitirim A. Sorokin. A Russian who served in the provisional government after his country's ignominious withdrawal from World War I, Sorokin was condemned to death by the Bolshevists, but luckily was exiled instead. The three thousand pages of his *Social and Cultural Dynamics* argue that a civilization may be too complex to be based on a single idea, but does arise out of violent chaos with a set of fanatically held beliefs that justifies whatever leadership structure it possesses, and organizes vigorous activity to build a great world power.[10]

For the first few generations, Sorokin argued, a civilization is largely "ideational," considering reality to be essentially spiritual rather than material, and basing loyalty on faith. As the years pass and the successful civilization consolidates its gains, it begins to deemphasize fanaticism in favor of comfort. Faith fades and the culture becomes "sensate," believing that reality is whatever the human sense organs perceive. It may become hedonistic, commercial, and secular. Sorokin said that Rome collapsed when it became highly sensate. The new, Christian civilization that arose on its wreckage began with an ideational culture, then evolved into its present condition, which is sensate. Sorokin did not say that Western civilization is about to fall, although a collapse as devastating as that suffered by ancient Rome is always a possibility for an advanced sensate society such as ours. Rather, he asserted that we are entering a major transition period that is bound to be grim, cruel, bloody, and painful. In a century or two, Western civilization may pass successfully through that gauntlet and regain its confidence and power.

Applied to the first decade of the twenty-first century, Sorokin's model would note that the West and Islam are two competing civilizations that are in different points in the ideational-sensate cycle. While Western Europe languished in the Dark Ages, Islam rose to heights of civilization, mellowed, and began to decline when Europe was still rising from its renaissance. Now, he would say, the West is declining, just when Islam may be poised for a new upsurge. If Sorokin were around today, he would be a controversial figure. He would be telling us that Islamic fundamentalism was not some small, terrorist aberration, but the very birth of a new civilization, fired up with faith and ready for conquest. Modern scholars, such as Mansoor Moaddel, would disagree with Sorokin, noting that Islam possesses a modernist movement as well as fundamentalism.[11] Whether history proves Sorokin right or wrong, his ideas illuminate issues not only in the real world but also in World of Warcraft.

The Alliance and the Horde are two competing civilizations, temporarily in a truce with each other, yet contending for dominance. They are locked in what political scientist Samuel P. Huntington called a "clash of civilizations"—a competition for power, land, and other resources—drawing their sense of identity from different cultural and religious traditions.[12] As Christie Golden reports in her novel *Rise of the Horde*, only two generations ago the Orcs were a tribal society that had never been part of a civilization.[13] Malignant supernatural intervention, or leaders who risked conspiring with magical forces, forged the tribes together and impelled them to invade the world of Elves and Humans. Reading Golden's book from the standpoint of a cultural anthropologist, one notes that the original tribes were endogamous—they did not intermarry across tribes—so the process of unification was bound to be difficult. But this is one reading of anthropology in general: the history of humanity is the difficult struggle to create ever larger social groups, starting with the wandering hunter-gatherer band of half a hundred souls and building through kingdoms modeled on the family to modern societies of a hundred million or more.[14]

Violent war, and the necessity of finding allies, has built the Horde into a coalition of five races, having little in common except their interest in opposing the Alliance and a host of lesser enemies. To succeed in the long run, according to Spengler or Sorokin, the Horde needed an ideational commitment to one or more key ideas. What their core might be was suggested by Durotan, father of Thrall: "You want us to be strong as a people, rather than as individual clans, and we cannot do that without a code of honor that is inviolable."[15]

The Alliance, in contrast, represents an association of older societies that are far past their ideational youth. As we see in chapter 3, the Night Elves retain some faith in their ancient culture, but the Humans, Gnomes, Dwarves, and Draenei are sensate societies. The core of the Alliance is actually the Humans, who organized the opposition against the Horde invasion. Just as ancient Athens felt it deserved hegemony over Greece because it had led the defense against the invading Persians, the Humans claim hegemony over the Alliance. However, as explained in Aaron Rosenberg's novel *Tides of Darkness*, the Human kingdoms had great difficulty uniting themselves and seemed to lack overarching moral principles. In chapter 3 of this book, we see that the religion of the Holy Light has some potential to provide an ideational basis for the Alliance. As Human paladin Turalyon brooded: "How could the Holy Light unite all creatures, all souls, when something as monstrous, as cruel, and as purely evil as the orc Horde walked this world?"[16]

## The Warcraft Trilogy

The three generations of Warcraft strategy games need to be considered here because they set up the prehistory and the range of cultures of the Warcraft universe, upon which World of Warcraft builds. In the three fictional decades covered by the trilogy, each game represents one of the three great wars that led to the social chaos and cultural fragmentation of the world.[17] A chronology published in the encyclopedic book about the tabletop card-playing version of World of Warcraft counts years, starting with zero, from the first infiltration by Orcs that led to the outbreak of the First War in year 1, and its conclusion in year 4. The Second War took place in year 6, and the Third War was fought in year 25. The present time is year 30.[18]

Warcraft III is the culmination of the trilogy, and the predecessor of World of Warcraft, but it was not rendered obsolete when the massively multiplayer virtual world was launched in 2004. Rather, it is a highly developed and still viable strategy game that happens to cover a period in the history of its world immediately before the action of World of Warcraft begins.

Given that it is set just five years before World of Warcraft, Warcraft III sets up some of the key conditions for its world, notably the system of interrace connections that became the Alliance and the Horde. Rather than two factions, Warcraft III has four: the Human Alliance, the Night Elf Sentinels, the Orcish Horde, and the Undead Scourge. Both the Humans and the Orcs have already invited other races into their faction. The Alliance already includes Dwarves and a few Elves, although the Elves are High Elves rather than Night Elves. The Horde already includes Trolls and the Tauren. Thus, combining the Warcraft III Alliance with Sentinels, and the Horde with some of the Scourge, nearly completes the two factions of four races with which World of Warcraft begins.

In the single-player version of the game, each of the four factions must carry out a major military campaign including several quests, some of which are required for progress, and some of which are optional. These campaigns reveal much about WoW's historical background.

The Human campaign starts out normally enough, as the forces of the Human kingdom of Lordaeron skirmish against Orcs, murlocs, and gnolls. Then it rapidly devolves into a grinding conflict, as a plague spreading through the food supply transforms living citizens into Undead members of the Scourge. The plague began in Andorhal, Lordaeron's agricultural shipping center, and in World of Warcraft that town has become a ruin infested by living corpses and skeletons. The second major military objective is Hearthglen, north of Andorhal, which is retaken from the Scourge. By the time of WoW, the broader collapse of Lordaeron has left this strong point in the hands of a radical Human cult, the Scarlet Crusade.

The leader of the Human army is Arthas, who at first responds rationally to threats but who becomes progressively more desperate, and, some judge, even insane. A key turning point is the conflict with his colleague Uther, and the names but not the deeds are reminiscent of two characters in the story of King Arthur, Arthur himself and his father, Uther Pendragon. The final point of dispute between them is Arthas's plan to kill the villagers in Stratholme before they can be subverted by the Scourge, the preemptive murder of a hundred innocent people. The ultimate result can be seen in WoW, where Stratholme is the capital of Scourge forces in Eastern Plaguelands, and Arthas has defected to the Scourge, becoming one with the Lich King. One of the game manuals even employs the language of Star Wars to say that "Arthas has turned to the dark side."[19]

The net result of these Human campaigns is the complete ruin of Lordaeron, with the retreat of Humans to Stormwind and the zones adjacent to it, and to a small area across the Great Sea around Theramore. The territory including Andorhal and Hearthglen becomes the Western Plaguelands, and the territory including Stratholme becomes the Eastern Plaguelands.

The Undead campaign begins with the former Human capital city having been ravaged by the plague, and Arthas taking command of the Scourge's legions and turning in the direction of the High Elf nation of Quel'Thalas, driving toward the capital, Silvermoon City. Silvanas Windrunner, ranger-general of the High Elves, put up stiff resistance, but the city is ravaged and she is captured and transformed into a banshee servant of the Scourge. The campaign comes to a climax with the siege of the sorcerer city, Dalaran, and the summoning of the Scourge leader, Archimonde. In the original version of WoW, Dalaran had become inaccessible beneath a magic dome—we could only wonder what took place inside—and with the Burning Crusade expansion, half of Silvermoon had been rebuilt by the Blood Elves. In the Lich King expansion, Dalaran was moved to or rebuilt in the air, floating over Northrend.

The Orc campaign describes their first months as refugees in Kalimdor, including their mutually beneficial pact with the Tauren against the centaurs, dislodging Humans from a number of camps, and the invasion of Ashenvale, a Night Elf zone. This last conflict begins with a mere attempt to obtain lumber from the sacred Elven forests but escalates to the assassination of their forest demigod, Cenarius. The Orcs eradicate Human settlements around Stonetalon Peak, but the political situation shifts dramatically, and the Humans become Thrall's allies against the Warsong clan of Orcs. The action ends before the Orcs have fully established themselves in the new territory, but they have a solid alliance with the Tauren to the west and an uneasy truce with the relatively small remaining Human settlement to the south.

The Night Elf campaign begins with contingents of the Orc and Human forces inside the Elf territory of Ashenvale. As if expelling them were not enough of a challenge, Archimonde establishes a foothold for the Burning Legion, and nearly kills the Elven leader, Tyrande Whisperwind. She escapes to the well-protected, sacred Moonglade, and informs her Elves that the sleeping druid, Malfurion Stormrage, must be awakened from his thousands of years of magical slumber, to sacrifice himself to defeat the Undead. She is especially concerned that Archimonde intends to attack the World Tree, which is the source of Elven vitality. Archimonde attacks and defeats Human and Orc bases, thereby impelling those races into a de facto alliance with their earlier opponents, the Night Elves.

The Warcraft III expansion, IIIX, includes a campaign called "Legacy of the Damned," which reintroduces Sylvanas, now leader of the banshees, who are Undead Elven women, and the schism that led her group of Forsaken to leave the Scourge and join the Horde. The campaign "Curse of the Blood Elves" concerns the fifth race that joined the Horde in the World of Warcraft: The Burning Crusade. This campaign also features the Draenei, the fifth race that joined the Alliance in that WoW expansion. Missing as active units are the Gnomes, but they provided military technology to the Humans in Warcraft II and must be assumed to have done the same again.

Warcraft IIIX ends with a bonus campaign, describing how the Orcs completed their takeover of Durotar under the leadership of their charismatic and wise chief, Thrall.

Importantly, it is programmed in the role-playing style, rather than strategy-game style, thus forming a bridge to the virtual world. A notable episode involves attacking a fleet of Human warships, and a player in World of Warcraft can swim through the wreckage of those ships, proving that the Orcs were successful.

## Quests for Knowledge of the Past

Someday, it will be possible for characters created in one virtual world to travel to another, for example, experiencing the events of Warcraft III before those of World of Warcraft. Today a WoW character can gain knowledge of the past chiefly by reading books that can be found all over the older regions of Azeroth, and by undertaking quests that deal with history or prehistory. At the Ruins of Eldarath, one quest had Maxrohn taking rubbings of runish inscriptions, using an archaeologist's drawing kit. Another time, he was sent to a remote corner of Silithus to collect fragments of clay tablets, so geologist Larksbane could better understand the presence of Twilight's Hammer cultists in the zone. Translation, however, required another quest to obtain the Twilight Lexicon.

NPCs occasionally impart snatches of historical lore, as when Corithras Moonrage spoke to Lunette about her race's great catastrophe: "After the Battle of Mount Hyjal, we were without direction. Nordrassil smoked from the fire it unleashed, and our immortality—the very essence of our beings!—was lost. It was in this trying time that the Betrayer was freed from his prison, and Shan'do Stormrage disappeared." He explained that Arch Druid Staghelm filled the leadership gap and inspired other powerful druids to grow a new world tree, Teldrassil. Later he admitted, "Without the blessings of Alexstrasza the Life-Binder and Nozdormu the Timeless, Teldrassil's growth has not been without flaw." Several days later, Staghelm himself told Lunette, "I fear my work on Teldrassil shall never be completed, and our immortality never restored."

An ironic historical quest, Data Rescue, sent Etacarinae into Gnomeregan, the high-tech city that the Gnomes had been forced to abandon, in search of lost data of great significance. The Gnomes were technologically the most advanced race, but their metropolis was invaded by the troggs, who were the most primitive humanoids. As explained in the 1970 sci-fi movie *Trog*, troggs are troglodytes or cave dwellers, representing an earlier phase in Human evolution. Since Gnomeregan was underground, apparently the troggs had some advantage in the battle, so in desperation the Gnomes released radioactive wastes, which unfortunately failed to kill the brutish troggs but rendered the city uninhabitable. The quest required Etacarinae to use a series of colored computer punch cards in reader punchers—white, yellow, blue, and red—ultimately to get a prismatic card and bring it to Master Mechanic Castpipe in the city of Ironforge.

The first irony here, of course, is that computer cards have been obsolete for decades. Developed by Herman Hollerith at the very beginning of the twentieth century, they were still in use when I did my quantitative study of science fiction literature in 1978.[20] More properly called Hollerith cards—or IBM cards, after the company he founded— they were wide pieces of cardboard with eighty columns in which rectangular holes could be punched, in patterns representing numbers or letters. My science fiction study was based on data from a questionnaire asking respondents to rate 125 science fiction authors. To avoid results being distorted by the placement of items, I produced five versions of the questionnaire with the authors in five different random orders. I entered the data by operating a punch-card machine, which incidentally deadened my hearing until I realized what was happening and started to wear earplugs, producing five different card decks, one for each ordering of authors' names. Then I wrote my longest computer program to that point in my career, reordering four of the sets to match the fifth, and automatically repunching the data on new cards. Finally, I merely had to physically combine the five sets of cards to get the full data set I analyzed for my book. Three years later, when I bought an Apple II personal computer, punch cards had become a historical curiosity.

The second irony is that the information on the Gnomeregan cards, once deciphered, turns out to be quite unimportant. As Etacarinae entered cards into one reader after another, binary data appeared on her screen like this:

01001001 01100110 00100000 01111001
01101111 01110101 00100000 01100011
01100001 01101110 00100000 . . . and so forth. . . .

These are eight-bit binary numbers, each representing one byte of data. One would immediately guess that they represent letters, in the ASCII code standard that developed in the early 1960s. It requires only seven bits per letter, but the leading (leftmost) bit in each of these groups is always a zero, so only seven bits are meaningful. Notice also that the sequence 00100000 appears three times. In binary, this represents the number 32, which stands for a space in ASCII, and thus divides words. Indeed, translated via ASCII, the above says, "If you can . . ." The full message Etacarinae saw was "If you can read this, you're standing too close." Other decodable binary messages included: "Tell your friends to play WoW." "Kiss me, I'm gnomish!" "Help! I'm trapped in a binary punch card factory!" When Etacarinae took the ultimate, prismatic card to Castpipe, he thanked her profusely and exclaimed, "Vitally, critically, immeasurably important data that we could not live another moment without!" In fact, the last message said, "Your laundry's ready for pickup."

Several areas and quests go beyond history to natural history and paleontology. In Un'Goro Crater there are sailed reptiles called Diemetradon, similar to Dimetrodon except having two sails rather than one on their backs, and boasting six legs. There is also a Tyrant Devilsaur, reminiscent of tyrannosaurs. Whelgar's excavation site in the Wetlands is infested by raptors, and thus reminiscent of two science fantasies of the late twentieth century, *Jurassic Park* and *Indiana Jones*.[21] Before *Jurassic Park*, the Michael Crichton novel and blockbuster movie, the word *raptor* was not commonly used. In Latin, the word means "plunderer," and in English it meant "bird of prey." But *Jurassic Park* popularized the velociraptor, the "swift thief" dinosaur whose name combines velocity with plundering. Indeed, it looks something like a running bird of prey, and dinosaurs are believed to be relatives of today's birds. Raptors are widely dispersed in World of Warcraft, for example, living also across the sea in the Barrens and down south in Stranglethorn Vale.

A version of Indiana Jones can be found in catacombs under a Troll temple complex, the Drakil'jin Ruins in Grizzly Hills, Northrend, locked in a cage and scheduled for ritual sacrifice. His name, Harrison Jones, is of course a combination of the fictional character's name and that of Harrison Ford, the actor who played him in the movies. The player's character enters the catacombs while on a quest called It Takes Guts, which requires collecting five Canopic jars, the containers for mummified Human entrails found in ancient Egyptian tombs. This reminds us that Indiana Jones behaves more like a tomb robber than a scientific archaeologist, and "guts" refers to intestines rather than to courage. Each time a Canopic jar is looted, the spirit of a Troll attacks, complaining in a Caribbean accent, "Why ya wanna mess wit me innards, mon?" A quest called Dun-da-Dun-tah!—a rendition of the musical theme from the Indiana Jones movies—helps Jones escape from the cage, rescue a fair maiden, and battle a huge serpent. When he sees this gigantic reptile, he exclaims, "Aww, not a snake!" In the movies, Jones had a severe snake phobia. Harrison Jones even looks like "Indy," compete with his trademark fedora (see figure 2.4).

Widespread but unconfirmed speculation says that one of the real-life models for Indiana Jones was the paleontologist Roy Chapman Andrews, who obtained great publicity for hunting dinosaurs in the Gobi desert of China in the 1920s.[22] The character in the movies took on various assignments to track down lost artifacts with magical powers, a common kind of quest in WoW. Some of the quests involve seeking information from the past that might explain why the world is experiencing such chaos. Whelgar himself seeks four fragments of an ancient tablet, but is too afraid of the raptors to keep looking. As he explains, "The text speaks of a 'divine plan' and a 'doomed prophecy.'"

### The Mystery of Time

All quests in WoW involve goal-directed action over time, but many concern the distant past, and a few even seek to change history. History is about time. Of all the mysteries of life, time is the most mysterious. For example, the mystery of individual

**Figure 2.4**
Harrison Jones (whose name is a combination of those of the actor Harrison Ford and a character
he played, Indiana Jones), facing his most dreaded enemy, a huge snake.

identity seems to be dependent in some way upon time. The ancient Greek philosopher Heracleitus raised this issue when he said we cannot step into the same river
twice. Alfred Korzybski, the twentieth-century philosopher who founded the General
Semantics movement, expressed this in the non-Aristotelian axiom that A does not
equal A.[23] This was a rhetorical way of saying that the identity of a thing is purely
conceptual, because the real world is constantly changing, even over short spans of
time. Nothing remains the same, so nothing is really itself. We cannot step into the
same river even once.

   One of the greatest science fiction novels, *The World of Ā*, by A. E. Van Vogt, imagines a future society based on principles of General Semantics.[24] The fundamental
axiom of this school of thought is that our language deceives us about reality as much
as it makes it possible for us to think about reality. A short distance into the book,
the hero is killed. Then what? The hero reappears, as characters do after death in
World of Warcraft, and the adventure continues. There may be several copies of the

hero, taking turns in living his life. Interestingly, the hero's name is Gosseyn—"go sane," the opposite of "go crazy"—implying that somehow the hero's apparently bizarre experience of life is actually natural.

People die, empires fall, and whole solar systems are engulfed by black holes. And yet, the physicists tell us that matter and energy can neither be destroyed nor created, but only reconfigured from one form to another. Consider a bolt of lightning. It flashes in an instant, yet every single electron inside it has existed since the very beginning of the universe. The key to this paradox is the fact that every electron is indistinguishable from every other. They differ only in their relations to one another, notably where they are in space and how their position is changing over time. What dies at the end of a flash of lightning or a human life is a structure of electrons and protons, not the electrons and protons themselves. For a century, biologists and medical doctors have philosophized that death is the price we pay for complexity, because every single-celled creature alive today, every paramecium and bacterium, has lived for a billion years.[25] The simplest things are eternal, whereas complex things, like ourselves, are ephemeral.

Phenomenologist Alfred Schütz argued that humans conceptualize the future as a kind of past, imagining future events as if they had already happened.[26] He also suggested that humans may experience multiple realities, largely distinguished from one another in terms of how we experience the flow of time.[27] Thus, it is possible to say that the mystery of time is merely a subset of the mystery of consciousness. Recently, philosophers, cognitive scientists, and leaders in the field of artificial intelligence—such as Daniel Dennett, Paul Bloom, and Marvin Minsky—have suggested that the very idea that a human has a unified consciousness may be false.[28] Our brains are complex assemblages of somewhat autonomous parts, and we are not aware of how they function because there was no evolutionary advantage to be gained by having such an awareness. To the extent that we are conscious at all, it is a chaotic swirl of impulses and reactions, not very far advanced over the "blooming, buzzing confusion" that philosopher and psychologist William James thought described an infant's consciousness.

At the extreme, time could be nothing but the human way of arranging our memories. However, if you think back on episodes from your past life, I believe you will find that you remember people, objects, and locations far clearer than the exact time when they occurred. Once, when I was a small boy, I was digging in the dirt behind our house, and I discovered a toy plastic car. I had never seen it before, so it must have been lost by previous inhabitants of our home. As an adult, I know that the house was built in 1743—yes, a real antique! I know I was born in 1940, and this was my first home, so the toy was lost by another child no later than the 1930s. It was made of plastic, so my adult mind tells me it must have dated from the twentieth century. When I dug the car up, I was surprised by the kind of plastic, because it was brownish with swirls of faint color, which I came to believe was an old-fashioned kind of plastic. In my memory of the episode, I am wearing short pants and a shirt, and the sun is warm, so it must have been summertime. I neither recall nor can deduce which year it was, although it could not have been later than the summer of 1949, because we moved away a few months after that. However, I know the location in space to an accuracy of perhaps one or two yards, because I recall I was facing the kitchen extension of the house, with the living room to my right. Unlike documents saved on a computer, my memory lacks a time stamp, and only our most recent short-term memories may really have a direct connection to our perception of time.

Episodic memories are little stories that tell who, what, where, and only by implication when. They are narratives that can be communicated from one person to another.[29] Indeed, the human mind functions largely in terms of narratives, in which a protagonist (such as yourself) seeks to achieve a goal that requires overcoming challenges, often with the aid of other people. Thus, the quests in World of Warcraft are models of human action. Among the great frustrations of life are incomplete lines of action, like quests that remain in the WoW quest log week in and week out, without being completed. My grandfather lived his early teenage years during the early 1880s in a cottage high on a Rhode Island hill, overlooking the sea. His family moved away, he completed medical school, the years passed, and finally in 1911, he was engaged to be married and brought his bride back to the cottage on a voyage of nostalgia. Asking her to wait for a moment, he ran into the barn and retrieved a toy he had left there decades before. All those many years, the desire to retrieve that toy had festered in his own personal quest log, and now he was able to complete it.

*Citizen Kane*, a movie fictionalizing the life of newspaper tycoon William Randolph Hearst, tells the story of Kane's life from the perspective of a journalist trying to understand his last word, spoken at the moment of death: "Rosebud." The journalist never learns what the audience sees in the film's last frames, that Rosebud was the most meaningful object in the protagonist's early life, a sled that represented his lost youth. These old stories are reminiscent of a WoW quest series in which Catullus retrieved the painting of Tirion Fordring's beloved family, which led to Tirion's reunion with his son, but only a moment after his son had been killed. Tirion's tale of damnation and redemption is told here in chapter 8.

While a good case can be made for the claims that time is a function of consciousness, and that consciousness is fragmentary, there exist competing conceptions of time based in classical physics and contemporary information science. When H. G. Wells wrote his tremendously influential science fiction novel *The Time Machine*, in 1895, time was conceptualized as the fourth dimension.[30] Today, cosmological string theorists suggest there might be eleven dimensions, not merely four, the majority of them far stranger than the three that define our perception of space. But if time is the fourth dimension, why can't you simply travel along it? This raises a contradiction: When you travel along a spatial dimension, you consume time to do it. What do you consume when you travel through time?

Inspired by seventeenth-century philosopher René Descartes, classical physics was in the habit of graphing any measurable quality in terms of a dimension, whether or not it really involved a direction in space. Graph the height of a hundred people against their weight, and you have a two-dimensional graph, in which one (height) is one of the three spatial dimensions, and the other (weight) represents the nonspatial dimension of mass. I like to joke that we social scientists are richer than the physicists because we have hundreds of dimensions.

As I mentioned earlier, the main section of my 1978 science fiction questionnaire consisted of 125 items, each of which asked the respondent to rate how much he or she liked a particular author on a seven-point scale. Mathematically, each of these scales can be treated as a separate dimension. For example, I could graph the 595 respondents in terms of how much they liked H. G. Wells versus how much they liked Jules Verne. Indeed, there turns out to be a strong correlation between these two ratings; people who like Wells tend also to like Verne. So, the author preference data gave me fully 125 dimensions, one for each author, although some of them were "leaning" toward each other and thus might be combined. Factor analysis is a method for finding a smaller number of dimensions in which the data can be graphed while minimizing the error.

My best factor analysis gave exactly four dimensions. The first was the kind of science fiction often called *hard science*, stories based solidly on real physics or other hard sciences, with an emphasis on logic and plausibility, usually rather optimistic about the ability of technology to make a better future. The second dimension was what was called the *New Wave* at the time, fiction closer to the humanities and social sciences, concerned with psychological conflicts or literary style, and rather pessimistic about the future of technology. The third dimension was the *fantasy cluster*, a set of related genres—like action/adventure, sword and sorcery, and horror and weird—that believed the world was awash in magical forces and that saw hope in the heroic actions of individuals rather than in scientific and technological progress. This is the genre of World of Warcraft, but note it is a dimension of science fiction rather than being completely unrelated to science and technology. We see more of this connection in chapter 3. The fourth dimension of science fiction, appropriately enough, turned out to be *time*. It was anchored by classical writers like Jules Verne and H. G. Wells.

Two features of Wells's classic *The Time Machine* deserve to be mentioned here. First, the time traveler is primarily an observer. There is no evidence that his actions taken a few hundred thousand years in the future influence the world he finds a few million years later, and, except for returning to his own time, he does not enter the past. Second, the human society he finds in the future is fractured into two classes or species. The Eloi, who seem to be the descendants of the upper classes from our society, are beautiful but stupid, indolent and passive, whereas the cannibalistic Morlocks maintain the machines that sustain the society and are presumably descendants of the working class. The novel, therefore, has elements of sociopolitical allegory, employing the metaphor of time travel to criticize the social arrangements of 1895. The novel ends with the death of the last living thing on Earth, thus driving home the question of whether we today have the power to steer history in a different direction.

This is where the other conceptualization of time, based on information science, enters the equation. A computer goes through a series of calculations, starting with input and producing output. Suppose it adds seven numbers: $1 + 2 + 3 + 4 + 5 + 6 + 7$. The result will be 28. Can we run this process in reverse? Suppose we told you that 28 was the result of a set of mathematical instructions—an algorithm. Given 28, could you tell us what the input was? No, you cannot. Perhaps the input was $4 \times 7$. Wrong. Now we give you a clue: The input consisted of seven digits. Perhaps, now you say, the input was $4 + 4 + 4 + 4 + 4 + 4 + 4$. Wrong again. Now we give you a different clue, saying the seven digits were all different from one another. Perhaps, with some measure of frustration, you say the input was $7 + 6 + 5 + 4 + 3 + 2 + 1$. Yes, we say, but you have the digits in the wrong order. How can you possibly guess what order they were in?

This is a simple example of the informatics way of distinguishing the past from the future. The past implies a unique future, but the future does not imply a unique past. Sometimes this is stated in terms of the theory of entropy, which bridges between information science and physics.[31] Entropy is a measure of the loss of information that takes place over time in the universe as a whole, which is equivalent to the idea that differences like those in temperature across different regions of the cosmos eventually even out.

While an individual WoW character may progress upward from level 1 to level 80 over time, progress for the virtual world as a whole is very difficult. When running one character, I often needed to repeat a quest already completed by another. Tanya Krzywinska describes this timeless quality of WoW:

Complicating both linear chronology and the sense of being in the world in temporal terms, some aspects of the game have a rather complex recursive time structure; you may, for example, have killed the dragon Onyxia, but you will still find her alive in human form as Lady Katrina Prestor in Stormwind Keep at the side of the human boy-King, and encounter her repeatedly in multiple visits. In this sense, the game does not have a consistent linear chronology; as with retellings of myths, battles are fought over and over again, and in this there is a cyclical organization of time—a kind of "eternal recurrence," to use a phrase from Nietzsche.[32]

However, the world of WoW does change, notably every Tuesday morning when server maintenance is carried out, in the frequent upgrades when parameters are tweaked and a new instance may be added, or at the two major expansions: The

Burning Crusade and Wrath of the Lich King. A visit to Stormwind Keep on December 21, 2008, revealed that young Andruin Wrynn was no longer king, but a prince, and he stood beside his father, King Varian Wrynn, not Lady Katrina Prestor. The only other named character in the throne room was Emissary Taluun from the Exodar, who joined the alliance at the time of the Burning Crusade expansion in early 2007. King Varian Wrynn had been missing for years, until he washed up on the Durotar shore in late 2008, just in time to play a key role in the defense of Stormwind when the Lich King attacked. He had been a victim of amnesia, a catastrophic loss of memory comparable to erasure of a computer's hard disk, but he was eventually able to recollect this lost information.[33]

On the evening of Monday, November 10, 2008, after weeks of probing raids, the Lich King's forces attacked both Stormwind and Orgrimmar—and naturally, I had characters in place to observe both battles! King Varian led the spirited defense of Stormwind from the expansive harbor, which had not been accessible before that time, whereas the Horde leader, Thrall, suffered a measure of disgrace and played only a secondary role in what followed. On November 13, invasion ships began leaving Stormwind to attack the Lich King's bases on the previously inaccessible Northrend continent, and zeppelins began flooding from Orgrimmar to do the same. One of my level-70 characters joined nearly a hundred other members of his guild in assaulting Northrend as a spearhead battalion. Thus, historical shifts can happen in World of Warcraft, despite the technical difficulties they can pose for a game-world that constantly welcomes new players, and that cannot possibly change in response to all their individual actions.

At the beginning of 2006, WoW added the first of a series of world events, episodes that require great effort from players but lead to a substantial change in the world. This was the opening of the Gates of Ahn'Qiraj in the high-level Silithus zone, which was accomplished separately on each realm (server) through extensive quests and attacks against the insect Silithids.[34] Another example is the addition of the Quel'Danas Sunwell Isle between the two major expansions, on which the Shattered Sun Offensive slowly made real progress against the legions of Kael'thas. More recently, several localities in Northrend are designed to change as the result of just one individual player's actions—although other players will not see the changes until they themselves have made them happen. For example, when first visited, the Shadow Vault in the top-level Icecrown zone is held by the Scourge, but completing a series of quests captures it for the invasion force.

Information technology has a way of surprising us, just when we thought we had everything figured out. The principle of entropy may apply to the universe as a whole, but it need not apply to small parts. Indeed, inside a computer, travel backward in time may really be possible. If you back up your data periodically, you can "back up" in time by means of reboot, reset, or restore. You cannot save the current state of the universe because you would need memory storage larger than the universe to contain the information. But in principle you could preserve, rewind, and relive World of Warcraft.

## Time Travel Quests

Time travel appears at several points in World of Warcraft. Notably, the Plaguelands were affected by dislocations in time. When Maxrohn entered the inn at the ruins of Andorhal, he found it in a condition as decayed as the rest of the town, except for one room upstairs that was untouched by the ravages of time. There, he met Chromie, who looked like a cute little female gnome but was actually a dragon in disguise, a member of the bronze dragonflight led by Nozdormu, the Aspect of Time. She gave him quests such as A Matter of Time that required luring fifteen temporal parasites through a temporal rift, and destroying them. Sometimes, too many of these huge, pink slugs would attack him, and when he tried to run away they slowed his time frame to reduce his chances of escape. Another of her quests, Counting Out Time, required finding five watches in the ruins, all frozen at 3 o'clock, reminiscent of the clocks of Hiroshima, that ceased counting time at the instant a hundred thousand people died. Eventually, Chromie explains, the watches Maxrohn gave her will naturally return through time dislocations to the point in time and space where he found them.

To very advanced characters, around levels 72 and 80, Chromie offers two connected Northrend quests, Mystery of the Infinite and Mystery of the Infinite, Redux. They bring together two versions of the player's character from different points in time to help each other penetrate a time storm and learn the identity of the leader of the Infinite Dragonflight, who maliciously seeks to alter time. The Hourglass of Eternity seems to indicate that it is Nozdormu himself, but Chromie dismisses this heretical idea immediately, failing to realize that only he could both know the nature of his own future doom, and strive to change the past to avert it.

Partly out of nostalgia for many lost opportunities in the past, and partly to connect his personal transformation to the broader flow of time, Maxrohn arranged to reach level 60 in Chromie's room. Prior to the January 2007 expansion, level 60 was the maximum possible, so it was an important benchmark. In the ruins of Andorhal, near the inn, he destroyed several Undead minions of the Scourge, until he was very close to leveling. Then he lured a soulless ghoul into Chromie's room and destroyed it before her very eyes, beginning with a blast of holy fire.

Chromie implied that those who sought to travel through time to change history were mistaken: "While the past is set in its ways, the future is always changing. The decisions you make in the here and now help guide that change." However, in another of her quests, the possibility arises that it is possible to change the past by influencing the future's interpretation of earlier events. Perhaps the saddest encounter of Maxrohn's adventuring was when he found Pamela Redpath, the ghost of a little girl, lurking in the blasted ruins of her home. At her request, Maxrohn found the scattered remnants of her doll and returned it to her. Then she sent him in search of her aunt Marlene and uncle Carlin, each of whom initiated a quest series; the series intertwined in the hope of saving Pamela's father, Joseph Redpath, not from death, because it is too late for that, but from corruption and dishonor in the Battle of Darrowshire.

At Marlene's command, Maxrohn took the wedding ring of Joseph Redpath to Chromie, who tells him to retrieve the Annals of Darrowshire, which contains the story of the battle. Chromie uses her magic to add pages to this book, thereby rewriting history. When Carlin reads these pages, he requires proof, so Maxrohn must undertake other quests to find physical evidence in the form of relics. Eventually, he takes them to Chromie, who says that if he places the relics in the town square of ruined Darrowshire, the battle will be refought, leading to Joseph Redpath's honorable death. Maxrohn finished all these quests alone, except the last one, which requires five players. After several failed attempts to organize a group for the Battle of Darrowshire, he gave up, keeping the quest unattended in his quest log for several months.

Maxrohn returned to the Plaguelands at level 70 for one last try. He placed the relics, stood back, and prepared to call upon all his hundreds of hours of experience to complete this group quest alone. Gradually, the warriors of the battle appeared, including Joseph Redpath, but they were translucent ghosts, rather than the solid bodies one might expect from physical time travel. Several times Maxrohn faltered, but he preserved Redpath past the point at which he would have been corrupted, and began to lose only when he was facing the final enemy. At the last instant before defeat, a level-56 female Draenei mage named Skyance appeared on the scene quite by accident and assisted Maxrohn, apparently out of the goodness of her heart. A few moments later, he was able to tell Pamela that her father had been saved. History had been changed, if not time. Pamela's father was still dead, as Pamela herself was, but now he had died honorably.

For Catullus, the most impressive time-travel experience in WoW was the rescue of Thrall in the Caverns of Time instance. Intruders, who appear to be dragons of unknown origin, are trying to change the course of history by reaching back seven years to the moment when Thrall escaped from Durnholde Keep, with the help of Taretha. They have kidnapped Taretha, thereby preventing her from playing her assigned role in history. If Thrall cannot escape, most Orcs will remain in Human captivity, the modern Horde cannot be created, and all major historical events will turn out differently. Because he was a member of the Horde, Catullus naturally has no doubt that Thrall must be liberated, so he and four companions enter the Caverns of Time, travel backward seven years, and enter Durnholde Keep in disguise. With difficulty, they liberate Thrall and escort him out of the fortress, killing many enemies along the way. Rather than rush off to free his fellow Orcs, however, Thrall rides to Tarren Mill in search of Taretha, seeking her in the church but finding her captive in the inn. Terrible struggles with her captors eventually free Taretha, who greets Thrall with respect and fondness. Once history has been restored, tragically Taretha and Thrall lose all memory of the events, and she must return to Durnholde Keep to suffer beheading.

The mutability of computer time was illustrated by the fact that Catullus needed to do this instance twice. The first time was fully successful for him and three of his companions, but one member of the group had failed to get the escort quest from Thrall, and thus did not get credit for the success. Disappointed, this person asked Catullus to help her try again, so they recruited three other people and repeated the effort, this time quite familiar with what to do but thoroughly exhausted. The computer term *instance* is used to describe the caverns, because several copies may exist simultaneously in a single realm, with different teams at different points during this roughly two-hour activity. Instances, therefore, represent separate timelines, in which somewhat different events unfold.

I personally found the Caverns of Time remarkably impressive. The scene represents about half of one of the most familiar WoW zones, Hillsbrad Foothills, surrounded by impenetrable mists. Because the time is seven years ago, buildings that I had come to know as ruins were in mint condition. The Horde town of Tarren Mill is dilapidated today, but was pristine then. Disguised as a Human, Catullus was able to visit the Alliance town of Southshore, attending a meeting at the inn where he met Tirion Fordring before his disgrace and exile, and overheard the local elite discuss weapons that might be used in the coming wars. Now, of course, those wars are over, and their immense cost in lives can no longer be prevented. The subjective experience of traveling back in time and seeing earlier days in a well-known place was thoroughly exhilarating.

The most time-consuming example of time travel is not a quest series or instance but the The War of the Ancients trilogy of WoW novels by Richard A. Knaak.[35] Ten thousand years ago, the unified Elven civilization ruled a single continent in a vast sea. Queen Azshara and her Highborne elite were not content to draw spiritual energy from the Well of Eternity but foolishly sought more power by magically assisting a fallen Titan named Sargeras in entering the world, accompanied by his Burning Legion. Opposing them were three heroes of WoW legend: Malfurion Stormrage, his brother Illidan, and the women they both loved, Tyrande Whisperwind. Because Elves do not age perceptibly, she still lives today in the Temple of the Moon in the Night Elf city Darnassus.

The novel sends three minor characters from the present back in time—Krasus, Rhonin, and Broxigar—to assist Malfurion in defeating the Burning Legion, but at the cost of a cataclysm that split the continent apart. It is said that North America is drifting away from Europe at roughly the speed that a person's fingernails grow, due to the continental drift on Earth discovered a century ago by Alfred Wegener,[36] but the separation of the land on the WoW planet caused vast sundering of land and peoples in a matter of hours. The visible remnant today of the area around the ruined Well of Eternity is the huge Bay of Storms in the zone named after Azshara, but a swirling maelstrom in the center of the ocean between the continental fragments proves that the forces of the well have not dissipated even after ten millennia.

Historical events described in the trilogy of novels are not identical to those given in other WoW sources, notably the actions of the three time travelers. There are three plausible explanations. First, the books are historical novels, and a convention of that literary genre is to tell the story of historical figures from the perspective of secondary characters who cannot be found in the historical record. That allows the author to give these characters adventures beyond those experienced by the real historical figures.

Second, the novels may supersede earlier sources in the process that the creators of serial fiction call *retcon*—retroactive continuity—the replacement of earlier assumptions by later ones, in order to produce the most appealing recent episodes. A famous example of retcon was when Sir Arthur Conan Doyle brought Sherlock Holmes back from the dead, because his readers demanded more stories. Robert J. Sawer's remarkable short story "You See But You Do Not Observe" suggests that Doyle's manipulation of fictional events actually upset the entire real universe, preventing humans from discovering extraterrestrials.[37]

Third, the presence of the time travelers may have changed history, for example, making possible the victory of the Burning Legion, which they themselves must then prevent. One of the time travelers, the Elf mage named Krasus—who also was a transmuted dragon—became disoriented: "The mage no longer knew what was a part of the original history and what had been altered by his interference."[38] This may be how all time travel paradoxes end, or indeed, all meditations about the meaning of time, with the confounding of fantasy and reality.

When Catullus first entered the Caverns of Time, the Custodian told him, "There are only two truths to be found here: First, that time is chaotic, always in flux, and completely malleable[,] and second, perception does not dictate reality." It is terrifying to think that the Custodian may be correct. Perhaps the universe really is a manifold of possibilities, a Twisting Nether, in which a chain of random events gave birth entirely by chance to intelligent beings who wrongly imagine there is something profoundly meaningful about their lives. We are the children of chaos. The fact that everything is in flux does not give us the power to create the future merely by imagining it. Indeed, even the most vigorous, concerted action may be incapable of mastering the chaos.

**Epilogue: Decline of the Trolls**

When Papadoc, the Troll priest, first visited the Echo Isles off the southeast coast of Durotar, he was deeply saddened by what he saw. The terrain itself was beautiful, dotted with palm trees, around which tropical birds circled, and even the local tigers added their brown and orange colors to the scene. His sadness came from beholding the ancient ruins that spread across the islands, and the primitive huts of the barbaric Trolls who inhabit this site of their ancestors' former glory. The ravages of time have scattered the stones, which were incised with hieroglyphs that no one can read today, but here and there an arch or a wall still stands. A colossal head stares out to sea, one red eye suggesting that the sculptures may have been brightly painted originally. Stylized malachite statues of tigers imply that nature may not have changed much, despite the decline of the Troll civilization. The modern huts are made of tree branches, raised above the ground to ward off bugs and rats. Instead of rebuilding their ancient town and temple, the lazy inhabitants toy with Voodoo and allow themselves to be hexed by their witch doctor chief. Perhaps it would be easier to travel back in time and prevent the fall of Troll civilization than to convince its primitive descendants to become civilized.

# 3 Religion

I am Lunette of the Night Elves, priestess to the Moon goddess, Elune. Having reached the twentieth level, graduated from the starting zones of my race, and undertaken a great adventure, I take this opportunity to reflect upon the many spiritual blessings I have received through my service to Elune.

While I am tolerant of the other peoples of the world, I pity them for their ignorance of Elune. She is, in fact, the only deity, as the other faiths openly admit through the fact that they cannot name a living god, nor do they worship one. To be sure, the primitive Tauren revere their Earth Mother, but she is merely the superstitious personification of the Earth's ecology, and not a fully developed deity. I have some respect for the Humans and others oriented toward the Holy Light, but I pity them for lacking any god or goddess. The Light has no personality, no will, no awareness. How can one have deep feelings about an abstraction that itself has no feelings? I have visited the Cathedral of Light in the Human capital of Stormwind, and I find it a peaceful place to meditate. But it completely lacks sacred symbols, and its light gray walls of stone do not speak to me. Contrast that with our many hieroglyphs of the Moon, the sacred owls, the moonwells, and the stones sculpted with spirals that symbolize both Elune and the great trees.

Ah, yes, the trees! The greatest of all is Teldrassil, the immense tree that forms the island on which I was born and that holds our capital city, Darnassus. Our architecture blends into the trees and is built in the flowing shapes of natural wood. Giant walking trees called the Ancient Protectors patrol the main roads of Teldrassil. These marvels would not be possible had Elune not nurtured a close relationship with nature. At the very least, the trees should prove to any skeptic that Elune actually does exist, not as a belief but as a reality. The flag of our nation shows a broad tree reaching up toward the Moon, and the Moon bending her bow down to embrace the tree. We Elves are like trees ourselves, tall, lean of limb, and connected together spiritually like the many branches of a family tree.

I pity most of all our estranged kinsmen, the Blood Elves. They no longer worship Elune, having become fascinated by the technical aspects of magic and selfishly using it for their mundane advantage rather than seeking to gain spiritual insights through restrained practice of spells. A constant challenge for me has been to ponder how to reunite these two twigs of the same branch that have grown in such different directions. We belong to the Alliance, and they to the Horde. One result is that we speak different languages, and thus cannot engage in economic exchange with each other except through the impersonal auction houses and cannot even send each other written messages. Unity will need to grow on the spiritual plane.

I recall with great satisfaction that one of my earliest duties as a novice priestess was to collect small samples of holy water from all around the island. Tenaron Stormgrip told me, "The moonwells hold the waters of the Well of Eternity, the ancient source of magic that has wrought so many horrors upon our world." He then sent me to the moonwell north of Aldrassil to partially fill a crystal phial (see figure 3.1). This I took to Corithras Moonrage at the moonwell in Dolanaar, who told me some of the gloomy history of our race's tribulations. Moonrage then gave me three phials to obtain water from other sacred sources: a jade phial for the moonwell at Starbreeze Village, tourmaline for the one near the Pools of Arlithrien, and finally amethyst for the Oracle Glade. When I returned from these brief

**Figure 3.1**
Lunette, a priestess of the moon goddess, Elune, at a moonwell on the Night Elf island, Teldrassil.

quests, he reminded me we had long ago lost direct aid from the supernatural dragons, saying, "Without the blessings of Alexstrasza the Life-Binder and Nozdormu the Timeless, Teldrassil's growth has not been without flaw." He mixed the waters together, symbolic of the unity of our tree-borne land as well as magically effective, and asked me to take a filled vessel to Arch Druid Fandral Staghelm in Darnassus, giving me my first opportunity to visit the capital city of the Night Elves.

From Darnassus, I voyaged to Darkshore, where I gained my first experiences on the Kalimdor mainland. There I carried out quests for two Elven gentlemen I met who were oppressed by tragedy. One was Cerellean Whiteclaw, whom I found brooding by the side of the dock, as he apparently had been for a very long time. Originally, of course, Elves were strictly immortal, but even today we live as long as many lifetimes of the ephemeral Humans. Thus, grief is rare but lasting. Cerellean's beloved, Anaya, had been killed when Ameth'Aran was devastated in the wars after the destruction of the Well of Eternity. Her spirit still haunted the ruins of that city ten thousand years later. He begged me to set her spirit free. I found her there, surrounded by the ghosts of Highborne Elven women, the perfidious upper class that we banished from Kalimdor seven thousand years ago, and I focused a barrage of lethal spells upon her.

When I returned to Cerellean with her pendant, a miracle occurred. Her spirit appeared before us, and the two lovers conversed one final time upon this planet. Cerellean asked Anaya if she hated him for having me destroy the specter that was her last living form. She replied, "Let it not trouble your heart, beloved. You have freed me from slavery, and for that I love you all the more." Then she departed this world, bidding her love farewell until he should join her in the beyond.

The other tragic figure was Asterion, a mage who had been imprisoned for centuries in a shrine surrounded by moronic sprites and depraved satyrs. I helped him seek the cause of his imprisonment, eventually discovering that one of the satyrs had found the ancient moonstone seal that the leading Highborne mage, Athrikus, had used to bind Asterion. I took it to the same ruins where I had found Anaya, and there destroyed it in a holy blue flame. Asterion's last words to me were "Already my feelings of hopelessness will give way into thoughts of vengeance." Thus, I had used my spiritual gifts to liberate two men whose spirits had been trapped in the past—one by love, and the other by hate. How many of us are similarly the prisoners of grief, revenge, or guilt?

An especially traumatic episode for me was when two Blood Elves, our kinsmen but enemies, killed me. I was trekking along the main north-south road in Ashenvale, when I received a message that the zone was under attack, but it did not say where. A few minutes later, when I was just north of Maestra's Post, word came that here was the exact point of attack. I rushed to the scene and found they had assaulted Lilandris Moonriver, a level-42 Night Elf. The Blood Elves were two paladins, one level 26, and the other 28, so she was able to hold them off. But I was concerned for her safety, and immediately began applying my limited healing powers, hoping her two attackers would see the futility of what they were doing and desist. Because I had taken her side in the struggle, I was no longer protected by the truce between the Alliance and the Horde. I was only level 19 at the time, so when they attacked me, they easily killed me.

I regained consciousness at a graveyard, and my spirit ran back to my corpse. When I resurrected, I found that Lilandris was perfectly all right, and her Blood Elf attackers had gone. I searched the campus and discovered that they had killed Delgren, the Purifier, who, like me, had been only level 19 and thus easy prey for them. I did my best to resurrect him, but my powers were insufficient, so all I could do was weep over his body. Not seeing the two Blood Elf paladins around, I climbed the observation tower, and spotted them just at that moment returning, as if they intended to attack Lilandris again! I rushed over to the entrance of the main building and found them confronting her, but they had not yet actually begun their attack. As I reached the entrance, so did a level-24 Draenei paladin, a member of our alliance, so we had the Blood Elves outnumbered, and they slunk away. The Draenei commented, as if he knew the rage rising in my soul, "They're garbage."

But how could he know my shame? Unlike me, the Draenei was not tortured by the rift that split Elves into the two factions, Night Elves in the Alliance, and Blood Elves in the Horde. He could not understand I was profoundly mortified by our alienation from our own kin. As the unholy pair left, I made a rude gesture at one, laughed at the other, and shouted: "Elves should unite!" The first of them yelled in the Orcish language, "*Rega osh'kazil.*" The second yelled, "*Zug zug. Nogah.*" Our shame extended to the appalling fact we did not even share a language! The Draenei yelled, "*k e k,*" because the Alliance believes this translates into Orcish as "lol" or "laugh out loud." I rather lamely said, "*k e k*" as well, but in my heart I resolved to find some way to heal the rift between the two factions of our race.

## Religion in the Social Sciences

Among the most sensitive of topics, religion has traditionally been handled with great care by social scientists. The result has generally been a polite discussion that preserved mutual respect but failed to make much scientific progress in understanding the topic. In recent years, however, new developments in sociology, anthropology, and cognitive science have added energy as well as unpleasantness to the debate. Here we follow the controversial principle that the fictional religions in World of Warcraft actually can teach us much about the facts of religion in the real world. Consider the following four theories:

**Supernatural theory**  Divine beings actually exist, and religion is the direct result of their action upon the souls of human beings.

**Societal theory**  Religion is a reflection of society, functioning to sustain societal institutions, community unity, and shared values.

Exchange theory  Humans interact with one another to get rewards and avoid costs, based on socially constructed beliefs, and when a valuable reward cannot readily be obtained, they will encourage one another to believe in divine exchange partners.
Cognitive theory  The human brain evolved to facilitate social interaction and to deal with predators or prey, so it naturally assumes that complex phenomena result from the actions of aware beings, incidentally favoring belief in gods.

The supernatural theory, of course, is the theory that believers in a religion apply to their own faith. It does not preclude the possibility that social scientific research can learn something interesting about how church congregations or religious institutions operate, as purely social phenomena, but it assumes that science has no role in explaining religion or evaluating the claims of their faith. Consider the remarkable fact that every WoW player sees magical phenomena practically every day in Azeroth, and that many of them have the actual power to resurrect deceased characters. Thus, while the truth of religious beliefs is controversial in the surrounding world, within WoW there can be no doubt.

The second theory, called either societal theory or functional theory, is more ambivalent. This has been the traditional theory in the sociology of religion since Émile Durkheim propounded his version of it a century ago, but usually in diluted form.[1] Durkheim himself seemed to imply that religious beliefs are always false because God is merely a metaphor for society in his formulation of the theory. When a priest says that God prohibits such and such, he really means that society does, and our only real hope for immortality is the good memories of us that remain in the minds of our survivors.

However, after Durkheim's own death in 1917, functionalism adapted to the implicit demands of the surrounding society and retreated from the troubling idea that religious beliefs might be valuable but false. Thus, it was easy for many scholars of religion to combine in some way the first two theories, believing that religious beliefs were true and that the human institutions of religion served the needs of the society. For many years, this was the dominant theory in religious studies, which after all was staffed largely by religious scholars. In the 1960s, functionalism lost plausibility in sociology, both because empirical research failed to give very much support to its assumptions and because many critics argued that societal institutions supported the interests of the power elite more than of the society at large. However, functionalism remained influential in religious studies, and the field became rather stagnant.

The third perspective, exchange theory, became prominent in social science in the 1980s, through a series of publications by me, Rodney Stark, and students who rapidly developed to become our peers and colleagues. Stark and I published three books together presenting this perspective, *The Future of Religion*, *A Theory of Religion*, and *Religion, Deviance and Social Control*.[2] Working solo, I published two intensive field studies of radical religious movements, *Satan's Power* and *The Endtime Family*, plus three conceptual overviews, *The Sociology of Religious Movements*, *Across the Secular Abyss*, and *God from the Machine*.[3] The last of these, published in 2006, is based on artificial intelligence computer simulations, almost as if I were creating a community of WoW NPCs, then watching them develop their own religious cults. Exchange theory is especially relevant here because it focuses on social, economic, and communication interactions like those that take place in WoW.

As I conceptualize the theory today, it applies the computer-science concept of "algorithm" to human life. An algorithm is a set of instructions for achieving a given goal in a finite period of time. When you do a long division by hand, you are following an algorithm. But when you bake a cake, you follow an algorithm, too, although we traditionally call it a *recipe*. An algorithm has a series of steps that often must be followed in a particular order. If you cook the eggs first, it will be hard to mix them with the flour and milk for the cake; the ingredients must be mixed before baking rather than afterward. One of Rod Stark's favorite jokes is in a cartoon of Hagar the Horrible that shows two rather glum Vikings standing before a flaming town, as one angrily corrects the other: "It's loot *then* burn! Loot *then* burn!" That's an algorithm.

In exchange theory, religion arises not from supernatural beings, nor from the needs of society as a whole, but from interactions among individuals. In pursuit of desired rewards, humans exchange rewards with other humans. Indeed, this is a fundamental human algorithm: "When in need, seek help." To get help, we often have to be willing to give something in return, either now or at some time in the future.

Humans seek many kinds of rewards, some of which cannot readily be obtained by any lone individual. Rewards like food or fun get used up and must be sought again and again. Thus, we learn to seek particular rewards through exchanges with particular other individuals or categories of people. Someone who is a frequent source of rewards, and to whom we give rewards in return, is an exchange partner. When we need a reward of a particular kind and cannot readily provide it for ourselves, we go to a valued exchange partner, especially one who has provided similar rewards in the past.

Human action is directed by a complex but finite information-processing system that functions to identify problems and seek solutions to them. We commonly call it the *mind*. One very important kind of reward is information about how to obtain a desired reward. This is another way of saying that algorithms can be valuable, and humans often seek them. Frequently, the best source of information is another person. Thus we have the algorithm: "When in need of an algorithm, ask a valued exchange partner."

It would be nice if we always got what we wanted, but only a spoiled child expects that to happen. Some desired rewards are limited in supply, including some that simply do not exist. Rewards that do not exist at all are unavailable even to rich and powerful people. A familiar example is eternal life. Man, that would be rewarding! At least we imagine it would be. Both inequality and unavailability create frustration. However, it is impossible to know for certain that a given reward does not exist.

In the absence of a desired reward, people will often accept algorithms that explain how to get the reward in the distant future or in some other context that cannot be immediately verified. These algorithms are *compensators*, in that they compensate the individual psychologically for lack of the reward. Typically, they are promises that the reward can be obtained.

Rewards vary in terms of how specific or general they are. Correspondingly, some compensators are relatively specific, for example, promising the cure of a particular disease or providing compensatory esteem for low status in society. Other compensators are more general, such as the hope for eternal life. Stark and I found it useful to distinguish magic from religion in terms of the specificity of the compensators they provide.

*Magic* is defined as specific compensators that promise to provide desired rewards without regard for evidence concerning the designated means. *Religion* is a system of general compensators based on supernatural assumptions. Both are based on faith, but magic requires faith only in one specific situation, whereas the scope of religious faith is vast. Thus, the defining difference between magic and religion is the generality of the compensators they offer. There is no categorical dividing line between the two, they blend into each other, and religion historically arose on the basis of earlier magic. These points are worth emphasizing because the difference between magic and religion is subtle in World of Warcraft, as it actually also was in the history of the real world. Modern religious denominations tend to distance themselves from magic because magical beliefs can often be disproven—for example, when a witch doctor manifestly fails to cure a disease—and clergy need to protect the faith of their congregations.

The fourth general theory of religion, the cognitive theory, has several variants, but the most influential ones argue that religious faith is a cognitive error. Of all the theories, this one is the most hostile to religion. Although cognitive science is a new field, and cognitive theories of religion arose only in the past decade, Sigmund Freud's psychoanalytic theory is a precursor. Freud and his disciples viewed religion as an illusion, a shared neurosis or even a shared psychosis, involving infantile wish fulfillment.[4] When humans are small children, they cry to their parents for help. An adult enduring pain or grief will spontaneously cry, regressing to the instinctual habits of childhood. A mature adult either has seen the death of his or her parent, or has learned to view them as relatively helpless elderly people. Humans displace their desires for infantile nurturance onto imaginary parents, such as God the Father, or in some traditions the Mother Goddess. Psychoanalysis claimed it could cure neurosis, and the psychoanalytic movement implied it could cure religion by helping people mature beyond their childhood complexes, to deal with the world the way it really is for adults, rather than as children.

Ironically, modern cognitive scientists dismiss Freud as a hack or a pseudoscientist, even as they emulate his disdain for religion.[5] Two variants of cognitive theory especially deserve mention, one focused on God, and the other on the human soul. Belief in God may merely be the result of a human propensity to assume that some kind of person is responsible for any complex events that occur. In prehistoric times, our remote ancestors evolved the cognitive ability to think in terms of another person's perceptions, feelings, and intentions. Most animals cannot do this, and our ability to do so may account for a major section of our larger brains, essentially wired in to our neurons. Pascal Boyer writes, "Our minds are not general explanation machines. Rather, minds consist of many different, specialized explanatory machines . . . more properly called *inference systems*."[6] The human inference system devoted to what many cognitive scientists call *mind reading* was tremendously useful, allowing us to predict the behavior of predators, prey, and partners. Belief in supernatural beings, from this vantage point, represents hyperactivity of this mind-imputing function of the human brain. This is the idea Justin Barrett uses to answer the question in the title of his book *Why Would Anyone Believe in God?* Humans have a "hypersensitive agency detection device" in their brains, defining an agent as a "being that does not merely respond mechanistically to environmental contingencies but initiates action on the basis of internal, mental states."[7]

If God is an illusion, so is the immortal soul. As Boyer notes, our brains appear to be complex assemblages of components serving different functions, including numerous inference systems. Thus, the sense of being an integrated consciousness may be false, perhaps nothing more than a reflection of how small our short-term memory is.[8] Paul Bloom explicitly says the idea that humans have souls is a delusion, resulting from the fact that the brain is not aware of its own operation.[9] Warlocks in World of Warcraft see direct evidence that souls exist, because they need to collect soulshards from dying enemies to be able to summon occult minions like the big blue voidwalker or the seductive succubus. But too many residents of the real world have watched elderly relatives lose fundamental attributes of their personhood to senility, leaving them to wonder how impoverished an immortal soul can be.

The nearest thing to a theory of religion presented inside World of Warcraft is the description offered when a player is getting ready to create a new priestly character: "Priests guide the spiritual destiny of their people. Through their unique insight into the mind, they are able to shape an individual's beliefs, whether to inspire or terrify, soothe or dominate, heal or harm. Just as the heart can hold both darkness and light, priests wield powers of creation and devastation by channeling the potent forces underlying faith." Note that some words sound like magic, but this description describes something grander than the mere magical cure of a disease or two. This sounds rather psychological, referring to how a priest may influence a believer's mind, suggesting either exchange theory or cognitive theory.

However, there is a place in Kalimdor, a mountaintop near Crossroads in the Barrens and directly west of Wailing Caverns, that expresses a religious hope, not in words but images. There, the Shrine of the Fallen Warrior is a memorial with the runic initials MK, standing for Michel Koiter, a real-world artist who died unexpectedly of heart failure at the age of nineteen, in 2004, while helping to create World of Warcraft.[10] Over the monument hovers a spirit, of exactly the form that provides resurrection in graveyards but unable to resurrect, identified with the name "Koiter" (see figure 3.2).

Imagine, for a moment, that the most heroic players of WoW earned a special right to be reborn within Azeroth. When one of them died, a suitable NPC would be renamed after the deceased person, or would take on the identity of that person's

**Figure 3.2**
Participants from the May 2008 scientific conference, celebrating the life of Michel Koiter, at the Shrine of the Fallen Warrior.

main character. Furthermore, imagine we are twenty years in the future when artificial intelligence techniques can realistically emulate the person's playing style and allow the NPC to become a posthumous playing character. Opinions may differ, of course, about what a person fundamentally is and what would constitute an afterlife. Speaking entirely for myself, I would consider a continued existence for my main WoW character, behaving as I would behave if I still lived, as a realistic form of immortality. This train of thought brings us to the brink of a radical realization: Ultimately, virtual worlds may evolve into the first real afterlife, not merely critiquing religion but replacing it.

## Elven Elune Religion

The worship of Elune is what social scientists call an *ecclesia* or an *established church*. For the Night Elves, it is the one official denomination, demanding adherence from all members of the society. Kings can be found in throne rooms of both Stormwind and Ironforge, but Darnassus has no throne room. Rather, high priestess Tyrande Whisperwind can be found in the Temple of the Moon. As her WoWWiki article explains, she "is the high priestess of Elune, Mother Superior of the Sisters of Elune and the official head of the night elf government." Night Elf culture lacks the concept that there should be a state separate from the church; the government is theocratic.

A classic quiz question asks the contestant to name the longest legitimate word in the English language: antidisestablishmentarianism. This jawbreaker means being against the separation of church and state. All Night Elves are antidisestablishmentarians. Indeed, it is hard to see what state exists among the Night Elves, apart from the complex relationships between the priesthood of Elune and the Cenarion order of druids, which we consider as a possible separate denomination in the section on Druidism.

In a journal article about World of Warcraft, Tanya Krzywinska explains that the mythic richness of WoW gives it the cultural depth needed to qualify as a genuine world:

The Night Elves for example worship the goddess Elune, and sickle moons, the totem of Elune, are carved on the walls of many of their buildings. Night Elf characters have a range of voice emotes (activated by the player and heard in the game) that invoke the goddess Elune, such as their cheer: "Elune be Praised!" (accompanied by some rather wild arm waiving). It is only in those races aligned with a nature-based worldview, such as the Night Elves or Tauren, that the druid class exists. The Night Elves are aligned with real-world symbolism relating to the moon and the use of nature-based magic, assigning the race its cosmological worldview and activating a mythologically resonant frame of reference.[11]

When Etacarinae visited the Temple of the Moon in Darnassus, none of the Night Elves actually exclaimed, "Elune be Praised!" This phrase may have been removed from WoW, along with wild arm waving, because it is more in style with a revivalist sect than a dignified ecclesia. Etacarinae did hear the following five religious blessings: "Elune light your path." "Elune be with you." "May the stars guide you." "Goddess watch over you." "Goddess bless you." Priests in an ecclesia have a monopoly on at least some sacred knowledge, which therefore a student priest must acquire. As priest trainer Laurna Morninglight said to Lunette, "Teaching young priestesses the ways of Elune gives me great satisfaction." A sect, in contrast, often has lay preachers, and every member can learn all the sacred teachings without the need to become clergy.

Two of the standard sociological theories of religion seem to fit Elune worship especially well: the supernatural theory that the religion is factually true, and the societal theory that the religion serves essential functions for the society. After all, a newbie Night Elf sees ample proof of the ancient legends in Teldrassil island, a gigantic tree holding the Night Elf newbie zone and Darnassus city a thousand feet above the ocean. It must be impossible for a young Night Elf to doubt the faith when she first sees one of the Ancient Protector giant trees walking along the road near Dolanaar, and other walking trees in abundance elsewhere.

The functionalist theory would emphasize how adherence to an ancient tradition could sustain a unified society in the face of disruptive historical events. Classical French sociologist Émile Durkheim argued that God is merely a symbol for society, so Elune would represent the Night Elves themselves. It is noteworthy that Night Elves have silvery eyes, a reflection of the silvery Moon, helping them see themselves in Her. Wherever there are Night Elves, across the vast geography of the four continents, there are moonwells reflecting the light of the Moon, symbolically connecting their race and hearkening back to the Well of Eternity that used to confer immortality. The tapestry of symbols around them constantly reminds Night Elves they are the superior race, with the most ancient and stable civilization. As Richard Knaak writes, "Elune offered the night elves strength and confidence, for she was always there in the heavens, watching down on her favored children."[12]

There are actually two moons in the sky over the Night Elves.[13] The brighter one, called the White Lady, is associated with Elune. The dimmer one is called the Blue Child, reminding one of the expression "once in a blue moon." An anonymous comment in WoWWiki reports, "For some reason, the 'Blue Child' is not visible in WoW, it once was but was removed from the game."[14] In the sanctum of the archivist, in the corrupted city of Stratholme in the Plaguelands, there is a picture clearly identified as the two moons. The painting shows two round celestial bodies, one partially covering the other, and it appears to depict the planet Jupiter as seen from a point in space just beyond one of its moons, perhaps Europa. Removing this painting to find another painting hidden underneath is the goal of the quest called Of Love and Family. Indeed, the painting shows the lost family of the quest giver, Tirion Fordring, and thus suggests that beneath all our myths lies the emotional reality of lost love.

A functionalist would note how Night Elf religion strengthens respect for the natural environment, thereby preserving the world in which their society lives. At Aldrassil, only a few paces from where she entered the world, Lunette saw a modest circle of stones arranged around the statue of an owl. A white light glowed in one of the stones, suggesting it was a sacred place for Elune, and three other glowing, ethereal lights reinforced a feeling of transcendence. Possessing the spiritual sensitivity of a priest, she concluded that owls were sacred to Elune, and soon she encountered real owls flying peacefully through the Teldrassil air.

When Lunette was still only level 6, and thus innocent in the ways of the world, she encountered a quest giver named Zenn Foulhoof, who promised to make her very happy if she would bring him three nightsaber fangs, three swatches of webwood spider silk, and three strigid owl feathers. This alerted Lunette that something was wrong, because she could not get the feathers without killing owls. She saw several other clues that Zenn was not legitimate. First of all, because he was a satyr he looked rather like a devil. Second, he commented rather suspiciously, "Lucky for you a day never goes by that I don't wish I had a fledgling priest to perform my bidding." The last straw for his credibility fell when he insisted she "keep this our little secret, night elf." Had Lunette done this trick quest, she would have gained 450 experience points but become an enemy of Teldrassil, and Zenn would have exclaimed, "Three cheers for the naive and gullible!"

Respect for nature does not mean that Night Elves cannot kill animals. Rather, they need an appropriate reason to do so. Lunette's very first quest had an assignment from Conservator Ilthalaine to kill nightsabers and young thistle boars, not to serve some selfish motive but to reestablish the balance of nature. Ilthalaine explained that heavy rains had caused some species in the forest to multiply at the expense of others. Later, a half deer, half woman named Tarindrella, serving as woodland protector, sent her to determine if creatures called *grells* had become tainted. When we English-speaking humans personify nature, we tend to use the feminine term *Mother Nature*. Elune is similar to Mother Nature, but elevated above the Earth so that she, herself, cannot be corrupted. Elune is the eternal, nurturing feminine.

The fact that the Temple of the Moon is run by priestesses, not priests, emphasizes that Elune is a female deity, although male characters can become priests. Indeed, while male characters may enter the temple and are treated equally, every NPC in the temple is female, including the numerous Sentinel guards. It is worth noting that all seven Night Elf priest trainers in WoW are female.[15] In contrast, just three of the five Human priest trainers are female, only one among the six Dwarf priest trainers, and none among the five Draenei NPCs that serve this function. Female religious teachers are rare but not unknown in the Horde: two of the four Blood Elves who teach religion and one of the five Trolls. The situation among the Undead is debatable because while all five conventional priest trainers are male, a sixth trainer is the female banshee

Aelthalyste, who at level 60 is equal in rank to the top male Undead priest trainer, Father Cobb. The male Undead priest trainers all appear to be former Humans, but Aelthalyste appears to be a former High Elf.

For the present discussion, the most striking comparison is with druid trainers. All eleven Night Elf druid trainers are male, whereas four of the seven Tauren druid trainers are female.[16] Thus, while gender opportunities in religion vary across races, among the Night Elves there is a nearly complete separation of the genders, females worshiping Elune directly, and males doing so indirectly as part of the Cenarion druid movement. The one glaring exception is the fact that there are two arch druids, one of each gender. Arch Druid Staghelm runs the movement from his tower high above the Cenarion Enclave in Darnassus, whereas the female arch druid, Renferal, appears to be suffering some kind of exile in the distant and largely inaccessible Alterac Valley battleground.

## Druidism

In pre-Christian western Europe, druids were a priestly class, reportedly revering nature and capable of divination. The ancient Roman Cicero was personally acquainted with a druid named Divitiacus, reporting: "He claimed to have that knowledge of nature which the Greeks call 'physiologia,' and he used to make predictions, sometimes by means of augury and sometimes by means of conjecture."[17] Caesar said of the druids he had seen in Gaul, "Beyond all things they are desirous to inspire a belief that men's souls do not perish, but transmigrate after death from one individual to another; and they hold that people are thereby most strongly incited to bravery, as the fear of death is thus destroyed."[18] Sadly, we know little about the real druids of yore, and modern attempts to revive Druidism are based largely on hopes rather than knowledge. For example, it would seem unlikely that druids had anything to do with building Stonehenge and similar standing stone monuments I have seen in both Britain and France, because these are more than a thousand years older.

In WoW, Druidism is an ancient religious movement among the Tauren and Night Elves exclusively. It is connected to the Elune faith of the Night Elves, which is unknown among the Tauren, and may be an offshoot of it, in the same manner that Christianity is an offshoot of Judaism. Concrete evidence of this connection is the fact that Moonglade, one of the zones of Kalimdor, is managed jointly by both Night Elf and Tauren druids, and druids of both races can teleport to Moonglade whenever they wish. The Night Elf influence predominates in Moonglade, and we can speculate that the movement arose among the Night Elves, then spread to the Tauren, with some mythological simplification along the way.

Among the Night Elves, Druidism could be described as a messianic religion, because it arose historically from the ministry of a charismatic Night Elf, Malfurion Stormrage.

Here, exchange theory fits especially well because messiahs mediate between a deity and the mass of humanity, almost like middlemen in an economic system. Legends tell that "Furion" was trained in the beliefs and methods of Druidism by a demigod, Cenarius, who dwelled in the great forest in harmony with nature and had the form of a manlike stag. In Moonglade and at Stonetalon Peak, a Night Elf outpost maintained by druids, can be found sons of Cenarius, half stag and half Night Elf. The Tauren claim they were taught Druidism directly by Cenarius, rather than by Furion. It is worth noting that centaurs are the hereditary enemy of Tauren, half man and half horse, and gods often have attributes of an enemy as well as savior. As already noted, the organization of Night Elf druids is described as Cenarion.

Competing views exist about the parentage of Cenarius. His father was a white stag named Malorne by the Night Elves or Apa'ro by the Tauren. The official version, given in the encyclopedia for the WoW card game, says, "Cenarius is the son of Elune and Malorne."[19] One debate concerns the identity of the mother of Cenarius. Some say his mother was Ysera, one of five dragons which the Old Gods left to rule the world after they had created it.[20] Others say that Elune herself was the mother. Still others reconcile these claims by saying Elune gave birth to Cenarius but wanted him to live on Earth rather than in the heavens, so Elune gave Cenarius to Ysera to be raised. In any case, dragons are central to WoW Druidism, as well as the Moon. Note that Lunette received much of her earliest training from Corithras Moonrage, who instructed her about two of the dragons, then sent her to visit the arch druid.

As author and dragon enthusiast Richard Knaak notes, "Among the elves, it had been said long ago that there were five great dragons, five leviathans who represented arcane and natural forces."[21] Sometimes called the Five Aspects, they are Alexstrasza (life), Ysera (dreaming), Malygos (magic), Nozdormu (time), and Neltharion (earth).[22] As so often happens in WoW mythology, Neltharion became corrupted by the lust for supernatural power, becoming Deathwing.

The transformational episode in Furion's training was when Cenarius taught him how to walk the Emerald Dream.[23] This is Ysera's domain, a plane of existence separate from but influencing the world of WoW. It is the same world, but without any history of habitation by intelligent creatures, so it is uncorrupted: "Nature is in perfect balance in the Emerald Dream."[24] By walking the Emerald Dream, one may gain understanding of our own world and its relation to eternity, even traveling swiftly to another region of our world.[25] Such travel is dangerous, however, because it is possible to become trapped in the dream, unable to return to waking consciousness. This is the current fate of Furion, who is believed to wander the Emerald Dream near the Stormrage Barrows in Moonglade, but who may return in a time of extreme danger, again to be the savior of his people.

When she was only level 2, Adalgisa, the Tauren druid, received a note inviting her to begin instruction from Gart Mistrunner in Druidism. It said they would discuss "nature, the spirits, the Earthmother, and even the night elves." Much of her training in fact concerned practical spells, like Moonfire to burn the enemy, Mark of the Wild to strengthen a friend's armor, and Rejuvenation to heal.

While taking druid training at level 10 from Turak Runetotem on Elder Rise in Thunder Bluff, Adalgisa learned to read the cloth books of lore that hung around the vast tent. One passage helped her understand the Tauren context for her faith: "The Earthmother's eyes shone down upon the lands she had breathed into creation. Her right eye, An'she (the sun), gave warmth and light to the land. Her left eye, Mu'sha (the Moon) gave peace and sleep to the stirring creatures of the dawning." Other passages described her creation of the Tauren upon the land, then their wandering into wickedness. Unable to bear the sight, the Earthmother tore out her two eyes and sent them spinning across the sky. Another legend told how a proud stag was chased by the Tauren, then leaped into the sky to escape them. There he mated with Mu'sha, the Moon, and she gave birth to Cenarius. This demigod taught Druidism directly to the Tauren, without any intermediary like Malfurion Stormrage among the Night Elves. This difference reflects the fact that Elven civilization was more complex and bureaucratic, and operating on the basis of elaborate exchange networks, in religion as well as in commerce.

## Shamanism

It is said that all societies possess religion, but faith was far less formal before the rise of the great world civilizations established state religious bureaucracies. In so-called primitive or tribal societies, theology was not codified, and a host of alternative supernatural beliefs and practices existed. This *archaic stage* in the evolution of religion is represented within World of Warcraft by shamanism, which is practiced by the Tauren, Orcs, Trolls, and Draenei. The Tauren and Orcs lack priests because their cultures have not yet evolved beyond shamanism. Although the Trolls are a largely tribal society today, they once possessed a high civilization, so both primitive and advanced features mark their culture. Historically, the Draenei had developed an advanced technological civilization, but after the profound disasters that brought them to this world, a revivalist movement arose to rediscover the shamanistic roots of religion. As fellow members of the Horde in the same general geographic area, the Tauren, Orcs, and Trolls share the same brand of shamanism. Therefore, one of our Tauren research team members, Minotaurus, will represent Horde shamanism. Draenei are trained in shamanism through an entirely different set of experiences on the distant archipelago they currently inhabit, so we need a second character, Etacarinae, to complete the picture.

The Trolls are the only Horde race with both shamans and priests, and the religion practiced by their priests seems like a kind of spiritism. Although some Trolls say, "Stay away from the Voodoo," this may be the form of religion they practice privately while concealing the fact from their allies, the Orcs. Papadoc's first priest trainer, Ken'jai, said to him when he had reached level 4, "Ah hope da spirits have protected ya thus far, mon." The spirits had told Ken'jai that Papadoc was coming, and the training involved learning to control the spirits, "but only if da spirits agree." Soon afterward, Papadoc earned some juju hex robes. We consider Trolls more closely in chapter 7, on identity, rather than speculating about the differences between their shamanism and priestly traditions here.

The fundamental principle of shamanism in WoW is personification of the elements of nature. In particular, a shaman must come to terms with beings representing the four primary elements in the following order: earth, fire, water, and air. Tauren provide the best example because they are the indigenous inhabitants of their land rather than refugees like the Orcs and Trolls, so their culture has suffered less disruption. Tauren shamanism exists side by side with a mythology based on deification of the Earth that could possibly evolve in the future into a state church.

The description on the character-creation screen begins, "Always the tauren strive to preserve the balance of nature and heed the will of their goddess, the Earth Mother." Lunette and many players wrongly assume that only Night Elves possess a deity. Thus, Tauren shamans undergo two parallel sets of initiation rites, one to allow them to "commune directly with the elements," as the same screen explains, and the other to become adults in harmony with the Earth.

The first thing one notices, when being born at the Tauren newbie area, Camp Narache, is that their architecture is reminiscent of the cultures of the indigenous people of the western United States and Canada, or at least the simplified popular image of those cultures. Many structures are large, conical tepees, made from hides stitched together with thick leather thongs, as one imagines the Navajo or Plains Indians using (see figure 3.3). Here and there stand totem poles, like those of the people of the northwest coast, such as Tlingit, Haida, and Kwakiutl, described a century ago by the classical anthropologist Franz Boas.[26] Boas was a leading proponent of *cultural relativism*, which in its extreme form claims that all cultures are equally good, which functionalists often interpret to mean that very different kinds of religion are best designed to support social solidarity in societies experiencing very different conditions of life.

Tauren training in both work and religion is nature-oriented and initiatory, consisting of a number of stages of work punctuated with rituals. Indeed, the hallmark of primitive religion is that it is integrated with the other institutions of life, and that common principles ideally permeate all of a unified and coherent culture. Chief Hawkwind said to Minotaurus, "All members of the tribe share in the harmony of life."

As anthropologist Ruth Benedict demonstrated in her book *Patterns of Culture*, preliterate cultures differ greatly in terms of how intellectual versus experiential their

**Figure 3.3**
Bloodhoof Village, a Tauren settlement, showing affinities with Native American cultures of the Plains and northwest coast.

magic and religion are.[27] Nineteenth-century pre-existential philosopher Friedrich Nietzsche had already distinguished *Apollonian* (emotionally cool and individualist) from *Dionysian* (emotionally hot and collective) cults, and numerous other writers have made similar points, from Sigmund Freud (obsessive versus hysterical) to philosopher William James (tough-minded versus tender-minded), to anthropologist Anthony F. C. Wallace (control-oriented versus liberation-oriented).[28]

The training of a Tauren shaman could be described as Dionysian or even psychedelic because it requires drinking consciousness-altering liquids that allow the future shaman to communicate directly with the elements from which the world is formed. For many members of the counterculture of the late 1960s, the most effective vehicle for the fundamental idea is Carlos Castaneda's novel *The Teachings of Don Juan*, in which the author claims to have visited a Yaqui Indian sorcerer and gained an entirely new perspective of reality after ingesting psychedelic mushrooms.[29] After completing his initiations, Minotaurus received magical totems that could be used for offense or defense, but during them the emphasis was on seeing the elements in a new way and making them part of one's inner being.

Like the Night Elves, the Tauren devote great energy to environmental protection, specifically trying to block the polluting activities of technically more advanced people that had invaded their Mulgore homeland. Goblins working for the Venture Company tainted the sacred water sources, so Minotaurus collected the materials for cleansing totems, and then applied them to the Winterhoof, Thunderhorn, and Wildmane wells. When Minotaurus had cleansed the second of these, Mull Thunderhorn told him, "Ancestors of the Thunderhorn clan spoke to me in a dream, praising you for your actions near their well." He was told to stop a Dwarf archaeological expedition by breaking their picks. As Blaine Bloodhoof says, "They think secrets lie in the earth, and that is true, but hollowing and defiling the land is no way to earn its teachings." In completing these quests, Minotaurus of necessity killed many Goblins, their hirelings, and many Dwarves.

In her WoW novels, *Rise of the Horde* and *Lord of the Clans*, Christie Golden has defined *shaman* in contrast with *warlock*. Since ancient times, shamans had been the spiritual leaders of the Orcs, but the amalgamation of separate clans into the first version of the Horde was accomplished by a conspiracy centered in the Shadow Council led by Gul'dan. Dissatisfied with the extent of magical power available to him, he sought a "power that is not dependent upon the whim of the spirits of air, earth, fire, and water. Power such as that is feeble. It is not reliable. It can desert you in the middle of a battle and leave you helpless."[30] Through discipline and deceit, Gul'dan created an elite corps of former shamans who had direct power over their magic, calling them *warlocks*.

Shamanism "required a give-and-take relationship between the elemental powers and those who would wield them."[31] Warlocks, in contrast, gained the power to command supernatural minions to do their bidding without complaint.[32] The price, ultimately, was the loss of balance in the world, and abandonment by the nurturant powers of nature.[33]

The ultimate Horde leader, Thrall himself, was trained in shamanism after he escaped captivity and began to unite the Orcs. Initially, Thrall did not understand that there were fundamentally different kinds of magic. Grom, his friend and adviser, enlightened him:

Sometimes the effect is the same. For instance, if a shaman was to summon lightning to strike his foes, they would be burned to death. If a warlock was to summon hell's flames against an enemy, they would be burned to death. . . . But, lightning is a natural phenomenon. You call it by requesting it. With hell's fire, you make a bargain. It costs a little of yourself. . . . The warlock's way was quicker, more effective, or so it seemed. But there comes a time when a price must be paid, and sometimes, it is dear indeed.[34]

Thrall's spiritual tutor, the great shaman Drek'Thar, explained that a shaman's powers were based on a "primary agreement with the elements":

I am granted these things because I *ask*, with respect in my heart, and I am willing to offer something in return. I request only the barest needs for myself and my people. At times, I ask great things, but only when the cause is just and wholesome. In return, I thank these powers, knowing that they are borrowed only, never bought. They come to me because they choose to, not because I demand it![35]

Again, shaman and warlock characters inside the game are constrained by strict rules. Shamans use mana to power their totems, and warlocks expend soulshards to summon minions from the plane of reality called the Twisting Nether. The rhetoric of elite shamans and warlocks may differ, but it is not clear that the fates or ethical systems of rank-and-file characters belonging to these two classes really differ.

While Orc and Troll shamans have essentially the same experiences as Tauren, the same cannot be said for the only Alliance race that has shamans, the Draenei. The sudden crash of the spaceship carrying the Draenei on an archipelago of islands disrupted nature, but it also marked the fall of their prior civilization. They developed an interest in shamanism in part as an antiquarian attempt to recover their own distant past, and perhaps also to reestablish a proper relationship with nature, because their culture had long since evolved away from a shamanistic connection to the elements.

Etacarinae at first took a purely anthropological interest in shamanism. She was especially pleased to learn the language of the indigenous Stillpine Furbolgs as a narrowly linguistic exploit. Then, the Stillpine allowed her to pay homage to their sacred totems of Coo, Tikti, Yor, and Vark. Remarkably, after the first of these she was told to leap from a high cliff in the direction of the second, when angel's wings miraculously sprouted from her shoulders and allowed her to glide safely across. Like many anthropologists, she became sympathetic to "her tribe," and helped the Stillpine in many ways. They in turn wondered if she might be the Promised One to fulfill the Prophecy of Akida: "A hero will rise—not of furbolg blood—and save the Stillpine tribe."

Experiences like these did not erase her intellectual fascination with the anthropological approach, but they did orient her toward the profound and practical aspects of her own people's shamanism. She listened carefully, during her Call of Earth quest, when the Spirit of the Vale said, "The earth beneath your feet forms the foundation for all things. The sky, the waters, even great fire—all rest upon its shoulders. While those others often form chaotic tempests, the earth abides. It grants strength and fortitude to the core of your being." *Earth Abides* is the title of an influential 1949 apocalyptic science fiction novel, derived from Ecclesiastes 1:4 (New King James Version): "One generation passes away, and another generation comes; But the earth abides forever."[36] The Call of Fire quest required Etacarinae to burn a wicker man effigy—fire represents both destruction and renewal—and burning a wicker man was reputed to have been a ritual of the ancient European druids. Thus, in rediscovering her Draenei traditions, she also rediscovered our own.

## The Holy Light

In different degrees, the religion of the Holy Light is practiced among Humans, Dwarves, Draenei, the Undead, and even Blood Elves, all of whom have priests. It is the most secularized of the WoW religions, making the fewest demands of faith. While many social scientists have argued that religion may vanish altogether in technologically advanced societies,[37] a currently more plausible view is that religion will persist, but largely demythologized, individualistic, and rational.[38] That seems to be what has happened for Human religion in World of Warcraft, but it is also possible that the reality of the supernatural in the WoW world has caused religion to return to its magical roots, which ironically may bring it closer to modern science.

Depending on one's perspective, the Holy Light is either deeply mysterious or merely vague, but the word *light* certainly carries spiritual connotations. When we say, "I have seen the light," we tend to mean we have gained a new awareness, realized the nature of a mistake, or come to agree after a disagreement. Many images carry the metaphoric connection between light and wisdom: enlightenment, a flash of insight, and the lightbulb that traditionally appears over the head of a cartoon character who just had an idea. Light may also be a beacon that guides us, a torch that illuminates our path, or a warning sign of danger ahead.

In his WoW novel *Tides of Darkness*, Aaron Rosenberg describes the Holy Light in terms like those used for the Force in *Star Wars*: "The Holy Light, after all, resided in every living being, in every heart and soul. It was everywhere, the energy that bound all sentient beings together as one."[39] The analogy with *Star Wars* suggests there might be a Dark Side to this force, but how can one aspect of light be darkness? Perhaps the light at the end of the tunnel is an onrushing train.

To religious Christians in the real world, the light is provided by God or by his agent, Jesus Christ. For example, on January 2, 1891, my great-grandmother Lucy knelt to pray, in a mood of dark despair.[40] Her clergyman husband had abandoned his job as leader of the Brooklyn City Mission Society and all his ministerial duties, to work obsessively writing a grand book in sacred linguistics that would never be published, and Lucy's two children now had no one to support them. Thus, in her own words, she sought "light unto perplexity."

At the very depths of her agony, she sensed someone standing over her. A reporter for the *New York Times* later heard her describe this moment to a Christian audience:

"I was in great perplexity what the Lord wanted me to do. One day I was alone on my knees, and I fancied—strange fancy, you may think—I saw our personal Savior standing before me. 'Wait,' he said to me, 'wait and you shall know what to do.'

"At the very moment I was on my knees," continued Mrs. Bainbridge, while the room was hushed in silence, "Mrs. Brown, Superintendent of the Women's Branch of the New York City Mission, died suddenly. Next day her place was offered to me!"[41]

Lucy had no doubts of the reality of this epiphany, as she later told the mission ladies:

It was not a dream that came to me in a distant city, on the very afternoon of Mrs. Brown's translation, when, kneeling and alone, pleading for light upon perplexity, the Savior stood for a moment visibly at hand and spoke the needed words of comfort. But such experiences are not for the world, and can only be hinted at for the encouragement of our sisters, who sit with us around the same hearthstone of the household of faith, and to whom we repeat the text.[42]

The contrast with the religion of the Holy Light could hardly be greater. The religion has neither god nor savior. Being trained as a priest of the Holy Light generates flashes of light, but this is true of all magical training in WoW. It is said that God always answers prayers but sometimes the answer is "no." At the Cathedral of the Holy Light in Stormwind (see figure 3.4), no one prays. If anybody did, the answer from Heaven would be a recorded message: "Nobody home."

While he was on the Hellfire Peninsula, Maxrohn had in his hands a book titled *Mysteries of the Light*, but he was not permitted to read or copy it. A drunken priest named Malgor Devidicus had asked him to retrieve it from behind the Expedition Armory, which had been overrun by unyielding souls who refused to stop fighting despite having been killed already during the past twenty years of battles. The book was lying on the front step of a ruined house, not far from where the edge of the planet was crumbling away into gravity-free floating boulders and mountains, the very limit of organized reality. The priest had read the book many times, then lent it to a friend who died in the wars. Maxrohn was unable to learn anything about the book's content from its besotted owner.

As Humans practice it, the religion of the Light has been hollowed out of all divine significance and consists merely of a collection of magical spells connected to an ethical creed. An encyclopedia oriented toward the card game version of World of Warcraft says the religion of the Holy Light "is a faith that advocates purity, goodness, kindness and compassion in the face of adversity."[43] Elsewhere, the three cardinal virtues are said to be respect, tenacity, and compassion.[44] Respect must be granted to an enemy, even when killing him, and tenacity must be practiced even in the face of one's own death. Thus, the religion of the Holy Light is a highly secularized faith, expressed as an ethical code essentially devoid of supernaturalism.

**Figure 3.4**
Maxrohn, a Human priest, rededicating himself to the Holy Light, in the cathedral at Stormwind.

The Dwarves have a very down-to-earth view of religion, and are said to have fallen away from an earlier faith in the Holy Light. At level 2, Lusea received a letter from Branstock Khalder, her future priest trainer, speaking of the Light and faith in very practical terms:

With the Holy Light warmin' our backs and new discoveries being made every day, 'tis an exciting time to be one of Ironforge's daughters. The Explorer's League makes headway every day in its search for long-lost answers to even older questions. And now we have you among our faithful to aid in the battle against the troggs and any other threat to our borders.

In this day and age, it is hard to believe that any ancient knowledge could be of practical value, unless it is the religious teachings contained in an ancient book, like the Bible.

For the Forsaken, death is not a mystery but a grim reality they have personally experienced. This is an extreme example of the fact that inhabitants of Azeroth do not need religious faith, nor do they speculate about distant deities, because daily they experience the supernatural directly.

For Blood Elves, the Light is a source of power more than of ethics, aesthetics, or spiritual enlightenment. Matron Arena, Catullus's first priest trainer, told him the way of a Blood Elf priest was not a "path of pacifism," despite the priest's healing role, but often was "a fist of vengeance for those who would transgress against us." She further observed, "The Light gives us the strength and magic to triumph." In Silvermoon City, Catullus heard Initiate Emeline say, "When I was younger, I never once thought of manipulating the powers of the Light this way. What a fool I was." Priest trainer Aldrae in Sunfury Spire repeated the mantra to him, "The Light gives us the strength and magic to triumph." The priest's salon there is nearly identical to the Mage salon on the other side of the foyer; both are supplied with many books and laboratory instruments for the control of supernatural powers.

The early training received by Catullus stressed both the benefits of magic and its dangers. Arcanist Helion reminded him that knowledge is power but warned, "Control your thirst for magic. It is a thirst unending, Catullus." Another time, Well Watcher Solanian warned, "You must master your insatiable hungering for magic before it masters you." As the introduction to the Knaak-Kim graphic novel *Ghostlands* explains, "Grieving for the loss of their homeland, most high elves have adopted a new name and a new mission. Calling themselves blood elves, they now seek out and siphon magic from any available source, including demons."[45]

Thus, in the Humans and the Blood Elves, we see two possible directions a highly secularized religion can take. Neither values a personal relationship with God, and both take it for granted that people should exploit magic for their own purposes. The difference is that Humans try to limit their use of magic under the constraints of a set of ethical rules, whereas Blood Elves will do whatever it takes to increase their power. To translate this debate into terms appropriate for the so-called real world, one need only translate *magic* as "science and technology."

## Magic

As classical anthropologists like Bronislaw Malinowski and E. E. Evans-Pritchard showed, serious magical beliefs and practices were fundamental features of so-called primitive societies and laid the basis for the religious bureaucracies of modern times.[46] WoW novelist Richard Knaak observes, "Of all the arts, magic truly had to be one of the most contradictory, guided by laws all its own, laws quite changeable at the worst of times."[47] This is true, perhaps, in the real world and in some of the spin-off novels, but only half true in World of Warcraft itself. Magic inside the virtual world follows rigid rules, comparable to those of physics and chemistry in our world, a different but stable set of laws that are not at all changeable.

In part, this is the heritage of WoW, which was powerfully but indirectly influenced by a group of science-fantasy writers associated with the magazine *Unknown Worlds* in the narrow period between 1939 and 1943, including Fritz Leiber, L. Sprague de Camp, and Fletcher Pratt. The editor of *Unknown* was John W. Campbell Jr., who dominated science fiction during its golden age by editing the leading magazine of the field, *Astounding Science Fiction*, still published today as *Analog*. Late in his career, Campbell promoted pseudoscientific technologies such as psionic machines that (supposedly) detected telepathic influences and mechanical levitators that (supposedly) flew through the air without benefit of Newton's laws. Around 1950, he was instrumental in launching Dianetics therapy, which later became the Scientology religion and was created by one of his stable of authors, L. Ron Hubbard. While open to novel spiritual possibilities, Campbell demanded rationality, and he was at least partly responsible for Isaac Asimov's two most potent ideas, the three laws of robots and the idea that psychohistory could chart future dark ages. Science fiction writer and critic P. Schuyler Miller said that *Unknown Worlds* was a marriage of science and the supernatural. Traditional fantasy stories rested on actual belief in the supernatural, but because our culture had lost its faith, Campbell "introduced a fantasy of disbelief to replace the old outmoded fantasy of lost beliefs."[48] Most *Unknown* stories concerned discovering the rigorous, scientific laws by which magic operated.[49]

However, there is a second and more important reason why the magic in World of Warcraft follows rigid laws, rather than permitting free wish fulfillment. Late me state this as an unproven assertion: *No real universe can permit intrusions of supernatural beings or forces, because they would cause escalating chaos and an ultimate disintegration of reality.* Given a lifetime in which to develop a shared perspective and the language to discuss such issues, we might conclude that this was the most fundamental proof that all religions are false. Lacking an opportunity to weigh whether a benevolent God could somehow intervene in reality without destabilizing it, or to consider whether there is any empirical evidence about the rigor of natural law from the quantum on up to the cosmos, we can state a much more modest version of this principle: *A virtual world based on unconditional but consequential magic cannot exist.* The rules of a multiplayer online game must be incorporated into the mechanics of gameplay themselves, because many players will not follow a rulebook, and a system that permits individual players to change the rules will surely crash.

A century ago it was possible for a scientist to believe that spiritual phenomena operated according to a similar set of laws as those governing the phenomena of physics and chemistry. For example, physicist and radio pioneer Oliver Lodge believed that research in these fields would reveal that telepathy was a kind of mental radio, and that the immortal soul was somehow sustained by the ether that was then imagined to permeate the universe.[50] But the typical assumption of primitive magic and religious healing always has been that a willful supernatural being or unreliable nonmaterial process could circumvent natural laws.

The *cognitive* theory of religion expects this, because it understands faith as a cognitive error analogous to wishful thinking. Sir James George Frazer's classic treatise *The Golden Bough* explains the concepts of *sympathetic magic*:

If we analyze the principles of thought on which magic is based, they will probably be found to resolve themselves into two: first, that like produces like, or that an effect resembles its cause; and, second, that things which have once been in contact with each other continue to act on each other at a distance after the physical contact has been severed. The former principle may be called the Law of Similarity, the latter the Law of Contact or Contagion. From the first of these principles, namely the Law of Similarity, the magician infers that he can produce any effect he desires merely by imitating it: from the second he infers that whatever he does to a material object will affect equally the person with whom the object was once in contact, whether it formed part of his body or not. Charms based on the Law of Similarity may be called Homoeopathic or Imitative Magic. Charms based on the Law of Contact or Contagion may be called Contagious Magic.[51]

In fact, none of this is found inside the world of WoW. Jeff Grubb's short WoW-related novel *The Last Guardian* tells the story of Khadgar (a student mage who today can be found in his maturity at Shattrath City in Outland) undergoing training from the greatest mage of all, Medivh. At one point they discuss sympathetic magic, almost as if Khadgar had read Frazer and was reporting on it to Medivh.[52] But characters in WoW cannot create a voodoo doll or charm based on magical similarity or acquire an aura by touching something. The only contagion is that of infectious disease.

This brings us to the paramount principle of real-world physics: the conservation of mass and energy. Matter cannot be created or destroyed but merely transformed from one configuration to another, and one of those configurations we call energy. Notice that magic based on contagion would typically violate the conservation law, whereas similarity involves action at a distance without a wave or medium of communication between cause and effect. Thus, they represent wishes of the human mind, not real phenomena.

At one point, Medivh and Khadgar discuss one version of the conservation issue: "whether when you created a flame by magic, you called it into being or summoned it from some parallel existence." Calling it into being violates conservation, whereas summoning it from elsewhere may not. Medivh claimed that the correct answer was a combination of both: "when you create fire, all you are doing is concentrating the inherent nature of fire contained in the surrounding area into one location, calling it into being."[53]

Rationalizing magic, and encompassing it by natural laws like those that operate in electronic games, normalizes it. But Medivh called magic "the art of circumventing the normal." It is wise to remember what Khadgar did not then know—that Medivh was possessed by Sargeras, the demon who sought to become the god of the world—when reading what Medivh said next, about those who would constrain magic by natural laws:

They seek to place rationality upon the world, and regulate its motions. The stars march in order across the sky, the seasons fall one after the other with lockstepped regularity, and men and women live and die. If that does not happen, it's magic, the first warping of the universe, a few floorboards that are bent out of shape, waiting for industrious hands to pry them up.[54]

Some WoW magic uses equipment, and thus is analogous to engineering technology. Onu, the Ancient of Lore, gave Lunette a phial of scrying, with which she could prepare a scrying bowl to communicate with him as she completed quests. Later, Kayneth Stillwind sent her on a quest for the Chalice of Elune, which worshippers of the Moon goddess believed had healing powers. Much WoW magic uses spells, many of which consume the magical substance, mana, as if it were gasoline or a chemical ingredient. As Ronald Johnstone explains in a standard social-science textbook about religion, the Polynesian concept of "mana" describes a widespread primitive view of the possible source of magical powers:

Mana is a prime ingredient in magic. To those who believe in it there exists in the world, everywhere, and in everything, an elemental force, a primary energy—mana. Mana even exists—it floats, so to speak—in the very air we breathe. Often it is just *there*, not directly attached to anything, simply waiting to be grasped, harnessed, used. Though mana is in people, in things, in animals, in plants, and in the atmosphere, it is impotent until someone or something, or a spirit perhaps, activates it by discovering the secret key that unlocks its energies.[55]

When a WoW character uses mana, it regenerates gradually, somewhat more quickly if the character rests by sitting down. This process could represent the gradual flow of mana from the environment into the character, and yet it has another interpretation: the transmutation of time into mana. In principle, neither of these interpretations conclusively violates conservation of mass and energy. However, characters who are mages can conjure up liquids, using a little mana to do so, then drink the liquid to get a sudden boost of mana. Without doing an extensive research project, I cannot report the exact mathematical functions involved, but conjuring liquids and then drinking them appears to produce much more mana than is consumed, getting something for nothing and violating conservation. There are two reasons, however, which this violation does not cause the game to spiral into chaos. First, the liquids can be drunk only while sitting at rest, rather than in combat as can be done with magic potions, and both conjuring and drinking take time. Second, conjured liquids vanish when the owner logs out of WoW, so they cannot be stored up to the extent that they would damage the economic market for drinks.

Although magical potions can be drunk during combat—replenishing health or mana, depending upon their nature—they cannot be conjured up from nothing but require ingredients that are often costly. To explore this, I had Maxrohn select alchemy as one of his professions, and choose herbalism as his second profession so he could acquire many ingredients directly through his own labor. To achieve the skill level of

375 in alchemy, Maxrohn both mastered transmutation and produced potions of ever increasing power. Before he could do any alchemy, Maxrohn needed a philosopher's stone. The first step was to get the recipe from a Gnome alchemist in Gadgetzan, named Pestlezugg. Then it was necessary to collect the four ingredients: iron bars and black vitriol, which he could buy at the auction house, and two herbs for which his herbalism skill was sufficient, purple lotus and fireblooms.

Alchemy in WoW involves more elements than just earth, air, fire and water, but unlike in the real world does not transform uranium into plutonium. Four additional elements exist: mana, life, shadow, and might. Among Maxrohn's final challenges was to create primal might, using his philosopher's stone to combine the primals of earth, air, fire, water, and mana. Unfortunately, he could make only one unit of primal mana per day, because the philosopher's stone had a cooldown time of twenty-three hours.

High-level ingredients are very difficult to collect, although Maxrohn had amassed supplies from his advanced questing in Outland, and he was forced to spend about two hundred gold coins to buy other materials at the Stormwind auction house to complete his skill development. He accomplished this inside the alchemy supply shop in the Mage Quarter of Stormwind. To reach skill 374, he produced several units of Elixir of Major Defense, each consuming three ancient lichens, 1 terocone, and one imbued phial. Then he reached skill 375 by making a fel mana potion. Drinking this during a fight restores 3,200 mana, but at the cost of degrading spell damage and healing for fifteen minutes. Two herbs are required to make this potion, mana thistle and nightmare vine. Notice that all these procedures are very rigorous, as fanciful as they may be, and involve very little uncertainty.

### Epilogue: Corruption of the Dream

Of all the intense experiences in her druidic training, Adalgisa was most affected by her two expeditions into the Wailing Caverns. Situated near the center of the arid Barrens, these deep caves vent geothermal steam that causes a wailing sound that permeates the passageways and the vaulted rooms where corrupted druids lurk. When Naralex, a Night Elf druid, discovered them, he naively imagined bringing the waters to the surface to irrigate the surrounding dry territory. The only source of power available to him was the Emerald Dream, so he went into a deep sleep to channel its energies. His dream became a nightmare, the waters became corrupted, and his followers were transformed into serpent demons.[56] Nara Wildmane, in the Tauren druid house at Thunder Bluff, gave Adalgisa the quest that sent her on her first expedition. She and her team were asked to assassinate four fanglord druids who ruled the caverns during Naralex's troubled slumbers: Serpentis (serpent), Pythas (python), Cobrahn (cobra), and Anacondra (anaconda). Her second expedition was to waken Naralex and end the nightmare. The lesson that religion can be evil—even her very own religion—was troubling in the extreme.

# 4 Learning

It is said that we Tauren are prisoners of tradition, but I, Minotaurus, enjoy learning new things. It is good to gain skills and knowledge about the world around us, and it is also true that traditions must be learned rather than being born into us. We cannot truly revere our ancestors unless we know and understand them. We cannot properly celebrate the past without building a joyous future. There is an ancient Tauren saying: "gladly learn, and gladly teach."

When I entered the world at Camp Narache in Mulgore, it was raining. Perhaps that was a good omen, suggesting I would have a special relationship with the spirits of the waters. A message, which I can interpret only as guidance from a spirit, told me to speak with the person standing before me, Grull Hawkwind. He said, "You have a promising air about you, and will prove yourself to the tribe." Thus, the very first words I heard identified a second of the four elements, air, which I was sure must be another omen. To begin to prove myself, Hawkwind asked me to help resupply the village by hunting, which I promptly did. He then gave me a note telling me to seek instruction in shamanism from Meela Dawnstrider, whose tent was in the camp.

She greeted me by exclaiming, "As quickly as water falls from the sky, here you are before me." I felt this confirmed my surmise about the water omen, and she went on to explain how important it would be to understand the elements and learn to communicate with the spirits of the Tauren. The instruction was not to learn by reading books and writing examination essays. Rather, I would need to experience chemically induced shamanistic initiations, involving quests to obtain the ingredients.

First, Seer Ravenfeather concocted a sapta drink, "created to bind our spirits to the elements," which I consumed while standing at the shaman shrine on Kodo Rock. A manifestation of earth appeared to me, and taught me that earth is the essential foundation, providing strength, stamina, and patience. The manifestation also explained that the elements are "dual natures, opposing one another."

Not as part of my extensive shaman training but as my early initiation to Tauren adulthood, I performed three rites of the Earthmother. First, in the Rite of Strength, I slew a dozen Bristleback enemies of the tribe. In the Rite of Vision, I consumed the Water of Seers at the tribal fire, whereupon a ghostly wolf appeared to me, howled, and began walking northwest. I followed it to a cave, where I encountered Seer Wiserunner, who praised me for completing the second tribal test. The seer told me, "Travel to Red Rocks east of Thunder Bluff and speak with the Ancestral Spirit."

When I approached Red Rocks, Lorekeeper Raintotem begged me to defend "our sacred burial ground" against Bristleback interlopers. After killing eight of these desecraters, I stood amid the ten-foot-tall wooden frames on which Tauren expose their corpses to the elements, wrapped like mummies. A spirit appeared to me, saying, "We, the Ancestral Spirits, represent the mighty Tauren who gave their lives bravely to found and protect our great city of Thunder Bluff." Having passed the third and last test, I now assumed the sacred duty of a defender of the Tauren people.

Soon afterward, when I reached experience level 10, I was mature enough to undertake the second set of shamanism quests. To learn the call of fire, the principle of destruction and chaos, I was required to trek to the Barrens, territory jointly administered by Taurens and Orcs, and meet an Orc named Kranal Fiss. He sent me to carry an unlit torch into the Orc zone of Durotar, climb one of the highest peaks, and ignite the torch at the Shrine of the Dormant Flame. The keeper of the flame proved to be a Troll named Telf Joolam, who explained that fire also represented life and creation. "Forces oppose one another, but at the same time, one cannot exist without the other." Whereas the manifestation of earth had peacefully conversed with me, the manifestation of fire attempted to consume me.

When I reached experience level 20, Xanis Flameweaver on the Spirit Rise at Thunder Bluff told me, "Long has it been since you were last tested, Minotaurus. You have shown patience thus far in your studies, but the time has come for you to learn more." Islen Waterseer, at the farthest point from Mulgore on the seacoast of the Barrens, told me I must learn the fundamental lesson that "water means rebirth." To accomplish that, I must find Brine in Southern Barrens, then follow her instruction to bring water to her from sources near and far: a pond immediately below her hill, the well in Tarren Mill all the way across the great ocean, and the ruins in Ashenvale back on our continent. Brine then blessed a phial of the water, and told me to return to Islen. She in turn sent me to use a few drops of the water, plus my combat experience, to defeat corrupted manifestations of water in a shrine on the west coast of the other continent, which had become polluted by the plague. Once I had succeeded in completing all those arduous assignments, Islen gave me my water totem.

I imagined that at experience level 30, I would need to undergo an exceedingly lengthy series of quests, even longer than those at level 20, to gain my final totem. But I was mistaken. Searn Firewarder in the Valley of Wisdom at Orgrimmar told me to seek Prate Cloudseer in a small cave on the northern cliff of the vast canyon called Thousand Needles. I wanted to prove myself worthy of the air totem, but after the rigors of the water totem quests I was terrified at the dangers that might lie ahead. To my astonishment, Cloudseer simply gave me the totem, without any further requirements. No quest, no danger, no learning! Then it struck me. This was a challenge even more difficult than all those that had gone before, because it required me to discern entirely for myself what it meant. I sat and meditated for a long time.

Gradually, the realization came to me. The ultimate lesson is how to teach yourself. Earlier, I had followed the instructions of my teachers, to the very last detail, with great dedication. Now, there were no instructions. I must decide for myself what goal to seek and how to achieve it. *Spirit* literally means a breath of air, and the final lesson for my spirit was how to breathe naturally, on my own volition, according to my own nature. All the earlier lessons had required me to learn the rules; this lesson concerned freedom from all rules. I stood and looked around me.

When Searn Firewarder told me where to find Cloudseer, he rather contemptuously said she was "hiddin' in a hole wit' her boyfriend." Firewarder was not merely being prudish, but expressing the widespread view that religious leaders must be pure, and that purity required celibacy. However, if everything natural were sacred, then sexual intercourse between Cloudseer and the man she lived with was sacred, and sullied her purity not at all. I looked for him.

Slightly deeper in the cave, I found him. Named Dorn Plainstalker, he commented, "So, you have sought me out, or perhaps destiny brings you to me? No matter." Yes! That is the insight exactly. The desire that drives me to seek enlightenment, and my destiny, are one and the same thing.

Plainstalker offered me a quest, Test of Faith, which would require me to leap from a precise spot on one of the stone pinnacles that gave this zone the name Thousand Needles. I stood there and looked down, a thousand feet or more, to certain death. I had a choice to step into empty air or not, free as the air to decide either way. Which faith would I test? It was not faith in Plainstalker, nor in ancient Tauren traditions, but in my own intuition. I moved forward, and suddenly I was falling. I fell, seemingly forever, until I saw the rocky ground rushing at me, certain death a fraction of a second in the future. Then, before striking the ground, I was teleported back to the cave with Cloudseer and Plainstalker, perfectly safe. Plainstalker offered me a second quest, to test my endurance, but I declined politely. I had no need to test my endurance, nor my strength or knowledge of lore that could be evaluated by other quests he would offer. For the time being, I had learned everything I needed to know, so it was time to begin to teach.

Once I had completed the quests to gain the totems of all four natural elements, and had gained the enlightenment that allows a mature student to take responsibility for his or her own further development, I was ready to become a teacher. I returned to my point of origin at Camp Narache and was assigned a student to mentor. Her name was Adalgisa, destined to become a druid, a class that has a spiritual quality comparable to that of a shaman like myself. I met her when she first arrived, introduced myself, and gave her a gold coin. I explained that she should learn frugality and that giving her the coin was a test. I hoped to see that she still possessed that coin when we next met, after her initial education. I left her in the trustworthy hands of the druid trainer Gart Mistrunner, who shared a tent with my first shamanism teacher, Meela Dawnstrider.

Adalgisa completed her early training quickly, and she had reached experience level 7 when she joined me at Bloodhoof Village, the town nearest her training grounds, still carrying the gold coin. I suggested she learn the same two professions I had learned many months before, skinning and leatherworking. Skinning is an excellent way to earn money, because one can skin not only the animals one kills in the ordinary course of questing but also the corpses of animals killed by people who lack the skinning skill. Furthermore, both druids and shamans wear leather armor, so leatherworking is a valuable skill to them personally, quite apart from its economic value.

I introduced Adalgisa to Chaw Stronghide and Yonn Deepcut, who made her an apprentice in both these professions. She bought a skinning knife from Wunna Darmane, the trade goods seller, plus some coarse thread. I then gave her some light leather I happened to have in my carrying bags. With four pieces of coarse thread, she was able to make for herself a set of hand-stitched leather bracers and a pair of boots. In her questing, she had looted bracers with an armor value of 15, and shoes with only 5. Her new bracers and boots had values of 21 and 31, so her first efforts at leatherworking had been a great success. This work had also increased her leatherworking skill from 1 to 3, which was admittedly a long way from the maximum of 375 that existed at the time.

Adalgisa then suggested we should both learn something together from scratch, and pointed to a fishing trainer, Uthan Stillwater, who was fishing in Stonebull Lake. That sounded like fun, so we became apprentice fishermen, bought rods and lures from a vendor near the bridge, and stood for a while on a large rock, taking turns casting our lures into the water. Between us, we caught eighteen brilliant smallfish and eleven longjaw mudsnappers, and she also caught a ten-pound mudsnapper. After all her exhausting work, Adalgisa went to the inn to rest. Inspired by Adalgisa's example, I decided to develop my own skinning skill a little bit. So, I traveled to the nearby Tauren city, Thunder Bluff, where I bought some materials from a vendor and the auction house, made myself some new armor, mailed some to Adalgisa, and raised my leatherworking skill from 134 to 145. Learning philosophical insights is uplifting, but learning practical skills is wonderful, too.

Adalgisa joined me at Thunder Bluff, where she received advanced training in Druidism and read some of the books describing the history of our people. We decided she should learn how to travel as widely as possible, giving her the greatest options concerning which quests to accept and which territory to visit. Through travel, she would learn many things, so learning how to travel was learning how to learn. Therefore, I showed her where to pick up the flight path to and from Thunder Bluff. In the Horde, we can ride wyverns, intelligent flying beasts with huge bat wings and features like those of a wolf or lion, but we cannot fly to a destination we have not first reached on foot. Therefore, Adalgisa and I ran to pick up the three flight paths in the Barrens, the zone between Orc and Tauren territory: Camp Taurajo, Crossroads, and Ratchet.

At Ratchet, we took a boat to Booty Bay in Stranglethorn Vale, at the southern tip of the other continents, picking up the flight path there. To get north from Booty Bay, we would need the flight path to Grom'gol Base Camp, but the beasts were too dangerous even for a level 30 like me to walk there, let alone Adalgisa, who was still only level 10. Therefore, we retraced our steps, sailing back to Ratchet, then ran north to Orgrimmar, the Orc capital. From Orgrimmar, we flew on a zeppelin to Grom'gol, where Adalgisa picked up the direct flight path to Booty Bay for future use. We then took another zeppelin to Undercity. The third of the three zeppelins could have returned us to Orgrimmar, but instead we used the Undercity teleporter to visit the Blood Elf city, Silvermoon.

After we had done some sightseeing in Silvermoon, Adalgisa explained that it was time for her to use a special spell to visit Moonglade, for druid training. This zone is unique among the areas of the world, because it is generally open only to members of the druid class. Above experience level 10, they can teleport there whenever they wish. Unable to follow Adalgisa, I wished her good fortune with her druidic education. She activated her spell, brilliant white light beamed from her hands as she held them partly outstretched on either side of her body, then she vanished.

Later, Adalgisa told me that her druid teacher Dendrite Starblaze had instructed her to seek out the Great Bear Spirit and learn about the nature of the bear, so that she would be prepared to take the form of this animal when necessary for her quests and battles. I could never talk with the Great Bear Spirit myself because I am not a druid, but Adalgisa did tell me one of its lessons: "Strength of the body is the power and swiftness of action." It is very good to learn from one's student. Gladly learn, and gladly teach!

## Character Learning

While Minotaurus is by no means unintelligent, he is not an intellectual who doubts, criticizes, and constantly analyzes the alternative positions he might take. Rather, he is faithful, trusting, and comfortable with the traditions of his people. It is worth noting that of all the ten races of WoW, the Tauren have been least affected by the wars, and thus their culture shows the greatest continuity. The Dwarves and Night Elves may be obsessed with their pasts, but the Tauren live theirs. Minotaurus's notion of learning emphasizes transmission of culture from one generation to the next, more than discovery of new ways. Note that he loves an ancient statement about education: "gladly learn, and gladly teach." In fact, these words are more than six hundred years old and can be found in the prologue to Chaucer's *The Canterbury Tales*, where they describe the Clerk from Oxford: "gladly wolde he lerne and gladly teche."[1]

To the extent that our imaginations assign personalities to our WoW characters, their learning can be subtle, but the computational facts are much simpler. When Minotaurus was escorting Adalgisa to get her flight paths, I engaged in some play-acting, pretending she did not "know" where the flight paths were and had never seen

**Figure 4.1**
For World of Warcraft's fourth birthday, each player received a cute Baby Blizzard Bear pet, here learning history from a Northrend warlord.

the places she visited. That may have been true for her as a character, but as a player I had already been everywhere. During their trek, I was in fact running both characters myself, using two computers and two WoW accounts, pretending that each character knew only what he or she had experienced inside the virtual world, during a short virtual life.

Neither Minotaurus nor Adalgisa had ever been to Booty Bay, although several of my other characters had been there, notably Catullus, who had walked there from Grom'gol when he had rather more experience than Minotaurus. The pair of Taurens met the Horde flight master on top of the Booty Bay inn, but they could not fly to Grom'gol because they had not already visited the flight master there on foot. That was the reason they needed to return to Ratchet, walk to Orgrimmar, and take the zeppelin to the camp. When they met the flight master in Grom'gol, they "learned" the flight point. What this meant computationally was probably a simple matter of a "0" being changed to a "1" in a memory register devoted to "Grom'gol flight point."

All the learning by characters takes place through similar simple changes of a byte or two in a designated variable inside the Blizzard database.

The details are not widely known, and there is no point in trying to deduce them. I once did "crack the code" of a video game, *The Wizard of Oz* for Super Nintendo, learning by experiment and logic what codes to put in what memory registers to conquer absolutely every aspect of this admittedly more simple game. Blizzard needs to keep the data on its own server because if players had the data on their own computer they could modify it in order to cheat. The same system applies to virtual objects that a character may gain. Presumably, each object has an identification number, and when that number is in one of the registers devoted to the character's backpack, the object is in the corresponding slot of the backpack. The graphics that display the object and the icon representing it are already on the player's computer disk, but they cannot be used unless the appropriate code has been unlocked.

The most important thing that characters learn is experience, starting at level 1 and ending (during the period of my research) at level 80. If I were programming this, I would use two memory registers. One, consisting of only one byte, would represent the level itself, because one byte can store the numbers 0 through 255. The second, larger memory register would store the number of experience points the character had earned within the given level. Later levels require a much higher number of experience points to complete. At the low extreme, level 1 requires only 400 experience points to finish, and can be done in less than half an hour. At the high end, completing level 79 requires 1,670,800 experience points. The time required to complete the levels does not differ by the same proportion because one earns more experience points at higher levels. At the highest levels, my characters might kill monsters giving more than 2,000 experience points, but even doing several high-level quests, advancing one level can take a couple days.

Of equal importance is learning class skills: shamanism skills, in the case of Minotaurus, and druidism skills, in the case of Adalgisa. As in the example given by Minotaurus, this occasionally occurs through completion of a quest. More often, a character pays money to a class trainer who communicates the instruction by casting a spell. About every two general experience levels, new class skills become available to buy.

Professions are learned primarily by practicing them, gaining higher skill levels the same way general experience is gained, but on occasion also from a trainer or quest. Skill in weapons is gained simply by practice, except that initial training from a weapon master NPC can allow a character to begin learning a new kind of weapon. Most of these forms of learning are limited by the general experience level a character has reached. For example, a rogue cannot advance in lock picking beyond a skill of 95 at level 19, while level 20 imposes a cap of 100. Thus, there is a mechanical quality to learning by characters, while humans may learn in many subtle ways.

One way of describing this is to say that contemporary game characters and NPCs fail to make use of what computer scientists call *machine learning*. Very complex examples of machine learning, such as the more advanced neural networks I employed for the research reported in my book *God from the Machine*, allow an artificial intelligence to learn how to classify entities or actions in their world, determine which courses of action on average lead to great rewards, and make decisions that are informed by past experience.[2]

An example from my own early work is a simulation of a mouse running up a simple maze in the shape of a **T**.[3] The behavior of the mouse was controlled by two memory registers, call them Left and Right. At the start, each register has the number 50 in it. The mouse runs up the **T** and reaches the decision point. Should it turn left or right? The computer generates a random number between 0 and 1, and multiplies it by the sum of the numbers in the Left and Right registers. If the result is lower than the number in the Left register, it turns left; otherwise, it turns right.

On one side of the **T** the mouse gets a rewarding piece of cheese; this adds 10 points to the number in the memory register for the direction it went. On the other side, it gets a punishing electric shock, and 10 is subtracted from the corresponding memory register (down to a floor of 10 points, below which the register cannot go). If you set the cheese on one side and the shock on the other, the mouse quickly learns which way to go. A slightly more complex version has one side (at random) be dark or bright, uses two other memory registers to represent these choices, and makes the mouse pay attention to which dichotomy is more informative, dark/bright or left/right. In fact, the mouse readily learns where you are putting the cheese—left or right, dark or bright—and if you switch the reward and the punishment, it will quickly unlearn old habits and adapt to the new situations.

That is a simple example of machine learning, but there are many other kinds, and WoW does not apparently use any of them, unless possibly in how an NPC decides which of two enemies to fight on the basis of the damage they had recently done to it. Humans have a number of different ways they learn, including different channels through which they gain information and different ways their nervous systems generalize from specific experiences.

Many authors have recently argued that virtual worlds can be excellent teaching environments for real-world skills, and that research on human learning in virtual worlds can tell us about learning in other environments.[4] For example, Anthony Papargyris and Angeliki Poulymenakou of Athens University of Economics and Business have argued that massively multiplayer games can teach many lessons useful in real-world organizations. These include "collaboration and team-work," "negotiating and trading (virtual) resources," "communicating knowledge," "developing and reassessing complex strategies," and "practicing leadership and administrative tasks (project management)."[5] Research on these topics is in its early stages, but for present purposes it is reasonable to assume that there is much to learn about learning from how people learn in WoW.

## Learning to Play

Learning by players is programmed to some extent, but it has many dimensions and degrees of freedom. Early stages of most popular RPGs, whether online or off-line video games, include explicit tutorials to get a player started. For example, when a player of *Castlevania: Lament of Innocence* enters the castle, all the game territory is to the right or straight ahead, while a few rooms to the left are explicitly a training ground. In the case of WoW, all characters start out in a protected area in the least threatening zone for the given race. The nearest beasts are docile, and single high-level characters of the opposite faction cannot enter past high-level guard NPCs.

For the very first levels, as the player moves forward and encounters new kinds of situations, buttons marked with an exclamation mark appear near the bottom of the screen. Clicking on one opens a small window giving a hint, first covering the basics and later addressing slightly more advanced topics. For example, one hint pops up as soon as the first quest has been completed, telling the player to return to the quest giver to receive a reward, and explaining that the quest giver will show up on the minimap when the player approaches closely enough. Another hint urges the player to team up with others and form a group when facing a difficult quest.

Many quests are examples of what might be called *embedded instruction*, training exercises that fit naturally into the gameplay and are not explicitly labeled educational. Some seem especially designed to get the character traveling out into the world and learning how to operate modes of transportation. For example, a young Night Elf like Lunette visiting Darnassus for the first time is likely to encounter Mydrannul, a salesman, standing near the entrance to the city. He asks for a package to be delivered to his colleague Nessa Shadowsong in Rut'theran Village. Although this village is on Teldrassil, it is impossible to walk there, so he explains, "to reach Nessa you must take the portal in Darnassus to Rut'theran Village. You will find the portal west of the Temple Gardens." This teleportation device is the only practical means to get on or off Teldrassil. It is possible to jump off the island, but doing so is fatal because the tree on which it rests is so high, and it is not possible to climb back on again.

In the village, Nessa asks for some fishing samples to be taken to her colleague Laird in Auberdine, which is a few miles across the ocean straits. There are actually two ways to get there, a boat trip and a flight. The first time Lunette tried this, she took the boat. However, Laird was not prepared to receive her, so she needed to return to the village and follow Nessa's precise instructions: "Bring my collection to our hippogryph master, Vesprystus, and speak to him about traveling to Auberdine." Vesprystus says,

"It is sound advice to speak with the hippogryph master in every town that has one. Once you speak to the master, you can then fly there from other towns." After Lunette took the flight, Laird was ready to receive her, asked her to take his response back to Nessa, and said, "If you wish to take the ferry, then one regularly departs from the dock to the northwest."

This is actually a chain of four quests (Mydrannul to Nessa, Nessa to Vesprystus, Vesprystus to Laird, Laird to Nessa). It acquaints the player with two modes of transportation, flying and sailing, and encourages the player to leave the zone where the character was born. In the town of Auberdine, several quests are available that take a young character all through the surrounding Darkshore zone. In the case of flying, the sequence alerts the player to the need to establish a network of flight paths across the world.

Humans' first experience with flight often comes after they meet Quartermaster Lewis at Sentinel Hill in Westfall, the second zone they usually enter. He asks them to deliver a note to Stormwind, saying, "The fastest way to Stormwind is through Thor, our gryphon master. He's just down the hill; bring him my note, and then take a gryphon to Stormwind." The gryphon master in Stormwind explains more: "The gryphon master in Westfall is Thor. If you've spoken to him before, then you can take one of my gryphons to him. That's a good lesson to know: gryphons are always trained to fly to their capital city, but they'll only take you to a remote gryphon master after you've already been there."

The same is true for practicing crafts and other skills. An early quest called Garments of the Moon sent Lunette south of Dolanaar to heal Shaya, an injured sentinel, giving Lunette experience with the healing and fortitude spells she had just learned. Embedded instruction is not limited to the lowest levels, although it is most prominent there, and the Shattrath City flight master on the advanced Outland continent not only sold flight tickets but also informed characters who were ready to buy their own flying mounts how they could learn flying skills.

**Verbal Teaching**

Research has confirmed that players learn much from other players, verbally asking questions and receiving answers. Bonnie A. Nardi, Stella Ly, and Justin Harris studied the ways players learn through text-based in-WoW chatting with one another, noting that this form of social learning had an emotional dimension, as well as a cognitive one.[6] These researchers distinguished three kinds of learning, as defined by what is learned: finding facts, developing tactics or strategy, and being socialized to the norms and values that constitute game ethos.

From my own observations of fact finding, here is a simple example. In Stranglethorn's general chat, one player asked, "Anyone know where is the tiger Sin'Dall?"

Another, immediately responded, "On top of a hill, in the middle of where the elder tigers are." A third confirmed, "Yes go where elders are and look for a mound."

A much more complicated example was when Kizamet asked fellow Winged Ascension guild members, "Does anyone know if there is a flight point in Alterac?"

Torchy answered, "There is, I think."

Hotstunty suggested, "Aerie Point?"

Kizamet disagreed, "That's Hinterlands."

Maxrohn chimed in, "Refuge Pointe. Aerie is in Hinterlands."

Torchy corrected him, "Refuge is in Arathi, not Alterac."

"Right, sorry!" Maxrohn admitted.

"Thanks for trying to help," said Kizamet.

Zott authoritatively explained, "Alterac has no flight path. The closest is Western Plaguelands. It's in Chillwind Camp."

"Thanks, Zott," said Kizamet.

"Good for you." Maxrohn commented. "That's right."

"I thought it was Southshore," Torchy interjected. "But that's in the wrong zone." Indeed, examination of the maps indicates that the closest Alliance flight point to the ruins of Altarac is at Chillwind Camp, but Southshore has the second closest, and Refuge Pointe is probably the third closest.

With respect to tactics, sometimes players share clever ways of completing quests. An example that shows how two apparently separate quests can affect each other was posted on the Wowhead website by Psonica in January 2007.[7] The quests both take place in the Bladespire ogre settlement in Blade's Edge Mountains, a zone of Outland for level-65 to level-68 players. One quest, The Trappings of a Vindicator, requires the player to retrieve a sword and a shield that are held by two level-66 ogres named Droggam and Mugdog. Unfortunately, each resides in a large hut, flanked by two elite guards, each of whom would be nearly impossible for an individual player to kill, and by two non-elites. The other quest, Getting the Bladespire Tanked, requires the player to entice five ogres to drink mugs of alcohol that attract them if placed in front of them, which does not work for a few labeled "sober." Psonica explains how to use the brew to get the sword and shield: "This quest is not marked 'elite' because you really don't have to kill the 2 elite guards to get the named ogre. Notice that the guards have 'sober' in their names? So what I did was this: 1. kill the 2 non-elites by pulling them out of the tent/hut. 2. go as close as you can get without pulling the elites and place a 'Bloodmaul Butebane Brew' on the floor. This will pull the named but not the two sober guards. 3. Kill named ogre. 4. Profit:) . . . easy as cake when you remember that most ogres are not able to resist the smell of some brew." Maxrohn confirmed that this tactic worked well.

On the level of economic strategies, my character Vadvaro reported an interesting conversation that he had with the master of his guild, Morskajak, about the business of herbalism. Morskajak reported he possessed six hundred gold coins, and commented, "Not bad for flower picking."

Vadvaro asked, "What part of the work actually gives you the gold?"

"Each herb has a zone where it is most plentiful," Morskajak commented. "For an example, the Hinterlands is the best zone for Sungrass. And there is the only one place where you can gather Ghost Mushrooms in any numbers. While Stonetalon Mountains is better than anywhere else for Wild Steelbloom. Plus, some herbs sell for a lot more than others. Ghost Mushrooms and Gromsblood sell for top prices. A lot of others pay so little they are hardly worth gathering."

"Do you sell the herbs directly," Vadvaro inquired, "or use them in alchemy or enchanting?"

"When the Auction House is paying well for herbs, I sell the herbs directly," Morskajak replied. "When the market drops or even crashes, I use them to make potions. I always sell them through the Auction House. Vendors won't give you nearly as much as the same item at the Auction House. The only thing you have to watch out for is the stuff that won't sell. For me, the in-game economy and the Auction House are a major part of the fun of World of Warcraft. . . . The gathering professions of herbalism, skinning and mining pay a lot better than any of the crafting professions if you learn the Auction House well. The problem with blacksmithing, leather working and such is that you have to pay for the materials. And often the materials cost more than you can get for the manufactured items. . . . When you are herbing, you not only need to find where they spawn, but you need to find where there aren't a thousand others gathering the same herb. And you wouldn't believe it, but you actually level pretty fast when you are herbing because of how many mobs you have to kill to get to the herbs that you want."

Learning game ethos depends upon their being an ethical code in the first place, and indeed one exists. WoW itself suggests nine basic rules of etiquette for players who are questing together in parties, which I will paraphrase and illustrate from my own experience:

1. Help everybody complete their quests, rather than quitting as soon as you have achieved your own goals. For whatever reason, party members frequently bailed out while other players and I were in the middle of an instance, leaving us too weak to continue.

2. When looting an area, the players who need particular kinds of loot most should get precedence in receiving it. I found this rule very difficult to follow in instances, because so much was happening so fast that I often could not think about what the loot was or whether I needed it. After a few other players had complained to me, I simply stopped taking any special items from the loot.

3. Do not loot dead monsters if your group is still in combat. Certainly the priority should be protecting your fellow group members, but some groups I was in were

constantly attacking fresh enemies, leaving no time to pick up the needed quest items.

4. Healers should give highest priority to healing other party members, and apologize when they fail. It is crucial not only to play your part in group endeavors but also to make sure other members know you are doing your best. Otherwise, group solidarity weakens.

5. Any player who becomes the target of enemy attacks and decides to retreat back toward the rest of the party should avoid drawing the enemies so close to the group that they attack a comrade. Actually, there were times as a priest when I found the best course really was to draw an enemy across in front of an inactive and well-armored member of my own party, because done with care this was a much quicker way of asking my comrade for help. Once Catullus was criticized precisely because he was not using his fade capability to cause enemies to attack stalwart party members rather than kill him. He felt this was unethical, but it was pointed out to him that other members could handle the enemy better, and he needed to stay alive so he could heal them.

6. Immediately before a battle or a difficult quest, members of the party should give one another protective buffs—shieldlike or strengthening spells—and they should pay attention to when those buffs need to be refreshed. Some buffs cost the receiver health, so the giver should be careful in applying them, and in extreme circumstances may want to give healing immediately afterward. Party members receiving the buffs need to be aware that those giving them may need a few seconds afterward to replenish their mana. In addition to buffs, party members may need to share quests and some resources. For example, mages may conjure extra food and drink, which other party members may then use at rest points to replenish health and mana.

7. When planning and conducting a battle, all players need to avoid arousing monsters that are just outside the area and do not need to be fought at the moment. For individuals as well as parties, the standard tactic for dealing with groups of enemies is to pull them off from their group, one or two at a time, to minimize the difficulty of the fight at any given time. In groups, this can be difficult, because individual members of the group may get different ideas about which monster to attack next. The leader of a party can mark targets, with symbols like a skull or star, and tell followers to avoid attacking any others.

8. Often a party contains two or more players with the same professions, who thus are seeking the same materials. For example, two skinners may each want to skin every animal corpse. They should take turns, or discuss between them who should get what, if their needs are different. This also applies when party members are doing the same gathering quest.

9. WoW's last rule of etiquette begins with a Biblical reference from Matthew 5:41 ("And whoever compels you to go one mile, go with him two."), saying: "Whenever

possible, go the extra mile to do things for your party. Play your best. Do whatever you can to help party members. If you impress them, they may look back on you with good memories. This can build good relations for the future."[8]

As the following chapter explains, game ethos is problematic, but here we can report that some norms are widely endorsed even in dealings with strangers. For example, a player who comes upon another who has been working on a quest should not rush in and take it away. When Vadvaro was at level 12, he returned repeatedly to a gnoll campsite in Westfall, where he could progress on two quests. One was simply to kill gnolls until he had collected eight of their paws as trophies. The other quest involved collecting sacks of oats to feed a horse named Old Blanchy, and he knew that one sack was in the very middle of the campsite. He had little hope of getting it, however, because it was guarded by several gnolls, whereas the best he could do was kill those who wandered far from the campfire one at a time.

Coming to the area again, he saw that a level-23 Human rogue had just killed the last of the gnolls, leaving the sack of oats unprotected. Figuring that at level 23 she would not be working on this low-level quest for Old Blanchy, and worried that gnolls might quickly respawn around the fire, he rushed in and took the sack. Then, feeling he needed to check if this was okay with her, he said, "Thanks."

She replied, "For what?"

"Unless you need it." He figured he could give the oats to her if she wanted them.

Her reaction was: "Huh?"

"Sack of oats for the horse," he explained.

"Ooo no, I don't need it at all."

Vadvaro then wished her good luck, and she replied, "You, too, friend."

Respect for other players can break down under conditions of stress, as Catullus found when he was repeatedly doing a dozen lightning-fast daily quests in Outland and Quel'Danas, to earn money fast for the May 2008 scientific conference. Other players were directly competing to kill the same beasts, and while they often assisted one another briefly, they also got in one another's way. For example, one of the Outland quests involved measuring flaming whirlwinds in a large open area, and these disappeared as soon as measured. Catullus was riding around on his huge flightless bird, spotting a flame in the distance, and riding rapidly toward it. But often a more advanced player with a flying mount would zoom ahead and "steal" the flame from him.

The fact that ethos must be learned implies that some players have not yet learned it. Two senior players were talking about the crazy antics of the youngest players. One commented, "They are okay for eleven year olds, but they are just too ADHD [attention deficit hyperactivity disorder] and high maintenance for me, and they are not intelligent at all. I guess I should say they have a few years to go, not socially mature yet."

The other older player replied, "Yah, they need to run together and make their own mistakes." This implies that a good deal of learning is experiential, rather than verbal.

## Nonverbal Learning

Players may learn nonverbally, either from their own experiences, by imitating what they see another player do, or by abstracting general rules from the data they have. We will call these modes of self-education *perception*, *modeling*, and *insight*.

Perception concerns being able to see and hear things, learning to discern distinctions that may not be immediately apparent. For example, the first two herbs that an herbalist needs to collect are peacebloom and silverleaf. Peacebloom is a white flower with a long stalk that is found only in the middle of open areas. Silverleaf is a tall bush that invariably nestles beside trees. An herbalist possesses an herb finder, which displays a yellow dot on the map at the approximate location of an herb, and mousing over it displays the name of the herb. But some of the more advanced herbs were especially hard to see, especially if there was a good deal of vegetation around them, prior to software update patch 2.3, which made them sparkle. Sungrass, which an herbalist cannot collect before acquiring a skill level of 230, gave Maxrohn a good deal of trouble. Sometimes he would be practically standing on it and still not see it if there were other grassy plants around. Mousing over an area where you think an herb is will often detect it because the cursor changes to be the clipper you use to harvest the herb, but scanning a wide area can be very time-consuming because the cursor changes only after a delay. Finding many herbs would be extremely difficult if the player could not employ both perceptual and cognitive cues. Yes, cognition tells you to look in open spaces for peacebloom and next to trees for silverleaf, but you still need to see them. After a while, looking in the right places becomes second nature, part of your perceptual apparatus rather than a verbal cognitive rule you have memorized intellectually.

Especially important is judging distance. A character that can kill at a distance, such as a priest with damaging spells or a hunter with a gun, will want to maneuver near enough to an enemy to attack, but not quite near enough to be detected. An enemy has an *aggro distance*, comparable to the *reaction distance* in ethology or the personal space in *human proxemics*. Visually estimating that distance becomes second nature to an experienced player. In the huge Maraudon instance, before fully preparing, Maxrohn often moved forward near the next enemy likely to be attacked so he would be ready to jump when his party attacked. A member of his party exclaimed, "Max, you're a nut, man, going to mana regeneration 10 yards from aggro, heh!"

Experienced players also learn to read the geography.[9] A set of enemies tends to be tied to a particular area, where some patrol short distances, others longer distances, and all adjust to the hills and other structures around them. Often, the player can spot a safe location, usually on a large rock or the low finger of a hill, where it is possible to stand without aggravating any of the enemies, while being close enough to strike out at them. When trying to peel one enemy away from a group, the player instinctively identifies the right direction in which to pull that enemy, where no other dangers will intrude from other directions. Without even consciously thinking about it, an advanced player has a plan of escape, to run in a particular direction or to jump into a river if the enemies mass too powerfully.

Although most of WoW's content is visual, some sound effects convey information. Many beasts and enemies emit a sound when they attack, and if the player is not looking in their direction, this noise may be the first clue of danger. A particular sound like a pair of dissonant musical chords alerts the player to the fact that an invisible or cloaked enemy is in the neighborhood. Thus, perception involves more than one of the senses, plus some cognitive preprocessing of information to make it maximally valuable.

Modeling is the learning that takes place when one person sees another perform an action or express an emotion, and then imitates it later. Albert Bandura, the great behavior modification psychologist, argued that adopting good behavior patterns is far more important than gaining supposed insights about inner traumas.[10] He said modeling was a powerful way of curing phobias, for example. If you are afraid of snakes, the best way to lose that phobia is not to undergo psychoanalysis to gain insight into the symbolic meaning of snakes for you, but to watch another person handling snakes successfully—why people would want to handle snakes is another matter. Much learning in WoW takes place through modeling, as it does in the surrounding world.

I remember when Maxrohn needed to kill some murlocs at a point on the south shore of Lake Everstill in the Redridge Mountains, early in my research when my skills were poorly developed. Murlocs are rather aggressive amphibious humanoids, who emit a disgusting gurgle of surprise when they discover your presence, as a prelude to attacking you. I had no trouble killing them one at a time, but they were bunched together, so the work was dangerous. As often is the case with murlocs, some were on the land where I could see them, but others were in the water unseen, ready to gurgle and jump at me if I got too near.

A warrior came along with the same task, and we began killing the murlocs side by side, attacking them two at a time. Then the warrior went into the water and disappeared from view. I had tried swimming, but was not very good at it. I was surprised to see the warrior put his head underwater, and I could not figure out how to do it. I imagined, correctly as it happens, that he could see the murlocs under the water, so

I followed him, clicking on the red labels that showed the approximate location of any murloc he battled, and added my spells to his killing power. This episode told me there was much more to swimming than I had imagined, and inspired me to look up the controls necessary to do what the warrior had done.

Once, Etacarinae took a Human warrior into territory he did not know existed, thereby teaching him lessons on many levels, several of them nonverbally. At level 13, she was in Stormwind for weapons training. Although she had an appointment to meet Alberich in Ironforge so she could give him examples of the Draenei language, she had time to waste and decided to kill some beasts in Westfall to hone her skills. On the way she met the level-8 Human and thought it would be amusing to impress him with the power of her flame totem and her general facility in combat. She helped him kill a Defias bandit, and he quickly invited her to form a raiding party with him. She agreed, then, ignoring the fact that he was formally the leader, she said, "this way!" and led him into the hills south of Stormwind.

Few players seem to know there is a remarkable mountain pass at Thunder Falls, where Defias bandits have a hideaway and it is possible to climb a peak that affords a marvelous view down onto Westfall. After showing him these sights, rather than descending the cliff on the Westfall side, she took him down to the Great Sea and began swimming north. She knew from Lunette's experiences that it was possible to swim along the edge on the continents, sometimes finding unknown sites, but she did not know what they might find in this direction. Logically, they might need to swim past cliffs sealing off several regions to reach Menethil, a Dwarven town, which she believed was the first zone with a passable shore. (This was before the Lich King expansion opened Stormwind Harbor, and indeed it is possible to swim there today.) They swam for more than twenty minutes, occasionally stopping for a brief hike in valleys that inevitably were closed off by high cliffs. Eventually, she saw a shape in the distance. Like many teachers, she wanted to appear more knowledgeable than she was, so she said, "Almost there." In a few moments, they had discovered Newman's Landing, a ruined house with a dock, where they paused for a while before continuing their voyage north.[11]

After another long swim, Etacarinae and the Human warrior followed the shore, turning east, and soon trees appeared along the shore. Knowing that Wetlands held many enemies that would be lethal for low-level characters like themselves, she told her companion to be cautious. After avoiding a dangerous murloc, she saw a dim shape on the northern horizon, guessed it was the thriving port town of Menethil, and began swimming across the bay toward it. Indeed, it turned out to be Menethil, and she showed him where the dock and flight path were, to help him in future travels. The whole expedition had taken more than an hour, and brought the warrior to territory far outside the scope of a level-8 Human. When he asked what other wonders she was able to perform, she looked at him for a second, then ducked into the nearest doorway, which she knew to be an inn, and disappeared from his life forever.

Insight learning involves abstracting a lesson from one's observations or by assembling information from multiple sources. A fundamental feature of insights is that they tend to exist in hierarchies, with later insights modifying earlier ones. First, a person develops a mental map describing part of the world, one that successfully achieves early goals. Then, he or she becomes aware of anomalies or contradictions that suggest a more sophisticated mental map is needed. For example, in the center of every newbie zone, where new characters enter the world at level 1, low-level animals are wandering around who will not attack on their own initiative, but will fight back when attacked. The newbie gets one or more quests to kill some of these animals, and their nonaggressiveness allows the newbie to gain skill in defense. These attackable but nonaggressive animals can be spotted by their names being printed in yellow, rather than red for animals that will attack, or green for NPCs that cannot be attacked. For the newbie, this nonaggressiveness allows him or her to learn how to get set for an attack, and protects against an attack by a second animal that happens to pass close to the fight. After leaving this origin point in the newbie zone, the player will stop seeing yellow-named characters and will assume that all other animals encountered at about the same level as the character will be aggressive.

This is a false conclusion, and before too long the character encounters other yellow-named characters who are equally nonaggressive but have higher levels, and thus could give the character experience points if killed. In fact, there are many areas around the WoW world where a number of nonaggressive animals live, with just a few aggressive ones wandering around them, that make excellent places for comfortably leveling-up. For example, Lunette found the areas around Maestra's Post in Ashenvale, especially the area to the west, abounded in nonaggressive buck deer at levels 18 or 19. There were also a few ghostpaw runners, aggressive white wolves at levels 19 or 20, but seldom more than two in a given meadow. Lunette would enter a meadow cautiously, spot the wolves, attack one as soon as the other was at a distance, and then kill the second in turn. After dealing with the wolves, she could relax and begin killing the deer. If she was fighting one, and another came near, it would either walk past or prance away, and never joined the fight as an aggressive animal would do.

Lunette also casually slew level-17 to level-19 giant foreststrider birds in Twilight Vale, the southernmost section of Darkshore, while she was hunting for fine pelts from the moonstalker tigers. Lunette gained nearly two full levels from this relatively comfortable hunting, when she was level 17 through 19. Later, when she had reached level 23, Lunette discovered a narrow valley with no aggressive animals at all, but many nonaggressive level-22 to level-23 stags, just south of Stonetalon Peak. Maxrohn happily harvested the level-30 to level-31 snapjaw turtles along the Misty Shore northwest of the Alterac Hills and along the water near Southshore in the Hillsbrad

Foothills. This principle goes all the way to the highest zones. For example, a large area of Crystalsong Forest in Northrend, a zone notable for its lack of quests, is inhabited with level-76 to level-78 stags and walking trees, who are ready for easy slaughter. Unless the player is lucky to stumble into one of these excellent upper-level hunting grounds early in his or her progress, or is told about them, their potential might not dawn on him or her for a long time.

## Learning and Unlearning Tenacity

We hope we learn from our mistakes, but sometimes the lesson is hard and the wisdom is ambiguous. My first explicit research goal in WoW was to get the last data I needed for a journal article on the religious implications of electronic games, which required interviewing fellow priests at the Cathedral of Light in Stormwind.[12] I felt nobody would respond coherently to a player who was a complete newbie, so I set the goal of reaching level 20 before the first interview. I had not yet decided to write a book about WoW, so I was not paying very much attention to many aspects of it, and to a newbie like myself the complex, dynamic environment can be quite overwhelming. Thus, I failed to consider at first the fact that the characters of many other players were Dwarves and Gnomes, and that their home territory was far away from the lands near Stormwind. I failed to ask myself how they got to the places I found them.

I decided to visit the Mystic Ward in the distant Dwarven city of Ironforge to study the religion there, which I thought might be culturally quite different from that in Stormwind. The maps seemed to tell me the way to go was through two very dangerous zones, the Burning Steppes and Searing Gorge, and I guessed that the direct route would start at the village of Lakeshire in the Redridge Mountains. I knew that area fairly well, and had often stood at a fork in the road looking north, wondering which path was the right one.

Unfortunately, both paths were blocked by vicious Blackrock warriors of various kinds, who were at combat levels between 19 and 25, often in groups, so there was little chance that I could defeat them alone. So I stood at the fork in the road, pondering. Along came a group of four players who asked me to join and help them on their quest. Seeing this as my chance to get past the cordon of Blackrock warriors, I agreed. The leader took us up the left-hand path, and we soon found ourselves at Render's Camp, where many Blackrock warriors infested a cavern. The goal was to kill fifteen Blackrock Champions, whose combat level is 24 to 25, an impossible task for an unaided priest at level 20.

The five of us were able to kill several champions right away, ganging up on them one or two at a time. But as we got deeper into the caverns, we found ourselves increasingly surrounded, and the job got much tougher. Soon we were constantly getting killed, appearing at the cemetery on the south shore of Lake Everstill, and having to run repeatedly back north a couple of miles into the caverns and look for a safe place to rez, where the Blackrock warriors would not immediately kill us. After killing about a dozen champions, we had stopped making any progress, and two of the five group members quit.

The leader and one other player, who happened to be a Gnome, were not quite ready to admit defeat. Recalling that one of the virtues taught at the Cathedral of Light is tenacity, I decided to stick with them. We found ourselves crammed together in a small alcove of the caverns, hoping a Blackrock Champion would not kill us before we had regained strength after resurrecting. But just before we were ready to defend ourselves, one would notice us and annihilate us. Finally the leader said he had an invisibility spell that would allow him to resurrect and gain strength unnoticed. He told me and the Gnome to wait until he had distracted the nearest champion. Then we would rez and get ready to help him. This desperate tactic worked, and with admittedly great further exertions, we were able to kill our fifteenth champion, and the three of us ran out of the cavern to our individual destinations.

This experience taught the value of tenacity, so I bravely headed north across the Burning Steppes. All the mobs in the Steppes had levels much higher than twice my own, from 48 through 57, and I soon discovered they could kill me in one or two whacks, and I could do nothing whatsoever to them. The land is literally blasted and burned, with ashes instead of earth, and only the most shattered ruins of houses. I tried to keep to the path, but at times it was lost under layers of ashes, and the monsters seemed to have no compunction against charging along the path after me. In places, the ground is cut by rivers of red-hot lava. When I reached the almost completely corroded ruins of Thaurissan, I lost the path completely.

The maps suggested I might get through to Searing Gorge at Blackrock Mountain, which was on the west side of the northern border of the Burning Steppes. I had entered near the southeast corner, so my journey was terrible in both length and in the trauma of constantly being swatted like a fly. The tunnel through the mountain is ominous, but surprisingly it contained no monsters, so I felt my plan was vindicated when I staggered through to Searing Gorge. As if to punish me for my optimism, a monster killed me as soon as I got through. Mercifully, another player at about level 50 was kind enough to resurrect me immediately, but he commented, "Aren't you too short for Searing Gorge?" At least the map was much clearer, showing a road cutting the full length of the zone to Stonewrought Pass in the northeast corner.

Misfortune dogged my steps, however, and it was only after many deaths that I finally reached Dustfire Valley and the entrance to Stonewrought Pass, knowing that pleasant lands with only low-level monsters lay beyond. Only then did I discover that one needs a key to get through the gate. I stood there a long time, hoping that someone would come along holding a key, but nobody came. My tenacious attempt, at the cost of a dozen hours of play, was a total failure. I rubbed the magic stone that would take me back to the inn at Goldshire in the Elwynn Forest, where I had originally entered World of Warcraft, feeling very much defeated.

Only then did I really think. How could the numerous low-level Dwarves and Gnomes I had seen have crossed the Burning Steppes and Searing Gorge? Before I had gone there myself, and discovered what horribly dangerous territories they are, I had vaguely imagined they had crossed in groups, combining their numbers to overcome individually stronger monsters. But that idea was no longer plausible. The monsters were too strong and too numerous over too wide an area. I took out my copy of *World of Warcraft Master Guide* and looked up *transportation*.[13] A small paragraph in this huge book explained that there was a subway running underground, linking Stormwind directly with Ironforge. From the inn, it was a pleasant, unimpeded stroll of perhaps five minutes to the entrance, a place I actually had seen before but it had looked ominous and unmarked by any sign. In five more minutes, without stress or cost, I reached my destination, thinking of all the horrible monsters crawling on the ashes above my head.

What is the lesson? Tenacity is good, but there can be too much of a good thing. Excessive tenacity is obsession. One must be flexible enough to think clearly about the evidence one sees, and imagine alternative routes to any important destination. Furthermore, one should learn as much as possible about one's environment, even when the information does not immediately seem useful. This highlights one of the flaws of behaviorist theories of learning; humans learn much that is not immediately rewarding or costly, because that knowledge may come in handy in the future. If I had fully realized that I did not understand how the Dwarves and Gnomes got to Stormwind, I simply could have asked one of them. One should be moderate in all things, including moderation. Fundamentally, therefore, all rules are at best tentative—including this one. Deciding when to follow one's habitual rules, and when to break them, is an art. Yes, one should often be tenacious, but only when it is right to be so. How one knows when to invoke an escape clause like that is another question.

## Arrested Development

To quest is to learn, and WoW characters cease learning only when they stop questing. Even active players often ignore some of their characters, and of course a character stops learning when the player stops playing. To get some insight into why a person or character might choose to halt the process of development, let us consider the stories of Aristotle, Vadvaro, Incognita, Zodia, and Annihila. The first four of these characters chose not to go beyond experience level 20, which means abandoning quests and refusing to accept new assignments. Annihila, an Undead death knight, entered existence at level 55 but refused to go beyond 57. Each of the five has a somewhat different mix of motivations and personality characteristics. They represent three of the ten races, and four of the ten classes.

Aristotle, a Human mage (see figure 4.2), was the first of my research assistants to be sent into Azeroth, but he was sidelined for a long time when I realized that healing priests could give me the best vantage point from which to understand society in a virtual world, and Maxrohn became my main assistant. Thus, Aristotle is the oldest of my characters, nearing the age at which many workers would retire or a traditional member of the upper classes in India might retreat into spiritual contemplation.

Other factors were the skills that Aristotle developed, which made him largely independent of other people. First of all, as a mage he could conjure up both food and drink. While this might make him valuable to a group in raids, because he could provision the other members, he never really developed the habit of questing with other people, and he belonged to guilds only to enjoy the little bit of intellectual banter he found in the chats. Second, Aristotle was always interested in nature, so he learned a

**Figure 4.2**
Aristotle, a Human mage and philosopher, lecturing about culture in the Stormwind art museum.

number of nature-oriented skills that added to his self-sufficiency, providing him with much to sell on the rare occasions that he needed to get his armor repaired or replenish his supply of manufactured goods. His main professions were herbalism and skinning, but he also learned fishing and cooking. Since he could conjure food in a few seconds, he really did not need to hunt or fish, but catching a nice fish and cooking it for his dinner gave a special sense of satisfaction that he enjoyed.

Given his maturity, he did not resent the fact that quest givers were sending him on missions that often had dubious goals and even more dubious means, but he was irritated that everyone around him took it for granted that one should accept whatever quests were given. He came to believe that the only genuine quests came from deep within the soul of the quester. Thus, the best way to seek quests was to know thyself. Put more simply, he was by nature a philosopher rather than a warrior.

His doubts clarified when he reached level 15 and met Captain Grayson, the ghost who haunts the Westfall lighthouse. The captain's ship was wrecked one dark night years ago after Old Murk-Eye, the leader of the murlocs, had scared away the family that tended the lighthouse. Consider this metaphor: What is worse than a dangerous coast that lacks a beacon? The answer: A dangerous shore that has a beacon that is not shining. Disaster is most likely when we wrongly think we are following trustworthy guidance. The family returned to the lighthouse and lit the beacon, but then Grayson's ghost had watched helplessly as the murlocs slaughtered them. He explained to Aristotle, "My afterlife plight is to see that no others follow my destiny." Given this compelling justification, Aristotle was happy to complete three quests, finding oil for the beacon, killing Old Murk-Eye, and thinning the ranks of the murlocs.

Aristotle took up residence in the lighthouse, ready to get more oil when needed, and happy to have Grayson for a companion. Indeed, for a philosopher, what better companion could he have? Being a ghost, Grayson had no personal need for material things. Existing on the other side of death, he had an interesting perspective that enlivened their discussions. Grayson was neutral to both Horde and Alliance, so he provided a certain detachment from all the politics that muddied analysis of the fundamental basis of ethics. Aristotle, being alive, was the more active thinker of the two, and he developed the habit of calling Grayson by the name of his former teacher, Plato. Shade that he was, Grayson had expressed doubts that Humans were anything more than shadows cast by firelight on the wall of a cave, and this reminded Aristotle that Plato used to say the same thing when in an especially foolish mood.

No, Aristotle said, Humans are real, and there are two senses in which they are real. First, Humans are part of nature, like the fire, like the cave, and like all the living things that are so vital and so fascinating. Second, Humans are real because they can transcend nature, because they can think about it, ask questions, and come to understand it. In short, Humans can aspire to discover truth if they study nature, if they study Human society, and if they do so with the tools of logic.

Aristotle did not really become a hermit. His interest in nature sent him out hunting and fishing far more than needed; then he would sell the loot he gathered to give it some use, while emptying his inventory. He would often visit Goldshire to do some business, hear the news, occasionally travel to other lands to study their governments, and debate with anyone willing to philosophize. When he reached level 17, he happened to meet Zaldimar Wefhellt, the mage trainer who lived in Goldshire Inn, who offered "further insight into the world of magic." Always interested in debating other people's supposed insights, Aristotle agreed. But rather than uttering a platitude as Aristotle had expected, Zaldimar told him to visit Jennea Cannon in the Wizard's Sanctum at Stormwind.

The city was in the middle of celebrating Brewfest, with drinking and singing that Aristotle found most offensive, but his mood improved considerably when he entered the Mage Quarter, the most beautiful district of the city, lush with foliage, framed by exquisite renaissance architecture, and largely devoid of people. Aristotle climbed the spiral ramp to the top of the Sanctum and passed through the portal.

Jennea, a level-40 mage trainer, had no time for philosophy. She gave Aristotle some new spells, including one that would help him detect magic in the environment, then sent him on a quest to clean up a mana rift disturbance at the tavern next door. When he returned to her with three rift spawn caged in containment coffers, she promised to make him a wizard's robe if he would bring her ten pieces of common linen cloth and six charged rift gems that could be found only in one mine far north in the Dwarven land of Loch Modan. In the end, Aristotle did have loyalties that could motivate him to undertake quests, loyalty to Grayson and loyalty to the Society of Mages. But Grayson gave him no new quests, and until the society called, he enjoyed a contemplative retirement at the lighthouse.

Vadvaro, a rogue, shared some characteristics with Aristotle, beyond the fact that both were Human. For one thing, both of them possessed powerful curiosities. But where Aristotle wanted to unlock the mysteries of the universe, Vadvaro merely wanted to unlock boxes, so he could steal their contents. Both liked hunting, however, Vadvaro did so not because he was fascinated by nature but because he needed raw materials for his leatherworking business. He preferred to pick people's pockets rather than their minds. Sometimes he dreamed about carrying out a major crime, a get-rich-quick bank heist perhaps, and sometimes he plotted with fellow rogues. However, the plans never rose to the level of action.

I suppose Vadvaro was lazy. For a while, he belonged to a guild dedicated to the fantasy novels Edgar Rice Burroughs wrote about the planet Mars, and he enjoyed the conceit that he was a reincarnation of one of the heroes. Such fantasies were pleasant to think about, but real questing was tough work. Reaching level 20 meant he was well trained in picking locks and pockets, and could handle the environment around Lakeshire. On a typical day, he can be found asleep on one of the comfortable beds upstairs at the inn. In late afternoon, he might go out for a couple hours, perhaps killing a helpless wild pig if he could not find a suitably full pocket to pick, then back to the inn where dinner and a mug of ale would be waiting for him. Only one thing might chase him out of this disreputable but comfortable lifestyle, namely, the police. The guards around the town were ready to defend against enemy attack, but given the constant state of emergency, there really were no police to hassle an honest thief like him.

Incognita, an Undead priest, may have possessed curiosity once, as she may have possessed a family and a community before the plague erased them, but she simply did not remember. The search for truth becomes hollow when memory fails. Suppose you had learned the ultimate meaning of everything, but could not remember it! Poised between life and death, she might be expected to hunger for life. For the Undead, this hunger took on a horrible meaning, however, because the quickest way one of them could recover from damage in a battle was to cannibalize the body of the defeated enemy. Aristotle may have been attracted to other people's minds, but Incognita did not enjoy the taste of their brains. The one great mystery she had solved, during her twenty levels of questing, was what happened on Fenris Isle. The answer was that corpses were being brought there by rot-hide gnolls for reanimation as soldiers of the Scourge. This was not a happy discovery, and it did not inspire her to explore other mysteries.

Whereas Vadvaro was lazy, Incognita was unmotivated, almost as if suspended in time. The Undead have the ability to swim underwater three times as long as any other race, because their metabolisms work more slowly and have less need of air. There was no immediate prospect of escaping this liminal existence between life and death. She had no idea how sociable she had been before the plague, but she certainly had few sociable instincts now. Losing too many loved ones is equivalent to losing the capacity for love. Without strong commitments, or any realistic future hopes, her sense of time was unstable, slow in some respects but fleeting in others, alternating between the quick and the dead. She sits today, on the ledge over the entrance to the Silverpine Sepulcher, motionless but ready to fall either out or in, depending upon the slightest hint of hope or despair, feeling nothing.

Zodia's story is quite different, yet touches upon the same themes. It begins with the crash of the Exodar, the spacecraft carrying all her Draenei people that broke up over an archipelago off the northwest coast of Kalimdor. As a priest, her first experiences were rushing to save injured Draenei, gathering moth blood to replenish the healing crystals, and helping to staunch the pollution flooding from the wreckage strewn across the landscape. Frantically, she learned a healing technique called the Gift of the Naaru and began applying it to injured survivors. Other tasks required her to gather scattered equipment, collect scientific data, and join in defense against an incursion by Blood Elves of the Horde. In time, she ventured out across the major islands of the archipelago, Azuremyst and Bloodmyst, visiting the city that was being built around the main fragment of the Exodar. There she discovered a dock where a ship could take her away from her desperate people, into Night Elf territory, and on across the new world.

Why, she asked herself, would she want to leave the islands? While she was exploring them, she had learned to love them. Fellow victims of the Exodar crash needed her here. To help others and to support herself, she learned five skills: first aid, cooking, fishing, herbalism, and alchemy. Zodia first saw the benefits of fishing when she learned the alchemy recipe for the elixir of water breathing, which requires the alchemist to have the oil from a fish. At the Exodar, she learned how to fish and bought a rod and reel from a fishing supplies vendor who was peacefully fishing in a decorative pool inside the Exodar. She tried fishing there herself, but was immediately told there are no fish in that water! Just outside, in the lakes near the entrance, she quickly caught twenty slitherskin mackerel. A short walk brought her to the ocean shore at Odesyus' Landing, on the south coast of Azuremyst Isle, where she tried her luck, catching several more but not yet getting a different species. Eventually, she discovered a spot where she could catch the needed oily blackmouth fish, and where she could also collect the stranglekelp that, combined with blackmouth oil, would give her the elixir. With her first bottle, she was able to swim underwater from Wrathscale Lair on Bloodmyst, around the east side of Azuremyst, all the way to diminutive Silvermyst Isle. School was for children, she told herself, and she now knew all she needed to make an adult contribution to her community, and live a satisfying life.

Perhaps the harshest lessons were learned by Annihila, an Undead death knight. Like others of her kind, she became conscious at level 55, in the citadel of the Lich King, having no notion of who she was or how she got there. The Lich King told her, "All that I am: anger, cruelty, vengeance—I bestow upon you, my chosen knight." Her first task was to take a battle-worn sword and forge it into a runeblade. Before long, it was spilling the blood of the Scarlet Crusade, one of whom vainly boasted, "You may take my life, but you won't take my freedom!" A feeble Human resident of New Avalon begged, as she plunged the sword home, "No, please! I have children!" She shared a dueling quest with a death knight member of Alea Iacta Est (AIE), and she joined that guild, without weakening her dedication to her master.

Annihila rapidly learned how to behave properly as a death knight of the Lich King, joyfully slaying his enemies without remorse, until suddenly a flash of light from the past illuminated everything in a new way. She was told to kill one of the prisoners being held in a barrack. This may have been a test of whether she had learned absolute loyalty, because the prisoners represented all ten races, and she was assigned to execute the only one of her own kind, an Undead named Antoine Brack. Before she could end his life, he spoke to her, revealing they had been friends in an earlier life: "Annihila, I'd recognize that decay anywhere. . . . What . . . What have they done to you,

**Figure 4.3**
Annihila, an Undead death knight, preparing to kill Antoine Brack, but learning they were friends before she became a servant of the Lich King.

Annihila? You don't remember me? We were humans once—long, long ago—until Lordaeron fell to the Scourge. Your transformation to a Scourge zombie came shortly after my own. Not long after that, our minds were freed by the Dark Lady" (see figure 4.3). Like the darkness that vanishes at the break of dawn, her loyalty to the Lich King vanished, and she refused to kill Antoine. Unable to rescue her old friend, she mounted her horse and fled, galloping swiftly through Tir to Light's Hope Chapel.

The Eastern Plaguelands were strangely vacant of all living things, and a mist prevented her from escaping to the wider world. Using guild chat, she sought the aid of fellow Alea Iacta Est members: "Any expert Death Knights on who know how to escape from the Lich King without doing battle for him? I refused to execute Antoine Brack, who was an old friend of mine before becoming one of the Undead."

Gradja whispered to her, "You have to, but I wouldn't stress over it."

Tasehires explained, "You can't leave the DK starter zone without doing all the quests."

Maui, the guild leader, asked, "Have we tried summoning a new DK?"

Tasehires replied, "I don't know of anyone who's tried but I doubt it will work."

Dills scornfully explained, "Just do the quests people, jeez! So many people are trying to circumvent the awesomeness Blizzard set up."

Annihila disagreed, saying, "We must always have the option of moral choice."

Maui supported her position, proclaiming, "I refuse to do Arthas' bidding."

Dills tried to convince her to do as she was instructed: "I don't want to spoil it but let me just say that everything works out in the end and you will be happy. The idea is that you are a servant of Arthas at the outset so role play that."

Incredihulk agreed: "The point is as a Lich, you don't have the power to do otherwise, you are under Arthas' control."

When Annihila said that Antoine had explained the truth to her, Gradja rejoined: "He explained A truth . . . not necessarily THE truth."

Dahkar, apparently irritated by the exchange, broke in: "Look by the time you finish the DK chain . . . things change bigtime for the Death Knights. BIGTIME. Just do the freaking chain already."

Annihila replied, "No, thank you. If any of you ever want to summon me, I'll be waiting in Light's Hope Chapel." Maui, the guild leader, would have tried to summon her to freedom, but the guild had few mages capable of doing the teleportation magic, and none was available for the experiment. Other members explained to her how she could use the chat interface to communicate with mages she did not know by name, and after three tries she contacted a Blood Elf mage, named Raeon, who was willing to help. Two of his friends, Eiga and Lokis, joined him in the Zangarmarsh zone of Outland, to provide the needed three summoners. Three times they tried, and this message appeared to Annihila: "Raeon wants to summon you to Zabra'jin. The spell will be cancelled in 2 minutes." Three times she clicked the "Accept" box, and three times the summoning failed. Realizing she must learn to love solitude, she sighed, saying, "I'll just live here in Light's Hope Chapel and pray for my soul."

## Epilogue: Learning to Doubt What You Have Learned

Lusea, the Dwarven priestess, had little idea what she was getting into when she took the Deeprun Tram to Stormwind, to help her Human allies in the battle to reestablish law and order in the surrounding territories. A first clue came when Etacarinae told her about a hideout of Defias bandits high above Thunder Falls and overlooking both Stormwind and the troubled territory of Westfall. In this latter zone, she quickly enlisted in the People's Militia, slaying Defias of many ranks, both in Moonbrook and the Dagger Hills above this outlaw-occupied ghost town. She intercepted a Defias message that referred obscurely to an overdue shipment from "BB" and instructed, "Send your supplies to the 'barn' this time." (She did not realize that "BB" refers to Goblin war profiteers in their pirate town,

**Figure 4.4**
Edwin VanCleef, leader of the Defias Brotherhood, learning there is a price to pay for rebellion.

Booty Bay.) Gradually, she learned that the Defias Brotherhood had been formed by Edwin VanCleef, the chief engineer for the rebuilding of Stormwind after the First War, who had turned traitor (see figure 4.4). In defiance of the Alliance, the brotherhood was amassing money and materiel for a vast project of unknown nature. Then a Defias informer led Lusea to a barn in Moonbrook that turned out to be the entrance to the Deadmines, formerly the greatest source of gold in Azeroth, and VanCleef's secret hideout. Only after she and a party of comrades had killed VanCleef and brought his head back to Stormwind did she learn the horrible truth. Stormwind city architect, Baros Alexston, told her, "When we had finished our duties, we were cheated. The nobles refused to pay us for our work. Some of the more senior of the Stonemasons were offered governmental jobs, but VanCleef refused it out of loyalty to all the Stonemasons. He led a riot and left the city, swearing revenge." Everything she thought she knew about the Defias Brotherhood was turned on its head, and she began to wonder if perhaps they were the heroes, and the leaders of Stormwind the villains.

# 5    Cooperation

I, Catullus, a priest, am a very cooperative fellow, not to mention talented, intelligent, and likeable. We Blood Elves are proud of our virtues, and our only vice is the failure to see that we have any vices. Indeed, I count among my virtues a certain self-critical stance, which causes me to be critical of other people as well, and to harbor doubts that those in the aristocracy really are superior to ordinary folk. Thus, while I am cooperative, I believe cooperation is highly problematic. With whom shall we cooperate, for how long, to accomplish what, and at how high a cost in spirit as well as gold?

The very first Blood Elf quest-giver I met in Sunstrider Isle, Magistrix Erona, gave me two fundamental goals: "Ever since the destruction of the Sunwell by Arthas and the Scourge, we have been a race adrift on a sea of oblivion. We teeter on the edge of uncertainty. This will change, priest, and you will learn and aid our recovery at the same time." I was anxious to *learn*, and it did not immediately occur to me that I might learn to doubt the Blood Elf leadership. Survival is a powerful motive for cooperation, but *recovery* implied more, a restoration of lost powers. This syllogism raised further questions concerning whose power and for what purpose. Over time I would learn most painfully what it meant to teeter on the edge of uncertainty.

My first quest for Erona was to help reclaim Sunstrider Isle by killing eight mana wyrms that had grown immune to our magical control, and the second was to kill lynxes that were upsetting the natural balance. Afterward, Erona told me, "Your continued successes shall be rewarded," and she passed me on to her assistant, Lanthan Perilon. Indeed, each quest I completed rewarded me with experience points, which had added together to take me to the middle of level 3, when I met Lanthan. Also, quests gave material rewards, either money or valuable articles or both. Thus, there were selfish motivations for cooperating with the quest-givers, quite beyond any altruism or commitment to the goals of the leadership. Erona also sent me to Matron Arena, a priest trainer in the Sunspire. From her I received my first training, learning spells in return for payment of money to "cover the training costs."

Immediately after a quest concerning unstable mana crystals, which raised questions in my mind about the dangers of magical technology, Aeldon Sunbrand, captain of the Blood

Hawks, told me, "The West Sanctum, one of our primary energy sources, has suffered a terrible malfunction and rumors of Darnassian sabotage are rampant." He assigned me to deal with anyone there who looked suspicious, and indeed I found a Darnassian scout, who was moving in a rather conspicuous manner. Anxious to learn more about the Night Elves, I tried talking with him. But he spoke only Darnassian, which had diverged histori- cally very far from the Thalassian spoken by us Blood Elves, so we could not understand each other. Perhaps feeling I was about to alert guards who were in the area, he attacked me, and I was forced to kill him. I found he was carrying documents, including maps of strategic locations in Eversong Woods, implying that the Night Elves were carrying out a major espionage operation in Blood Elf territory.

This did not, however, prove anything about sabotage. Two other motives could be behind their spying. First, each Elf government would logically want to know as much as possible about the other group, given their common heritage and affiliation with oppos- ing factions. Second, Night Elves may be worried about the Blood Elf obsession with advancing the technology of magic without concern either for its spiritual basis or its potential dangers to the surrounding world. When I reported to Ley-Keeper Velania, she commented, "Could elf saboteurs be behind this? I doubt it. With the load we've been putting on the West Sanctum it was only a matter of time until something went wrong."

Soon my increasingly difficult assignments had taken me into Ghostlands, where I was told to kill a dozen Night Elves who had seized An'daroth, a ley-line nexus that was crucial for transmission of magical power in that area. Then, an aristocratic Blood Elf named Dame Auriferous ordered me to steal secret plans from a base the Night Elves had set up on Shalandis Isle, just off the coast of Ghostlands. I found that a Night Elf ship had docked, tents had been set up, and two complete moonwells had been established on this island. I had never seen a moonwell before, and I found them extremely beautiful. The aesthetic styles of the two Elf races could hardly be more different. Whereas our buildings stand out from the landscape and appear to be built from brightly colored porcelain, theirs blend with nature and often take the form of trees.

Impressed by the beauty of the moonwells, I tried to steal the secret plans without killing any Night Elves. One set of plans was in a tent, guarded by a Night Elf standing at atten- tion in the door. I was able to sneak up to the side of the tent and get the plans without entering or disturbing the guard. A second set was lying on the ground at the entrance to one of the tree houses. Its guard had already been killed by a marauding Blood Elf. The third set was on a table on the high deck of the ship. I watched as other Blood Elves blud- geoned the crew to death, and felt like a murderer myself as I picked up the plans. At least I had no actual blood on my hands. Then and there, I resolved never to kill a fellow Elf again.

About this time I became aware that I was in communication by mysterious telepathic means with others who lived at great distances, possibly even in other worlds. My studies in old books in the priest salon at Silvermoon had uncovered a legend that some gifted people could communicate indirectly, via a being called a "player" and a channel called "Internet." Without giving this story full credence, I talked occasionally in a purely mental manner with priests and shamans of other races, including Maxrohn, Incognita, Papadoc, and Minotaurus. The spiritual link was especially strong with Lunette, a Night Elf in faraway Darkshore, and we often conversed about the sad history of the sundering that separated Night Elves from Blood Elves.

By a set of curious chances, I unexpectedly found myself the grand master of a guild called the Blood Ravens, and in a fit of enthusiasm decided to transform it into an instrument of Elven unification. The Blood Elf starting zones are at the far northeast corner of the Eastern Kingdoms, and low-level members of the Horde from other races almost never go there. Therefore, guilds that start in these zones tend to have predominately Blood Elf memberships to begin with, and this was true for the Blood Ravens. I joined with no thought of playing any leadership role, but I did do my part in questing and representing the guild to nonmembers. Then a fight broke out among the leaders, a period of instability set in, members were demoted without explanation, and the guild master left. A few days later, he wanted to return. I was the only other member online at that point, so I readmitted him to membership and shortly found myself promoted to chaplain of the guild. The next couple of days were somewhat farcical, as he regained grand master status, apparently thought I was an old friend of his merely on the basis of similarity of names, and defected again, leaving me in control.

By this point, I had developed severe doubts about the objectivity and the wisdom of the Blood Elf leadership. For example, while rank-and-file warriors were giving their lives to defend our territory just a mile from his mansion, Lord Satheril sent me on quests to collect hors d'oeuvres for a decadent social event he was hosting. My resolve strengthened when I watched helplessly as Magister Sylastor, a Blood Elf noble, commanded his Undead minions to kill a band of Night Elves.

With Lunette's psychic advice, I wrote a manifesto under the slogan "Today a Blood Elf, tomorrow simply an Elf." The full text reads:

When in the course of human events it becomes necessary for a sundered people to reunite, they have every right to undertake whatever dangerous or difficult quests are required to overcome the powerful opposition to their legitimate aspirations.

For thousands of years, the Elves have been split primarily into two groups, the scientific and technological Blood Elves who have mastered the power of magic but are in danger of losing their souls, and the mystical and aesthetic Night Elves, who seek to be at one with nature yet fail to understand the corruptions that are invading their forest. This situation is tragic. Through building a fellowship of Elves, a shared spirit and hope for the future, we can begin to repair the rift.

Ultimately, Elves will need to leave the Horde and Alliance, and create their own third, superior faction. We must recognize, however, that is impossible today. We were pure in the past, and will be again in the future. Until then, we must cooperate with the other races and sometimes accept distasteful tasks. To the extent possible, Blood Elves should avoid harming Night Elves, and Night Elves should avoid harming Blood Elves.

Our immediate goals should include:

- Building fellowship among Elves through quest parties and other shared adventures
- Helping every member of our guilds to gain experience, power, and knowledge
- Completing an inventory of all the Elven resources, every outpost and every population of Elves
- Updating each other concerning Elf news of all kinds
- Inventing our own quests—becoming our own quest givers—for example seeking to defend an Elf outpost of either faction against its non-Elf enemies, or gaining and sharing secret information from both Horde and Alliance that it would benefit Elves to know
- Increasing our collective magical powers, and providing our members with the armor, weapons and other material resources needed to succeed
- Developing a deeper appreciation for Elune, the Moon Goddess, the only genuine deity worshipped in all of Azeroth
- Sharing our own individual ideas concerning how to reunite the Elves while providing exciting, positive adventures for each individual Elf

I recruited a couple new members and began helping Blood Ravens with their quests. An especially rapturous experience came when I had reached level 23, assisting Quy, a beautiful blond, level-14 guildie on her quest to collect the secret plans from Shalandis Isle. "Careful, Night Elves," I said. "We should not kill fellow Elves, if we can help it. I think Elves should unite." I pointed to one of their sacred shrines, saying, "We do not have beautiful Moonwells, like this." She agreed, and I realized she had allowed one of the Night Elves to kill her, and she was lying under the water of the moonwell. I resurrected her, we talked about the magical beauty of the place, then I told her our history. "The Elves were one people, once. Then the Well of Eternity was destroyed, and the Sundering split us into two separate tribes. Now we are in the Horde and Alliance, but ideally we would be a third force, all the Elves together." We talked about the ancient days, the sadness of those who remembered, and the natural beauty cultivated by the Night Elves.

Quy began to cry, perhaps feeling guilty about the many Night Elves she had already slain, and said she wished she were dead. I tried to comfort her, but she walked over to a Night Elf guard and let him strike her. Despite all my healing abilities, I could not protect her forever, as she stood there, passively taking blow after blow. Quy died. "I'm still here," she said. "I'm just a ghost. You may join me, if you like, and we will be able to live together in harmony." What a beautiful idea! I let one of the guards kill me, and joined Quy in death. Death was surprisingly liberating; the Night Elves would not attack us, and we could swim under the water without needing to breathe. We played hide-and-seek under and around the ship, then she taught me how to dance along its rigging. I sensed that Quy was probably too young for me, and I felt bound to Lunette, but I shall always remember that hour playing dead with Quy as one of the happiest times of my life.

Lunette and I decided that we should meet, and the best plan was for her to come to Ghostlands (see figure 5.1). Because she did not belong to a guild, whereas I was grand master of one, we thought the Blood Elf territories would be a better launching ground for a mass movement to unite all Elves. I feel really ashamed when I think back on what followed, but it must be remembered that the only tie between us had been spiritual. We belonged to different races and factions, we had never communicated via chat or mail, we had never exchanged gifts or done business together, and we had never seen each other face-to-face. We had certainly never gone on a quest together nor depended upon each other for our very lives.

The standard way by which low-level people enter and leave the Blood Elf zones is by a teleportation link between Silvermoon City and Undercity, which is not accessible to members of the Alliance without the support of a small army. Lunette thought she could swim from the north coast of Tirisfal Glades to the west coast of Ghostlands. This would be a very long journey. In Darkshore, she took ship for Menethil in the Wetlands, across

**Figure 5.1**
In a shared dream, Catullus and Lunette imagine being together at Booty Bay, a tropical tourist area of Stranglethorn Vale.

the Great Sea. She then walked halfway across the zone, north to Thandol Span and into the Arathi Highlands. Moving cautiously, because this zone is recommended for those level 30 and above, she hiked west into the Hillsbrad Foothills. Crossing this zone, she entered Silverpine Forest.

Although Silverpine is for levels 10 through 20, and she was 25, she was very careful. This was her first experience crossing into undisputed Horde territory. She was not in fact loyal to the Alliance, but as a Night Elf she was automatically assigned to the Alliance, so any high-level Horde NPC might attack her without asking questions about her political or religious views. Without incident, she entered Tirisfal Glades, headed north, passed safely between Brill and the ruins of Lordaeron, and reached the coast. She dove into the water and began to swim east. Again and again, she telepathically told me she was still swimming, although for all I knew she was cozy at home in Darnassus. Finally, she said she had reached land, but it was the Hinterlands, south of Eastern Plaguelands, not Ghostlands. This made me really suspicious, because surely she would have had to swim through the solid land of Ghostlands to get there, and that was impossible.

To test her honesty, I suggested she hike up across the full breadth of Hinterlands and Eastern Plaguelands to the Thalassian Pass that led to Ghostlands. I felt sure she could not accomplish this feat, because Eastern Plaguelands requires level 53, more than twice her degree of experience, and its monsters could kill her with a single blow. Nonetheless, after a couple days, she informed me she had just arrived in Ghostlands and would go to Shalandis Isle for provisions and repair of her armor. Setting aside my doubts, I informed the guild that she had arrived and we would be launching the Elven Unification movement shortly.

When I got to Shalandis Isle, I frantically looked for Lunette, but I did not find her. Three young Blood Elf men claimed to have seen a Night Elf woman on the island, but when I tried to explain the manifesto to them, they scoffed, and one went so far as to block any further messages from me. Lunette and I argued telepathically, both claiming to be at Shalandis and unable to see the other. In a fit of anger, I said I doubted her whole story and would prove it a pack of lies by swimming south to Tirisfal. I dove in the water and headed down the coast. When I reached the southern border of Ghostlands, I encountered a swift current that prevented me from going farther. While this was not the problem Lunette said had prevented her from completing her swim, it did seem odd I could not either reach Tirisfal or circumnavigate Ghostlands.

Without Lunette, and burdened by my profound personal doubts, the Elven Unification movement collapsed. From time to time, travelers report seeing a strange Night Elf woman at Shalandis, shouting words to them that they cannot understand. Often, they say, she dances high up in the rigging of the enemy ship docked there, and they suspect she is insane. At times I wonder about my own sanity. I feel estranged from everyone, from fellow Blood Elves as well as from the Alliance. The future of the guild remains clouded. Logic tells me that I should forget idealistic notions of unifying peoples on the basis of culture or spirituality, and get down to the practical business of accepting quests from our leaders, building up experience points, and garnering gold coins.

At best, I must give up naive notions of fellowship, altruism, and love. Yet, I cannot help but think of Lunette. When I do, a verse comes to mind that I found in an old book: "He seems to me a god, yea more than a god, who sits beside you, watches you, and hears your sweet laughter."

## Programmed Alienation

There are two main reasons two characters may not be able to meet in WoW. First, they may exist in different realms—that is, on different computer servers—of which World of Warcraft has hundreds. For example, Maxrohn and Catullus could not readily meet, because the first was on Shandris and the second was on Earthen Ring—my research team was spread out across six servers. Second, characters may belong to the same player using a single account, and only one character per account can be online at any given time. Lunette and Catullus were indeed in the same realm, the role-playing one called Earthen Ring. However, both were on my first account, so they could not be logged in simultaneously. Eventually, I opened a second account, so that some members of my team could work together closely, and paid the extra charge to have some characters moved from one realm or account to another. Significantly, one is not allowed to move a character from a normal realm to a PvP realm, preventing players from perfecting a character in an easier environment, then invading the PvP world where the natives might be at a disadvantage.

Lunette's trek to Ghostlands is among the great heroic voyages in the history of World of Warcraft, because it required her to swim along a vast span of coastline depicted as unclimbable cliffs, as well as brave innumerable dangers in two zones way above her experience level. Her trek illustrates the way that virtual space separates people and places, and the variety of barriers to free communication that exist. As it happens, the Blood Elf zones were added to the virtual world in January 2007. They had already been depicted on maps, so it was widely known that they were attached to the continent. However, they are really a separate computer environment, reachable only through a pair of portals, one depicted as the Silvermoon teleporter, and the other as Thalassian Pass. Travel in the virtual world takes time, and many areas are practically inaccessible for most people.

When Lunette found herself on the east coast of the Hinterlands, thoroughly exhausted from swimming, she consoled herself with the knowledge that there were two Elf bases along her route, Quel'Danil in the Hinterlands and Quel'Lithien in Eastern Plaguelands. Quel'Lithien is near Thalassian Pass, and when Catullus had jaunted briefly into the high-level zone, the Elves there had attacked him, so it was reasonable to assume they were Night Elves, even though they looked like Blood Elves.

In fact, the two bases are the last remnants of the High Elf civilization, hostile to the Horde but indifferent to the Alliance. When Lunette reached both places, she was allowed to enter but given access to no resources of any kind. The virtual world is divided not merely into two major factions of players but also into innumerable subdivisions among the NPCs, having a wide range of relationships to members of the factions, from hostile to indifferent to cooperative.

The Hinterlands is doable by characters who have reached level 45, twenty steps above Lunette's status, so she had a terrible time in it, dying and resurrecting repeatedly. Her route out of the zone took her to the Dwarf outpost at Aerie Peak, where the good little men who operated the place sold her everything she needed. A brief run through a surprisingly safe route in Western Plaguelands, entering through Plaguemist Ravine, was a lucky break before the hell of Eastern Plaguelands.

Crossing Eastern Plaguelands was extremely difficult for Lunette, and she died many times. While she could readily resurrect, her equipment took a beating she could not repair. Thus, the greatest disappointment about Quel'Lithien was that she could not get her armor repaired, something that can be done only by friendly NPCs with the right skills, like one Dwarf at Aerie Peak. She would have been wise to cross Eastern Plaguelands naked, dying more quickly but preserving her armor, but she did not think of this. When she reached Ghostlands, her armor was totally useless, as were her mace and wand. The Night Elf NPCs on Shalandis Isle ignored her completely. She could not approach a Horde NPC capable of repairing her equipment, because it would immediately attack her. The best she could do, and it was not very good, was to get whatever fresh armor and weapons she could, plus food and drink, by killing animals or enemies and looting their bodies. In a hostile zone, she was completely cut off from economic trade.

The language barrier was also impenetrable. The WoW software includes modules that transform chat text into meaningless but pronounceable syllables, across faction boundaries. The social module has a "who" tab, which lets a player learn something about others he encounters, but it returns no information when they are members of the other faction. A player cannot open a trade window with a member of the other faction, nor send items and money via mail, nor invite them to join a party or guild. Under normal conditions, communications are limited to standard gestures like bowing and saluting.

The primary means of complex communication between characters is text-based chat. At any one time, a character may have several chat channels open, and their texts will run near the lower left-hand corner of the computer screen, some displayed in different colors and others identified by names. For each zone, there is a local defense chat channel that chiefly displays automatic alerts if members of the opposite faction attack NPCs of the character's faction. In Barrens, the message might be "Barrens is under attack," or "Crossroads is under attack." A channel labeled Trade is supposed to be used for buying and selling, almost any topic is appropriate for the General channel, but players often use Trade for joking and other noncommercial communications.

If one player wants to communicate privately with another, he or she sends a whisper, which opens up a dedicated channel between the two. Every questing party gets a temporary Party channel that vanishes when the group disbands. Similarly, every guild gets a Guild channel, open only to members, and leaving or disbanding a guild closes it. A guild that one of my characters belonged to uses the Guild channel only for in-role communications between characters, and it established an extra chat channel for real-world communications between the players who belonged.

Among the most interesting features of the text chat is the fact that—in theory, at least—characters speak ten different languages. All members of the Alliance understand the Human language, Common. All members of the Horde speak the Orc language, Orcish. But each of the other eight races also has its own distinctive language.

When Etacarinae met Alberich, a fellow member of the Alliance, they were able to communicate perfectly well in Common, which looks exactly like English on the player's screen. For example, they both acknowledge the following principle of the major religion of the Alliance: "The cardinal virtues of the Holy Light are respect, tenacity, and compassion." When Etacarinae spoke this sentence in the Draenei language, it looked like this to Alberich: "*Lok enkilzar gulamir il lok Parn Golad lok kieldaz mordanas ruk burasadare.*" And, when Alberich spoke it in Dwarvish, it looked like this to Etacarinae: "*Eft khaz-dum dun-fel ta eft Grum Dagum kha ganrokh mogodune gor midd-havas.*" If either of them spoke the sentence in Common, it would look like this to any nearby member of the Horde: "*Ras cynegold andovis va ras Dana Garde ra vassild landowar ash aelgestron.*" Here is how another sentence looks in English and all ten WoW languages:

English  The Horde is a mass of contradictions, and the Alliance is a marriage of convenience.

Common  *Ras Majis lo o uden va waldirskilde ash ras Landowar lo o endirvis va bornevalesh.*

Orcish  *Mog Ro'th ha g rega gi moth'kazoroth kil mog Ragath'a ha g zuggossh gi no'gor'goth.*

Darnassian  *Dor Falla ri o aman lo anu'dorannador nor dor Thoribas ri o d'ana'no lo fandu'talah.*

Thalassian  *Dor Fandu ri o aman lo anu'dorannador nor dor Thoribas ri o d'ana'no lo fandu'talah.*

Gnomish  *Zah Modor we g grum ti kahzhaldren gar zah Grumgizr we g dimligar ti gizbarlodun.*

Dwarvish  *Eft Skalf we a rand ta gosh-algaz-dun gor eft Mogodune we a thulmane ta dun-haldren.*

Draenei  *Lok Zekul il x maez il zennshinagas ruk lok Sorankar il x rukadare il mannorgulan.*

Gutterspeak  *Ras Majis lo o uden va waldirskilde ash ras Landowar lo o endirvis va farlandowar.*

Troll  *Fus Nehjo fi m skam fu fus'obeah sca fus Machette fi m zutopong fu or'manley.*

Taurahe  *Alo Ti'ha wa i balo wa awakeeahmenalo ich alo Porahalo wa i oba'chi wa aloaki'shne.*

The way the language-generation system works is both simple and subtle. Any common syllable in English gets automatically converted into another pronounceable syllable. Note, however, that both *is* and *of* become "*il*" in Draenei. Although Incognita could not understand what the agents of the Scarlet Crusade shouted at her in the Common language, her own Gutterspeak, ironically, sounds the same as Common to members of other groups. This reflects the fact that Undead characters are all reborn Humans. Notice, however, that the sentences are not exactly identical in Common and Gutterspeak. Darnassian and Thalassian are both languages of the Elf family, and the two sentences are very similar but not quite identical. Apparently the language generation algorithms occasionally add random complexities. Although the pairs of Human-origin languages look nearly identical, as do the two Elf languages, in fact members of one cannot understand what the other is saying. This enforces a strict communication barrier between Horde and Alliance.

To find out what the agents of the Scarlet Crusade had been shouting at Incognita, I sent Maxrohn into the very heart of the cult, the Scarlet Monastery. To obtain correct translations without being distracted by other goals, he entered alone rather than in the usual party of five. Because he had reached level 70, he was able to defeat as many as three level-34 elite defenders simultaneously, noting what they shouted at him. Then it was a simple job to analyze the patterns of words. In English, this is what the agents of the Scarlet Crusade had said to Incognita: "You carry the taint of the Scourge. Prepare to enter the twisting nether." "The Scarlet Crusade shall smite the wicked and drive evil from these lands!" "The light condemns all who harbor evil. Now you will die!" "There is no escape for you. The crusade shall destroy all who carry the Scourge's taint."

Perhaps the reader noticed that the verse with which Catullus ends his personal account was written by the ancient Roman poet, Catullus. But they were not original to him, having been translated from a poem by Sappho, a Greek woman who was tremendously influential on the Roman poet's life, but who lived hundreds of years before him. They never met because of the chasm of time between their lives. This quotation reminds us that all worlds, not virtual ones alone, impose barriers to intimate cooperation.

The story of the bond between Catullus and Sappho illustrates many other dimensions of intimacy and estrangement. Separated by centuries, the two could not cooperate through an equal give-and-take. By today's standards, his use of her verses was plagiarism, yet by the cultural standards of his day, it was an homage. She herself had once hoped, "I think men will remember us even hereafter."[1] Interestingly, when I take a screen shot of Catullus for use in a commercial publication, I need permission from Blizzard Entertainment, on the basis that they own all images in WoW. If it had been a photo taken in the real world, the issue would be whether I had taken it in a public place, or needed written permission from Catullus.

In a sense, the Roman poet Catullus tried to have an erotic relationship with the Greek poetess Sappho by proxy. The poem quoted is widely believed to have been written to the promiscuous but erudite Roman woman, Clodia, although some scholarly debate surrounds this point. Another poem in the series begins, *"Vivamus mea Lesbia, atque amemus"* ("Let us live, my Lesbia, and let us love"), using "Lesbia" as a synonym for Sappho, because Sappho lived on the island of Lesbos, an inhabitant of which is called a *Lesbian*. The modern English word, *lesbian*, refers to a homosexual woman, on the assumption that Sappho shared physical love with members of her own gender. This detail about the life of the poetess derives from particular interpretations of her works, in the context of the belief that homosexuality was common in classical Greece, and this claim, also, has been contested.[2]

Contemplating the connection between our Catullus, the Blood Elf; his namesake in ancient Rome; Clodia; Sappho; and Lunette offers a very long catalog of kinds of estrangement. People are often separated by the sands of time, different languages, incompatible preferences, ambiguities concerning ownership, and failure to make commitments.

## The Roots of Cooperation

Social scientists traditionally derived human cooperation from mutually beneficial exchanges between individuals, or from shared cultural beliefs and values. If I were writing an entire book today on cooperation, I would include chapters on at least two new theories based on the biology of the brain. One builds on the fact that erotic relations between people, and the breast feeding of babies, liberates the hormone oxytocin, which appears to increase trust and generosity between people.[3] The other biological theory notes the discovery of *mirror neurons*, a specialized structure in the brain that allows people to take the role of the other, perhaps therefore to empathize, and thus to pay attention to each other's needs. Both these theories would seem inapplicable to cooperation in World of Warcraft, because people cannot really touch each other in WoW, or see the other's facial expressions and subtle emotional gestures. The theory that shared values support cooperation may also not apply well because nobody really believes the religions of WoW, and the notion that values actually constrain behavior in the real world has only dubious scientific support anyway.[4] This leaves the more-or-less economic theory that people cooperate because it often is in their individual best interests to do so.

For a quarter century, we have known how to program very simple artificial intelligences that are capable of learning to cooperate, without benefit of oxytocin, mirror neurons, or religiously inspired values. The key factor is that the AIs need to be part of a system of exchange in which they repeatedly return to each other and thus develop reputations as good or bad exchange partners.

Today, we know many ways to represent this in computer programs. The classical example, reported in Robert Axelrod's 1984 book, *The Evolution of Cooperation*, merely had each AI agent remember what the other agent did the time before, and emulate that behavior.[5] Axelrod's experiment used the game called the "prisoner's dilemma," in which two people or software agents make an agreement. If they both fulfill the bargain, both gain. But if one double-crosses the other, while the other keeps the bargain, the double-crosser gains while the honest agent loses. Thus, short-term calculation of benefit favors double-crossing. Only if the agents interact repeatedly over time can cooperation emerge.

This may not be the case for lone WoW players, but it certainly is the case for members of guilds. WoW has an elaborate reputation scheme, but it measures how well the individual has been completing certain kinds of quests, not how well the individual fulfills obligations to other players. It is not what computer scientists call a *reputation system*. The most familiar example is the reputation system in eBay, the e-commerce company that facilitates buying and selling among many thousands of individuals. In the *Berkshire Encyclopedia of Human-Computer Interaction*, which I edited, Cliff Lampe and Paul Resnik note that a reputation system can serve three related functions.[6] First, it informs users about each other's trustworthiness. Second, it indirectly rewards people for good behavior. Third, it discourages *adverse selection*, the situation in which the best people leave the market because they cannot get adequate reward from the quality of their goods and services, leaving the market to shady characters. Thus a major function of guilds in WoW is to let trustworthy players earn good reputations that will encourage others to cooperate with them.[7]

My primary mentor, when I was a graduate student in sociology, was the behaviorist George C. Homans. I can recall the excitement with which he told me about Axelrod's book, immediately after it was published, when our separate paths converged in Harvard Yard. Homans had long argued that human society was based on cooperation between individuals for mutual benefit. His 1950 book, *The Human Group*, had gone a long distance in that direction. His later book *Social Behavior* had provided greater theoretical precision in its 1961 and 1974 editions. Homans's main line of analysis was exactly like Axelrod's, but his full argument was much deeper. He died in 1989, but I imagine his analysis would have deepened further over the past two decades.[8]

Humans are a social species, not the least because we are born helpless. Even mature adults need to rely on each other for protection, for food and water, during illness, and increasingly over the span of history for economic exchanges. Social interconnectedness is so important, and has been for so long, that evolution gave us a variety of mechanisms to support cooperation. Language is one of these social binding tools, but it also permits us to deceive one another. Thus, human social nature is chaotic and complex, relying on the interplay of many factors. Importantly, Homans repeatedly hinted throughout his work that processes beyond rational calculation of long-term self-interest were also at work. In *The Human Group*, he specifically argued that humans who interact repeatedly come to be more similar to each other and to value each other quite beyond the material rewards they exchange. There is a general, but not perfect, tendency for people who interact to become alike and to come to like each other.

A half century after *The Human Group*, and remarkably without citing it, Edward J. Lawler, Shane R. Thye, and Jeongkoo Yoon came to a similar conclusion:

Social exchange is inherently a joint activity in which two or more actors attempt to produce a flow of benefits better than they can achieve alone or in other relationships. . . . Productive exchange is a group-oriented coordination task in which actors seek to produce a valued result through their joint collaboration . . . commitment in dyads and larger groups may grow from expressive, as well as instrumental, foundations . . . social exchange has emotional effects on actors, and if these are attributed to social units, the social unit takes on expressive value or intrinsic worth.[9]

If he had joined a successful WoW guild, Homans would have immediately commented that he saw much pure socializing going on between members, such as joking on the guild chat, which cemented relationships quite beyond the strength of ties attributable to practical need. Much recent sociology research has shown that high-solidarity groups can create a generalized sense of trust among members, even beyond the validation of individual reputations (see figure 5.2).[10]

Thus, enlightened self-interest may be the core of human cooperation, but it is not the whole story. In WoW, as is true outside, other dimensions of social interaction are also important. Guilds function to evaluate individuals and authenticate their reputations, but they may have a host of other functions, as well. It is worth considering for a few moments the natural history of WoW cooperation, starting with its faintest forms, then introducing its formalization in parties and guilds.

## Evolution of Cooperation

Even without a formal agreement to cooperate, one player can benefit implicitly from the actions of another whenever their goals differ but overlap. A notable example

**Figure 5.2**
A chaotic group meeting on the roof of the bank in Orgrimmar, celebrating the new year.

benefits skinners, characters who have developed the skill to skin dead animals and then sell or use the leather they get. Most characters are not skinners, but must kill skinable animals to get through many areas, looting the corpses for some valuables, like fangs and eyeballs, but leaving the rest of the carcass intact. A skinner who comes upon a recent kill can take the leather very quickly with a simple application of a skinning knife, without the risk and effort of killing. This is a completely asymmetrical kind of cooperation, but it is not exploitation, because the character who killed the animal loses nothing. Once the leather is on the market, it adds to the total wealth and thus benefits everybody. On occasion, a skinner will kill animals just to get their leather, thereby clearing a path for other characters without specifically intending to help them.

Folwell first experienced implicit cooperation when he was just reaching level 5 in the Night Elf newbie zone. A quest required him to find a spider egg deep within caverns infested with adult spiders. These arachnids were spaced out along the corridors and needed to be killed one by one. He encountered Direnight, a level-5 Night

Elf druid, who was doing the same quest. They did not talk, gesture, or otherwise communicate with each other. But they quickly fell into a pattern of killing alternate spiders, thereby reaching their goal nearly twice as quickly.

Formal cooperation often rests upon the division of labor, in which different people specialize in accomplishing different parts of a complex task.[11] In WoW, as in many similar MMORPGs, there are three main roles in battle: tank (holds the enemy in pace), healer (sustains the tank), and DPS (applies maximum damage per second to the enemy). Having someone to play the tank role can be the difference between success and failure. Maxrohn saw this with his own eyes when a Human rogue asked him to help her kill Durn, the Hungerer, an elite in the level-64 to level-67 Nagrand zone. The quest calls for five characters, and the team was completed with a Human mage, a Dwarf hunter, and a Night Elf hunter. None of the five was well equipped to be a tank. The Hungerer has an estimated health of 120,000, which means he must be attacked severely to be killed, and the team had ample DPS members who could do this job. The problem was that the Hungerer aggressively stomped on the nearest of them, moving so quickly that Maxrohn could not heal them fast enough to keep them alive. A good tank capable of resisting damage could have been saved. After the team was swiftly defeated, the Night Elf hunter left, and the leader got a replacement. But the new team member was a priest, unsuited to be a tank. The leader decided to use one of the hunters' pets as the tank, but Maxrohn's attempt to heal it as the Hungerer stomped on it failed. After a second ignominious defeat, the leader said, "Oh well. Guess I'll just have to wait to get him later on tonight or tomorrow. Thanks anyway guys. I appreciate the effort."

Given the triad division of labor in battle, some classes can be hybrids. For example, paladins are a hybrid of warrior and priest. In Aaron Rosenberg's novel *Tides of Darkness*, Archbishop Faol of the Human church established this class, saying, "I chose these men for both their piety and their martial prowess. They will be trained, not only in war but in prayer and healing. And each of these valiant fighters will possess both martial and spiritual power, particularly in blessing themselves and others with the strength of the Holy Light."[12] In a sense, both hunters and warlocks are miniature teams, although only a single player is involved. A hunter has a pet animal, and a warlock has a minion spirit, which are assistant NPCs or secondary avatars. They are sent forward to hold the enemy, acting like tanks, while the hunter or warlock stands back and shoots at the enemy, also occasionally healing the pet or minion.

The designers of WoW needed to encourage commitment to social groups as a way of committing players to WoW itself, but they also needed to provide a variety of game experiences for a diversity of players, and for players running second and third characters who needed something refreshing after the experience of their first character. It is entirely possible to reach the top level of experience without ever joining a guild, or even cooperating with another player. However, the instances and battlegrounds that dominate play at the higher levels are group activities and cannot be attempted alone. Similarly, many particular quests require from two to five players to collaborate.

One tactic WoW's designers used to encourage solo players to become sociable is committing the player to a quest before informing the player that it is difficult or even impossible for a single player to win. Only after accepting a quest does the player learn it is a "group" or "dungeon" quest. Of course, the player can immediately abandon the quest, but many players feel that would be an admission of defeat, so they leave the quest on their list, intending to decide about it later. Easy opportunities to cooperate on the quest may come along, or the person may eventually decide to seek help actively.

Many quests that need two or three players to complete comfortably are not labeled "group" quests. For example, when Lunette was level 16, she attempted the quest Cave Mushrooms in the Darkshore zone, which requires entering a cave hidden behind a waterfall and gathering five scaber stalk mushrooms and one aptly named death cap mushroom. Unfortunately, the cave is filled with level-15 to level-17 Naga, intelligent green sea creatures who were apparently attracted by the Cliffspring River that runs over their cavern. Two Naga are posted immediately outside the cave, and two just inside, so getting past the entrance is a big challenge. Once a character is inside, the cave branches right and left, with the left branch heading downward into a large space. Lunette went left, and with great difficulty she was able to kill the Naga one at a time and get the scaber stalks. The Naga respawn rather quickly after being killed, and a priest like Lunette needs to pause between battles to rebuild mana as well as health, so it was vital to keep progressing away from the spots where they would respawn. Finally, Lunette reached the bottom level and could see death caps. Unfortunately, the cavern was filled with closely spaced Naga, whom she could not attack separately, bolstered by two Twilight Thugs standing right next to the mushrooms. Twice she died. She found it was possible to rez unnoticed in a pool of water in the center of the cavern, but very quickly one of the wandering Naga would detect her and attack before she had regained her strength, with fatal consequences.

The Wowhead and Thottbot websites carry extensive conversations between players about how to win this quest solo, some reporting it was easy, and others admitting they failed no matter how hard they tried.[13] Several suggested that a rogue character was best because he or she could sneak past some of the Naga in stealth mode. Others suggested a hunter was best because his or her animal companion could attack a Naga while the hunter stood back and shot arrows without taking damage. One noted that there was an advantage to being an herbalist, because the locations of the mushrooms would show up on an herbalist's map. Many reported a solo player's only chance was to take the right fork of the cave, not the more obvious left fork, because a death cap was hidden at the end, and there were fewer Naga to contend with.

Eventually, Lunette returned at level 20 to try again. She succeeded, but her sense of independent accomplishment was compromised by the fact that a level-21 Night Elf druid and a level-19 Dwarf paladin entered the cave beside her, so she had the advantage of their help even though she did not formally join their group. Cave Mushrooms begins a series of five quests, the other four of which cannot be started until all the mushrooms have been collected, so cooperation is very much to an individual's advantage.

Sometimes a series of solo quests feeds into a group quest. A famous example is Bride of the Embalmer. The series of eleven quests begins in Duskwood with the hermit Abercrombie, whom many believe is named after the Abercrombie & Fitch department store. The tenth quest involves taking a note to the mayor of Darkshire, Lord Ello Ebonlocke. He in turn offers two quests that require the player's character to have reached levels 21, 22, or 23. One is a simple solo matter of taking the note a short distance to be translated, but the other requires going to a grave northeast of Raven Hill Cemetery, digging up the Undead body of Eliza, the bride of the embalmer, and killing it, while she is protected by three guards. Each of the guards is level 18, and Eliza herself is a level-31 elite, which means she's more powerful than an ordinary 31. Thottbot and Wowhead carry extensive discussions about whether it is possible to solo this quest at level 30, perhaps by dying one or more times during the battle.[14]

Maxrohn tried this quest solo several times, when he was around level 30, and could not even come close to completing it. He returned at level 46, vengeance in his heart, and discovered that it was not easy even given the great power of 16 levels he had gained. If he killed Eliza first, and then the three others, Eliza would rebury and need to be fought all over again. After three unsuccessful attempts, he succeeded by killing Eliza and simply ignoring the damage being done to him by the guards as he cut out Eliza's heart. When he returned the beating heart to the mayor, the experience points he earned were insignificant, just 370, when the experience he needed to rise from level 46 to 47 was 123,200! The mayor did give him a Mantle of Honor and a Crest of Darkshire, which together had a cash value of about 69 silver coins. At that point, Maxrohn possessed 50 gold coins and 61 silver, or 73 times as much. He could not use the two items personally, because the Mantle of Honor was shoulder armor weaker than he was already wearing, and as a priest, he could not carry the Crest of Darkshire, which was a warrior's shield. These facts illustrate that little may be gained, other than a sense of completion, by soloing a group quest at a higher level than it was intended for.

## Guilds

Catullus received a lesson in the folly of trusting strangers, while he was battling Ogres in the Alterac Mountains. Over the general chat channel, an Undead mage asked,

"Can someone help me clear two yeti at Growless Cave? I'll pay 5 gold for your time." Five gold pieces sounded excessive, but Catullus was having difficulty saving up to buy a mount, so he agreed. A Blood Elf rogue also joined the party, and the three of them were able to complete the mage's quest very quickly. At that point, the mage thanked his two helpers and ran away, without paying.

"Well, we live and learn," Catullus said to the equally disappointed rogue.

The rogue replied, "Next time the money up front."

Catullus contemplated how that plan would merely put the onus of trust on the other party, and joked, "Or put in escrow with a priest!" In fact, because nobody believes WoW religions, there is no reason a priest would be more trustworthy than, say, a rogue. In fact the nearest thing to escrow in WoW is the guild vault, a place where guild members place valuables in the care of the guild master.

There seem to be three different routes by which people become members of guilds (see figure 5.3). First, they may form a guild from scratch, and often a successful guild

**Figure 5.3**
An example of a successful Horde guild, Alea Iacta Est, in the Earthen Ring realm, here celebrating its first birthday by seizing an Alliance tower in Elwynn Forest.

is formed by a group of people who are already friends, sometimes even members of the same real-world family. Second, guilds that are trying to grow may advertise on the guild-recruiting channel of the chat system; depending on how selective they are, even a halfhearted expression of interest may result in a formal invitation to join. Third, a member of a guild may share quests or other experiences with a nonmember, come to see that person as competent and trustworthy, and extend an invitation on the basis of extensive familiarity based entirely on in-game interactions.

During his long career, Maxrohn belonged to two successful guilds in the Shandris realm, the Shadow Clan and Winged Ascension. He found both to be friendly, active, and graced with good leadership. He left the Shadow Clan simply to expand the range of his social experiences, and Winged Ascension was somewhat larger. He had joined the Shadow Clan after encountering a Human paladin named Memra a couple times by chance and helping each other. On their third happy encounter, Memra called her Dwarf husband, Malius, and they both invited Maxrohn to join the Shadow Clan.

Before he had joined their guild, Max had added Memra to his list of friends, and the system always alerted him when she came online. When she and Malius moved to Winged Ascension, he remained in the Shadow Clan, but kept that other guild in mind. At levels 56 and 57, while he was in Winterspring and she was in Silithus, they exchanged messages in which she expressed satisfaction with her new group and he admitted he was doing mostly solo quests. She remarked, "If you want to come join us just let me know. . . . We're going to quest in the Blasted Lands. . . . Don't need to be in the guild for that." Shortly afterward, Maxrohn opened the social module of his user interface, selected his own name in the list of online guild members, and right-clicked to get a confirmation message, saying, "Really leave the Shadow Clan?" He clicked "Accept," then composed a gracious resignation letter personally thanking Dicola, the leader of the Shadow Clan.

The next step was to seek entry into Winged Ascension. While Maxrohn was traveling the snow-flanked road in Winterspring, he contacted Memra, saying, "Memra, I would like to join your guild. Is that still possible?"

She replied, "Give me a second, and I'll talk to the guild for you." She then asked whether he had any alts, which are secondary characters, and he replied that he did but he was the main, and the alts were not in the Alliance in this realm. "Ok. Whisper Aazenroth. He's the guild master, and he's expecting you." To Maxrohn's great surprise, Memra's friend and senior guild member Dreadmaul suddenly rode up on his warhorse and helped Aazenroth interview Maxrohn. Given that he was level 58, they said he should be in Outland. With his cautious temperament, though, he did not feel ready to go there until reaching level 60, and he may have seemed insufficiently aggressive to his interviewers.

When asked why he was changing guilds, Maxrohn explained, "Shadow Clan is okay, but not as vigorous as it had been. I get along with the people, but your guild

is bigger. There was no fight or anything like that between me and Shadow Clan."
Dreadmaul said he thought there would be no problem being accepted into Winged
Ascension, and Memra sent him the extremely useful gift of five large carrying bags
she had crafted. However, Aazenroth said, "I am looking for more end-game oriented
people." He seemed a little skeptical that Maxrohn had the motivation to join with
other high-level members in advancing quickly to level 70 and then attacking dungeons and raiding Horde cities.

A couple days passed, in which Maxrohn gently nudged the guild members. Then
he asked Aazenroth directly, "Did you and the other guild leaders come to a decision?
Do you want to invite me to the guild, or suggest I find another guild?" Aazenroth
told him to hang on for a few seconds because the level-70 guild leader was battling
a boss enemy in the Mechanar. As soon as the boss had been defeated, Maxrohn was
a member of Winged Ascension. A chorus of members welcomed him: Malak, Sathura,
Ulla, Brictorn, Kizamet, Mooncrusher, and Musicguru, plus Aazenroth, Memra, and
Dreadmaul. Lockness said, "You come well recommended," and Lethal said, "Welcome
to the family." Maxrohn's modest reply was "I'll do my best."

Most guilds may not be large enough to be adequate recruiting ground for raiding
parties. For many of the special environments called *dungeons* or *instances*, a group of
five is ideal, and each member must be above a certain level. A given guild simply
may not have enough members online at the time when one wants to organize a
group. For example, on June 2, 2007, Luisserare, a level-54 Dwarf paladin who belonged
to the Alliance Assassins wanted to raid the Sunken Temple in the Swamp of Sorrows.
His guild had only 35 members, and none was available, so he recruited two people
he had found reliable during earlier escapades: Gewyn, a level-54 Draenei mage who
belonged to the Druid Circle, which had 209 members, and our own Maxrohn.
Maxrohn's guild, the Shadow Clan, had 67 members. Luisserare posted a recruiting
message on the Looking for Group system, and periodically the party of three would
see the following automatic message in their chat window: "You are still seeking more
members through the LFG matchmaking system." Maxrohn sent a message on his
guild's chat channel and quickly recruited Aliizsa, a level-54 Draenei warrior. For
several minutes, the party was unable to recruit any more members.

An important criterion was the level of the character, because a level even a couple
steps below optimum would be damaged easily in combat and would contribute little.
The group figured that levels 52 or 53 would be best. Maxrohn himself was only level
50 when the recruiting began, but Luisserare said, "Well, Max is a 50, but he's a really
good healer." Maxrohn chimed in, "I'm about to level to 51," and indeed he did before
the group entered the temple. Gewyn commented, "Doesn't matter so much for the
healer. Honestly, we're lucky as hell to have any priest." For a while they discussed a
volunteer who was only level 49, but Luisserare already had turned down friends at
that level. Eventually, they were joined by a third member of the Shadow Clan,

Silence, who was a level-51 Night Elf rogue and had some experience in the temple already.

## Group Problems

The overwhelming majority of guilds fail, and many of the smaller ones are quite dysfunctional. When she reached level 7, Lunette was invited to join a guild by a member who explained, "[W]e have friendly people and we all help out." This sounded good, so she joined. After hearty welcomes from its two officers, she began receiving all the chat messages sent on the guild's private channel. She thought the chat was very encouraging, as members would exclaim "DINGGG" when they leveled up, and others would respond "grats" in congratulation. Then, one member began saying obnoxious things. Another member, who was a level-63 warrior and thus senior, proclaimed, "I will not take disrespect in this guild to ANY other member. Is that clear?" This stern warning brought an apology. The warrior warned, "Don't let it happen again," and was promptly appointed master of the guild. Lunette thought this was a good sign.

However, the former leader had been an Elf, whereas the new master was a Human, so Lunette inquired, "Does this mean we are a Human guild, instead of an Elf guild?" One member replied, "We are a mix, I think." Another answered, "We are an everything guild." Lunette wanted to be in an Elf guild, and the way she left the guild (although not race-related) was especially disheartening because she wanted Elves to be superior. Having reached level 10, she agreed to accompany a level-14 Elf warrior on one of his quests, despite being a little put off because he seemed to be something of a braggart. For the first time, she left Teldrassil on the boat to Darkshore, where he suddenly dove into the water without first checking whether she knew how to swim. Doing the best she could, she paddled after him into the Mist's Edge, while he carried on a sexually oriented chat with other members who remained at a distance and thus were not prepared to help them if they got into trouble.

They did indeed get into trouble, because the warrior swam down into a sunken ship without explaining what he was doing, and Lunette could not find him. When they finally rendezvoused on a nearby shore, after a quite harrowing time, the warrior vanished. Lunette waited for fifteen minutes, but he did not return—apparently the other player had left the game—and she realized she was alone in a strange land she had never seen before, far from safety. Angrily she informed the guild, "He asked me to help him on a quest, took me far away from my own area, then left. I am leaving this guild!" The replies she got were limited to "Ok, Bubi," and the other guild members chattered about selling a car one of them owned. Lunette exclaimed, "You people are not serious about WoW. Please tell me how to leave the guild." Three members laughed at her, then one explained, "Go to the guild window, right click your name and leave guild." Another laughed and said, "We have a life."

Catullus had an especially bad experience in a party with two fellow guild members, and he still wishes he could have handled the situation better. He had recently become grand master of the Blood Raven guild, and was desperately struggling to build its membership. He had succeeded in recruiting a couple low-level members, but had built an alliance with a smaller guild that amounted to nothing and repeatedly failed to recruit higher-level members who seemed friendly toward him but unwilling to make a commitment. Two fellow members, whom we will call Mack and Muff to preserve their anonymity, invited him to join a party for the Blackfathom Deeps dungeon. Soon, two female Blood Elves had agreed to join the party, bringing its membership to the ideal five, and Catullus had hoped to recruit them to the guild. In retrospect, Catullus recognized his goals were not those of Mack and Muff. They simply wanted to win the dungeon right away, while his eyes were on the longer-term goal of building the guild. Conflict often arises when people have different goals that prove to be at least partially in opposition, including differing on whether the goals were short-term or long-term.

One of the women, whom Catullus knew well from previous contacts, dropped out because of a real-world distraction. The remaining woman noted that that left only four and recruited a male friend of hers, who was busy doing business at another location. A ten-minute verbal tug-of-war ensued, as the woman tried to pull her male friend away from his business deal, and Mack kept urging them to come. The language got heated, with Muff saying, "You're a retard," and Mack exclaiming, "Ok, screw it!" Mack suddenly, and without consulting Catullus, kicked the woman and her friend out of the party, and recruited another male Blood Elf. This stunned Catullus, but Mack said to him, Muff, and the newcomer, "Let's go, guys, we can make it on our own."

Rather than follow Mack, Catullus sat down to ponder the situation, while communicating separately with both Mack and the discarded woman. She whispered to him, "Mack and Muff are asses."

Catullus told Mack he did not think that kicking the pair out was a good idea. Mack replied, "We can make it ourselves. They just slowed us down." Of course, this comment merely reinforced Catullus's awareness that he and Mack had very different goals.

Catullus told Mack, "More important to be helpful and friendly than always to win."

Mack replied defiantly, "We got another person, now. It's okay, and they were pissing me off."

Catullus responded, "But they were not bothering me. It often takes a long time. You were the leader, but not the dictator."

Muff shouted, "Let's go!"

Catullus disagreed, saying, "I don't think we should have given up on them." When both Mack and Muff urged Catullus to get moving, and again said the couple was just slowing them down, Catullus said angrily, "That is just not important to me, sorry." At that moment, he used the social interface to resign from the group.

Mack complained, "I know I'm not a dictator. But Muff was screaming at me on the phone, and they have to leave. I'm sorry, but they were no help. I tried to be nice."

Muff shouted at Catullus, "Fag! Homo!"

Shortly thereafter, because he was no longer a member of the instance's group, the dungeon system automatically teleported Catullus to his home inn, which at the time was in Tranquillien, very far from Darkshore, where he would have wanted to be.

In addition to the conflicting purposes of the different individuals, this incident is interesting for the role of communication patterns. Mack and Muff were friends sharing a telephone link, which the others did not even know about. This intimate communication naturally strengthened their solidarity. The woman was virtually present inside the dungeon, but her friend was not, and this probably reduced the influence of the party on him. In any case, he was in heated negotiation about some business with somebody else. At the height of the incident, not only were Mack and Muff communicating privately by phone but also the woman was whispering with Catullus, and Catullus was whispering with Mack, unbeknownst to Muff or to the woman's friend.

Shortly after the incident, Mack and Muff left the guild. Only one other member was online at that point, and Catullus somewhat defensively told him, "You might wonder why two people just left the guild. There was an argument in a dungeon between them and two other people. The two people from our guild expelled the others from the raid. I argued for reconciliation, and refused to go on unless the group talked through the conflict and tried to make friends. But that did not help." The other member commented that this news was sad. Catullus continued, "Don't know if I did the right thing. I did not expel the two members from our guild. I wish them well. People have different values, and some place a higher value on winning points than winning friends."

The best guilds provide inspiration, not merely material assistance. On that ominous day, Friday the thirteenth of July, the leader of Winged Ascension proclaimed in the message of the day, "Remember my dear family, the Ascension is about being better than ourselves, not others."

## Faction Relations

At the historical moment represented by WoW, the Horde and Alliance are in an uneasy truce, which is more peaceful on "normal" realms than on PvP (player-versus-player) realms. To explore this difference, I created two characters on the Emerald

Dream PvP realm—Llana, the Blood Elf paladin, and Folwell, the Night Elf druid—but I never took them beyond level 20, and thus they did not experience the chaos of conflict far outside their home zones. At one point, I had them meet in the inn at Ratchet, to do some of the language analysis reported earlier in this chapter, and Folwell needed to hide behind a pillar. When he had entered the inn, a Tauren named Sinslayer immediately beat him to death with a huge mallet. Wherever he went around this seaside town, Hordies would kill him on sight. He retreated to Ashenvale, near Maestra's Post, to grind deer for leveling, but gangs of Hordies kept running across him. I thought a paladin and a druid would be good characters for a PvP realm because they could be self-sufficient, but I now think I had it backward. Either a priest, who would travel with a group as their valued healer, or a rogue, who could hide even better than a druid, might survive.

PvP battles occur on normal servers, too, often when a group intentionally attacks NPCs of the opposing faction, but individual players can stay out of the fight if they avoid raising their battle flags. On June 20, 2007, Lunette entered Auberdine just as it was under attack from members of Horde's Celestial Gate guild. She instantly realized the attackers were far above her level, because she could not see their level numbers, and their pictures showed a skull as well as the red player-versus-player badge of the Horde. She stood helpless, watching them slaughter Night Elf NPCs, Flintbeard and Steelhand, as the two shouted in Darnassian for help. A level-23 Night Elf player exclaimed, "Absolute blood bath! I'm a level 23. No way am I fighting these, what? 70s or higher." Lunette knew there was nothing higher than level 70 at that time prior to the Lich King expansion, but she had to assume they were at least level 33 if the other Elven player could not see their numbers, and she was still only level 20. Eventually, she could not withhold her help any longer. She tried to heal a dying NPC, but this only switched on her PvP flag, and one of the Horde players attacked her. Although she dove into the nearby water, she was slain.

Wanton killing of another player's character is *ganking*. Maxrohn experienced ganking firsthand when he was around level 40 at a crossroads in the Swamp of Sorrows. A level-37 Horde scout was standing there, barring the way, so rather than go around, Maxrohn attacked him. This had the effect of turning Maxrohn's battle flag on, rendering him vulnerable to attack by Horde players. Unfortunately, the crossroads was between the Horde flight path at Stonard and the entry to the high-level Blasted Lands zone. Just as Maxrohn was bending down to loot the scout's corpse, a high-level Horde player killed him instantly. His last memory of the episode is the Horde player's laughter.

Many months later, Catullus happened upon the same spot when he was level 42. He watched as a level-42 Draenei warrior, belonging to the Alliance, proceeded to kill two Horde scouts. Horde loyalist that he was, Catullus found this offensive, but stood watching and calculating what to do. He felt sure the warrior could beat him in a duel, but he thought that the warrior looked vulnerable because the two scouts had depleted about half of the Draenei's health. He also noticed that the Draenei's name contained the word *killer*, and felt this was rather boastful. As soon as the second scout fell dead, Catullus slammed the Alliance warrior with holy fire, followed quickly by a mind blast and a smite. Before the enemy knew what hit him, his health was exhausted. As the Draenei fell, he raised his arms in a gesture of desperation. Not wanting to face the angry warrior after resurrection, Catullus walked the short distance to the protection of Stonard. He tried to tell himself that his actions were all justified, but in his heart he felt that ganking was a sweet, immoral pleasure he would not mind experiencing again.

Cooperation between factions during questing is very difficult, but not impossible. For example, one day when he was at level 45, Maxrohn was in the Hinterlands, working on a quest to kill green sludge and jade ooze mobs, a job that might have been easier with a partner but could readily be done by a single player. Then he saw that a level-46 Human paladin named Stelly had posted a message on the Alliance general chat for the area, seeking someone to help with a different quest in the same zone, the Altar of Zul. Having that quest on his list and knowing something about how to accomplish it, Maxrohn formally invited Stelly to join a party with him. They met just north of the altar, which was at the top of a long set of monumental stairs that were guarded by many level-46 or level-47 Troll mobs, including some level-48 elites, which means they were actually tougher than level 48. The pair found that they could just barely kill one of these Trolls if they worked together. Stelly would attack a single enemy. Maxrohn would use one or two spells to weaken their opponent, then concentrate on keeping Stelly alive, adding an occasional shot from his wand.

They noticed that another pair was in the neighborhood, two Blood Elves of the Horde, a level-47 warlock named Ballistics, and a level-59 hunter named Kaleen, who were both members of a guild called Respected Ones and thus presumably experienced in cooperating. The two pairs made no hostile moves against each other, and for a time they largely ignored each other. After completing one quest, Stelly mentioned he had some other quests in the area, and Maxrohn offered to help him. The Altar of Zul is a small part of a huge temple complex, rather like a maze punctuated by courtyards and monumental staircases. The two pairs of players found themselves working in parallel, and occasionally a member of one pair would assist the other pair in killing a difficult common enemy. These formidable Trolls stood in the way of both pairs, so it was in their interest to help each other kill them. Although Maxrohn frequently could use his priestly talents to heal Stelly, when he was injured he could not heal the two Blood Elves. He actually felt embarrassed by this, although the limitation was built in to the virtual world rather than being his own choice, and he wished he could apologize. Because they could not talk to each other, it was difficult for the two pairs to coordinate their actions and to agree to pursue the same goals.

One reasonably effective mode of communication was gestures. At one time, neither pair had any idea where to go. Stelly logged off the game briefly, and consulted the online Thottbot database, then logged back on. Naturally, he explained to Maxrohn exactly what he was doing through their party chat channel. But how could he communicate with the two members of the Horde, given that they could not understand each other's languages? When Kaleen said "*thrakk*" in the Orcish tongue used by the Horde, what did he mean? Stelly relied on the age-old human understanding of gestures, jumping up and down, then pointing in the right direction.

As they were beginning to cooperate, the two pairs exchanged gestures, and most gestures are accompanied by text that shows up in the chat window. Unlike regular chat text, this gesture text is legible to members of both factions. Here is one set they exchanged, as read by Maxrohn, who initiated it: "You bow before Kaleen. Kaleen thanks everyone. Kaleen asks you to wait. You salute Stelly with respect. Kaleen bows down graciously."

The teamwork between the two pairs lasted about an hour because there were many places to go and enemies to pass before achieving the quest goals. The two pairs could not form a four-person party, so each pair needed to complete each quest separately. After one pair did so, the other might need to wait for a few minutes for the quest goal to become active again. It is questionable whether either pair could have succeeded alone, although the Blood Elf pair did include a higher-level character. At the very least, their progress was made much easier by their cooperation with Stelly and Maxrohn. This would probably have been impossible if a member of one faction had shown hostility toward the other, as in fact is often seen. On several occasions, Maxrohn had been spat upon by a member of the Horde, without provocation, and a gesture like that would have prevented cooperation.

An interesting variant on interfaction cooperation is treason, practiced by some players who have characters in both the Horde and Alliance. For example, word came to Etacarinae that the Alliance city, Stormwind, was about to be attacked by the Horde. Like many others, she rushed to the main gate, glad that an Alliance spy in the Horde ranks had provided warning of the impending assault. The defenders milled around for a while, getting progressively more anxious, then rushed south when word came that the Horde army was advancing up the road from Westfall. This proved to be disinformation, spread by a traitor in the Alliance ranks. When she rushed back to Stormwind, Etacarinae discovered the invaders had nearly reached the keep, deep inside the city, before being crushed. Soon afterward, her guild began planning a counterattack against Orgrimmar.

Recognizing the value for our collaborative research, I had Etacarinae immediately inform Incognita, her contact in the Horde. This allowed Incognita to photograph the Alliance counterattack, from its entry of Orgrimmar through the West Gate to the death of the Human guild leader at the bridge to the flight tower. Incognita refrained

**Figure 5.4**
A Horde raiding party of the Alea Iacta Est guild, resting after success penetrating to the heart of the Alliance, the Deeprun Tram station in Stormwind.

from alerting the defenders that the attack was coming, and the Alliance spread disinformation, through its own mole in the Horde ranks, that the far city of Silvermoon was where the blow would fall.

## Epilogue

Nearly a year after Aristotle settled at the Westfall lighthouse, his repose was shattered by the startling rumor that a hidden city had been discovered beneath Ironforge, accessible only with great difficulty and the help of a mage. Overpowered by his scientific curiosity, he rushed to Northridge to find an apprentice who could help him launch archaeological research into that mysterious region. He recruited Ozma, a young Human mage, and soon the two of them were in Ironforge, following the intricate instructions contained in the rumor. First, they went to a precise spot near the bank, the only location in the city where dueling was possible, and challenged each other. This would allow Aristotle to use his polymorph spell at a certain other spot, turning Ozma into a sheep and rendering her small enough to pass through a hidden gap into the realms below. Unfortunately, they discovered they could not run fast enough from the edge of the dueling zone to the other spot to complete the experiment. Aristotle analyzed the situation and realized he had two courses of action open. First, he and Ozma could both invest the time to reach level 40 and gain mounts on which they could ride more swiftly than they could run. Second, he could seek a partner in the Horde, who did not need to be dueling with him to be sheeped, to replace Ozma as his assistant. Rejecting both alternatives, he wondered what other interesting research he and Ozma could accomplish if they left the confines of Ironforge and quested together out across the wide world.

# 6 Economy

We, Alberich and Stephie, are a married couple. We entered the world together in Coldridge Valley, the southwestern district of snowy Dun Morogh, and our home is nearby in Ironforge, the industrial heart of the Alliance. Alberich is a Dwarf hunter, and his professions are blacksmithing and engineering. Stephie is a Gnome warlock, and her professions are mining and tailoring. We do much of our traveling, questing, and working together, so we are a team (see figure 6.1). With our pet and minion, and with our uncle Maxrohn, cousin Etacarinae, and Alberich's cousin Lusea, we are also a family. Much of the time we function as an economic unit.

Stephie's mining provides raw materials for Alberich's blacksmithing and engineering. For example, she extracts copper and tin ore from deposits she finds in the hills, then carries them to a forge, where she smelts them into ingots. Depending on Alberich's need, she can also alloy copper and tin to make bronze. He, then, can make things for her, like pretty daggers. Both of us loot cloth from some of the humanoids we kill, then Stephie uses her tailoring skill to make useful things like cloaks and tote bags. Each of us has one or more assistants, because warlocks summon minions, and hunters tame pets.

Alberich tamed a snow leopard, which he named Pardner. When we went hunting, Pardner would pad along beside us, but when we came to the city, we would leave him in the care of a stable master. Pardner was rather costly to keep because he needed to be fed food frequently, which we often needed to buy from a vendor. Also his training cost us money, and frankly we tended to neglect it for that reason. But he was a great help in questing. He would rush forward and attack our prey, while we stood back and shot bullets and spells at it. Alberich came to feel that Pardner really was a kind of partner. By level 12, Stephie had both an imp and a voidwalker. They had names, Piptip and Huckgore, but she really did not think of them as friends. Rather they were rather spooky minions she could summon from the beyond when absolutely necessary. Both cost mana to summon, and Huckgore also used up a soulshard, which could not be purchased but had to be extracted skillfully from a dying enemy or beast.

One day, we decided to visit the Stormwind auction house and see how it compared with the one in Ironforge (see figure 6.2). As we had learned from Maxrohn, walking

**Figure 6.1**
Alberich and Stephie on a hunting expedition in their home territory, Dun Morogh.

through all the dangerous regions between Ironforge and Stormwind would cost us our lives, so we went to Tinkertown, to take the Deeprun Tram, a subway train between the cities. Cheerfully, Stephie said, "Alberich, I hope you enjoy the tram ride. This marvel of technology was built by a great Gnome, High Tinker Gelbin Mekkatorque."

"No, Stephie," Alberich replied, "King Magni Bronzebeard built the tram, because he hired Mekkatorque, so it is Dwarf technology."

Stephie insisted, "Mekkatorque was the designer! The honor belongs to us Gnomes!"

He growled, "Bronzebeard ordered the work to be done! We Dwarves deserve the credit!"

She screamed, "Dwarven arrogance again! Go take a hike!"

A stern expression on his face, he muttered, "I think I may just do that."

Indeed, Stephie went by train, and Alberich hiked along the tunnel through which it ran. Her journey took only one minute, whereas his took seven. In terms of money, both trips were free, and the tram apparently is public infrastructure operated by the govern-

**Figure 6.2**
The Stormwind auction house, the center of the Alliance economy, where members of five races buy and sell virtual goods.

ment of the Alliance. However, his journey was more costly in terms of time. As the rapacious Goblins say, "Time is money."

Using money sent to her by Uncle Maxrohn, Stephie bought bolts of linen cloth at the Stormwind auction house, and coarse thread from Duncan's Textiles in the Mage Quarter of the city. She made a number of belts and gloves, which earned her the right to pay Georgio Bolero four silver coins and seventy-five copper coins for training from apprentice-level to journeyman-level tailoring. She also bought the instructions needed to make green linen bracers, reinforced linen capes, and linen boots, each costing one silver and ninety coppers. She sold most of her products to the innkeeper at the Golden Rose, but stored some samples of her handiwork in her bank deposit box at the Stormwind counting house. She looked for bargains in the auction, but only after she had purchased many bolts of linen cloth did she realize she could buy individual pieces of linen and make them into bolts herself for less than half the cost. She bought eighteen more tailoring patterns for fifty-one silvers and seventy-six coppers, and proceeded to work her way through all the money Uncle Max had sent her.

When Stephie rendezvoused with Alberich at the Golden Rose, he was a bit distressed at how much she had spent. She explained that the money plus her hard work had raised her tailoring skill from 49 to 111, and that now every single one of the articles of clothing she was wearing had been made by her. Admittedly, her armor strength had dropped from 188 to 166, and her clothes did not really match each other, but she was proud nonetheless. Alberich's mood brightened considerably when she gave him the woolen cape she had made for him, plus an eight-slot woolen bag he could carry things in or use at the bank to increase his storage space. She also mentioned she had sent a woolen cape to Etacarinae, which was much better than the frayed cloak her cousin had been wearing. Alberich felt even better after Stephie gave him twenty-eight copper bars and twenty rough stones from her mining, and he generously gave her ten of the twenty gold coins Uncle Max had sent him. Hers, of course, had all been spent.

For fun, we decided to fly back to Ironforge, costing fifty copper coins each. We noted that the flight from Ironforge to Stormwind would have cost slightly less, only forty-five copper coins. This differential reflected the fact we had achieved honored status in Ironforge through our quests, but only friendly status with Stormwind. Vendors give discounts depending on the reputation the customer has with their group: friendly (5%), honored (10%), revered (15%), and exalted (20%). As we flew north on separate gryphons, a journey of three and a half minutes, we waved at each other and enjoyed seeing the various terrains below.

Stephie rested at the Stonefire Tavern in Ironforge, while Alberich made himself some nice copper mail–armored clothing at the Great Forge, then discovered that as a hunter he could wear only cloth and leather. While he was working, Tormus Deepforge gave him a quest to make and deliver 4 runed copper belts and 4 heavy copper mauls to Verner Osgood, the blacksmith in Redridge, which was west of Stormwind. He did not yet have the skill or instruction to make these two items, so he diligently labored with an additional 120 bars of copper from the auction house, reaching blacksmithing skill 78. He returned to Stormwind, this time taking the Deeprun Tram, then ran 10 minutes to make his delivery. His reward was plans for making Ironforge breastplates, 1,150 experience points, and 250 reputation points with Stormwind. Osgood sent him back to Stormwind, to the Dwarven District, where weaponsmith Grimand Elmore asked him to deliver a package to Mountaineer Stormpike in Loch Modan, for 7 silver coins, 1,050 experience points, and 250 Ironforge reputation points. The financial profit from this second delivery was reduced by the round-trip flight cost between Ironforge and the terminus in Loch Modan, which was 1 silver and 98 coppers.

Our three manufacturing professions were rapidly depleting even Uncle Max's wealth, so we asked our cousin Etacarinae to help us. At the time, she practiced no professions, concentrating instead on running a small number of shamanism-related quests that contributed to her anthropological research, and on grinding beasts. *Grinding* is the practice of killing one enemy after another, to gain loot or experience. In her case, grinding was a little more sophisticated because her chief interest outside of anthropology was martial arts, and she was developing her skills with six weapons—daggers, staves, maces, two-handed maces, axes, and two-handed axes—as well as her skill in unarmed combat. True, she had received elementary training in fishing and first aid, but she had never actually caught a fish or bandaged a wound. So we convinced her that she should take up mining, so she could send us bars of metal and valuable stones for Alberich's blacksmithing and engineering. She and Alberich would both send the cloth they found to Stephie for her tailoring. And all three of us would share the products of our manufacturing and also valuable things we looted from enemies that we did not ourselves need. For her second profession, Etacarinae selected skinning, both because she could sell the hides and because grinding low-level beasts would then be profitable without advancing her experience level too quickly for her to perfect her weapons skills.

We had little direct contact with Lusea because she was receiving priest's training, but we occasionally sent her a gift and enjoyed hearing the news of her spiritual progress. As with all other occupations, the role of a priest has an economic dimension, although we felt we all benefited from the honor of having a woman of the cloth among our close relatives. Anyway, much of our money came from Maxrohn, who earned it as a priest, so we could hardly deny some support to Lusea, even though we never received gold from her. What goes around comes around, so logically what comes around goes around. We thus became an economic unit, six individuals sharing their work and prosperity—Alberich, Stephie, Etacarinae, Maxrohn, Lusea, and Pardner—what also is more commonly called a *family*.

## An Economic System

The economic aspects of WoW seem secondary to the struggle for power and status in its essentially feudal society, yet they may be essential to its success. Scott Rettberg suggests WoW is so popular because

it offers a convincing and detailed simulacrum of the process of becoming successful in capitalist societies. *World of Warcraft* is both a game and a simulation that reinforces the values of Western market-driven economies. The game offers its players a capitalist fairytale in which anyone who works hard and strives enough can rise through society's ranks and acquire great wealth. Moreover, beyond simply representing capitalism as good, *World of Warcraft* serves as a tool to educate its players in a range of behaviors and skills specific to the situation of conducting business in an economy controlled by corporations.[1]

The economy is far too important to be left to economists. While economics is often called the dismal science, it is arguably more rigorous than cultural anthropology, sociology, or political science, but also more narrow. When asked why he robbed banks, Willie "The Actor" Sutton reportedly said, "because that's where the money is." The same logic explains why economists focus almost entirely on money-based markets, largely ignoring other kinds of human exchange and the human preferences that ultimately determine prices even in markets. I do not mean to say that smart people flock to the field of economics because they anticipate earning more money than sociologists do, although that may be true. Rather, the science of economics is attractive to people who like rigor, because money provides a precise metric that allows them to carry out rigorous studies.

Economists tend to focus on markets, in which people exchange things of value, rather than on how value is produced. By some definitions at least, markets are good places for determining the value of something, because we can see what people are willing to pay for it. But markets do not tell us why people have the preferences they do, nor do they explain how valuable things are produced in the first place.

Blizzard Entertainment created considerable wealth through World of Warcraft by learning from past experience and from solving a wide range of challenges that were simultaneously technical and artistic. As Paul Graham explained in his book *Hackers & Painters: Big Ideas from the Computer Age*, this is how much of the wealth can be created in an information economy.[2] How, then, do characters inside WoW produce wealth, given that they have only information to work with? They are able to convert time into work, and exchange the products of work for other valuables.

In his extremely influential 1944 book, *The Great Transformation*, Karl Polanyi argued that markets had become vastly more important in modern society than they ever were before.[3] His analysis identified two other kinds of economic exchange that remain important but no longer dominate in the way they once did: reciprocity and redistribution. *Reciprocity* is the form of economic exchange that takes place between individuals who have mutual obligations, whether arising from past exchanges between them or from the norms of the society in which they live. It is an open question how much sharing is based on reciprocity within intimate family groups, where parents sacrifice for the well-being of their children, rather than being an expression of some kind of natural instinct common among mammals. Reciprocity is the primary glue that holds together tribes in preagricultural societies and guilds in World of Warcraft.

*Redistribution* exists when a government uses political power to obtain resources, then invests them in particular people or projects. As some critics would put the point, a progressive system of taxation steals from the rich to give to the poor, in the fashion of Robin Hood. Or a government extracts wealth by whatever means to invest in public goods such as transportation systems and armies, which benefit citizens but might not arise spontaneously from markets or reciprocity. Presumably the example of redistribution in World of Warcraft is the provision of goods, services, and military defense by the NPCs in each faction, which at least in theory must be supported by some kind of hidden sales tax levied by vendors and trainers.

There exists something like a *phantom economy* in WoW, only sketched and not fully realized in hypothetical exchanges between NPCs. Every NPC vendor will buy materials and equipment from characters, often for far less than the auction house will pay, but nonetheless adding up, over thousands of transactions, to a huge cash flow to characters. Where does that money come from, and where does the vendor-purchased stuff go? One would imagine that the vendors make a profit reselling the stuff they obtain from characters, as well as from the stuff they sell to characters. We can imagine some of their income is taken by the local government to pay all the guards we see walking around and occasionally fighting rampaging beast and invading enemies. But this phantom economy exists only in our imaginations. For example, I have evidence that vendors do not resell the stuff they buy.

Qiff, an engineering supplier in the Outland town called Area 52, sells a number of items that are in limited supply including smoke flares, which sell for only ten silver coins. Catullus and Maxrohn tried a simple experiment with him, repeatedly checking what Qiff had for sale to either Horde or Alliance characters, as Catullus did business with him. First, Catullus bought the three white and two green flares that were available. Both he and Maxrohn found that this did indeed reduce Qiff to having no more left to sell. Catullus then sold one of them back to Qiff—at one fourth the original cost. Logically, this would mean that the supplier would have one to sell, but neither Catullus nor Maxrohn saw one for sale. Because Catullus could have retrieved the one flare from buyback, he logged off the server and then logged back on, at which point the flare vanished altogether from the display, and Qiff still did not have one for sale for Maxrohn.

Thus, the really important dimensions of economic exchange in WoW are markets, especially the auction houses, and reciprocity, especially inside guilds. Building on but also disagreeing with Polanyi's work, Mark Granovetter has argued that reciprocity is still central to the economic system of modern societies, and that all forms of economic exchange are embedded in the structure of social relations.[4] If that is true, the mixed system in WoW may be a fairly realistic model of the real world's, even though some aspects, notably the vestigial redistribution dimension, are not fully functional.

Some hint of the complexity of the economic system was provided by Alberich's first experience making a gun called the Deadly Blunderbuss. He could not get the necessary training until he had reached a skill of 105 in engineering. Achieving this excited him greatly because he knew that a major Horde quest series requires a player to have a Deadly Blunderbuss, but their only source was engineers who could make them. The quest requires collecting a variety of supplies for an Orc at Splinter tree post in Ashenvale named Locke Okarr. Oil must be scavenged from a dangerous satyr camp, and a logging rope must be looted from the corpse of a Furbolg. An axe shipment must be picked up on the Booty Bay docks at the southern tip of

Stranglethorn Vale. The only source of the fourth quest objective, warsong saw blades, is a Goblin trader named Pixel, who would exchange them only for a Deadly Blunderbuss. So Alberich set out to create one, hoping to make some good money in doing so.

He was in Ironforge at the time and had just received supply shipments from Stephie and Etacarinae, so he was ready to do the work. From a vendor who sells engineering supplies, he bought a wooden stock for one silver and eighty coppers, plus three units of weak flux for a total of two silver coins and seventy copper coins. Although he possessed a lot of copper, he could not counterfeit these coins, so he got them from selling things he had collected while hunting. First, he fabricated two copper tubes, each of which required two copper bars and one weak flux. Then he made four hands full of copper bolts, using one copper bar for each. Using the third weak flux, he combined the stock, tubes, and bolts with two units of medium leather that Etacarinae had obtained in her skinning. The result was one Deadly Blunderbuss.

Alberich ran to the Ironforge auction house in great excitement. He discovered that seven other Deadly Blunderbusses were already for sale by three engineers: Bibbity, Pharoh, and Hiiaka. Their buyout prices ranged from forty-five to seventy-five silvers, and their starting bids from twenty-five to fifty. Hoping to get a quick sale, he posted the gun he had made for a buyout price of forty-five silvers, and a starting bid of twenty-five, with a twenty-four-hour auction duration. Only then did he remember that the quest series giving this gun potentially great value was limited to Horde characters, and members of the Horde could not access the Ironforge auction house.

There are in fact three separate auction systems. The Alliance auction houses in Ironforge, Stormwind, Darnassus, and the Exodar are all connected to one another. Similarly, the Horde auction houses in Orgrimmar, Thunder Bluff, Undercity, and Silvermoon City are connected. The third auction system is operated by the neutral Goblins, with houses in Booty Bay, Gadgetzan, and Everlook. All three would be extremely difficult for Alberich to reach, because his experience had reached only level 18, whereas these Goblin towns were in regions for characters who had reached levels 30, 40, and 53, respectively.

Alberich convinced his uncle Max to support an attempt to launch a Blunderbuss business, making weapons in the Alliance for sale to the Horde. Maxrohn sent his nephew twenty gold coins as starting capital, then went to Booty Bay, a place he had visited many times and in which he felt quite safe, given his experience was the maximum level 70. The cost of going there from his current home at Stormspire in Outlands was forty-five silver pieces and sixty-seven coppers, not to mention the time involved. Precisely because Booty Bay's region was far below his experience level, Maxrohn could not earn a decent living there, so if the auction worked out, they would need to find a different way of selling the guns. When Maxrohn accessed the

Goblins' auction system, he discovered that not a single gun of any kind was for sale, and the whole stock of merchandise seemed very meager, compared with the abundance available from the Alliance system. With great difficulty, Maxrohn escorted Alberich to Booty Bay, so he would be able to handle the entire Alliance side of the smuggling operation, and they contracted with Incognita to handle the Horde side. In the end, they found the meager profits were simply not worth the labor, even when they had their system working at peak efficiency.

## The Value of Money

As the Tranquillien innkeeper said to Llana, "Everything has a price." This is one way of saying that the WoW economy reaches into most aspects of life in this virtual world, from the money earned completing quests or looting the corpses of humanoid enemies to buying and selling through vendors and auction houses, to the production of wealth by gathering or crafting professions. Money in WoW, as in the surrounding world, is valuable. From NPCs, one must purchase consumables like food and protective elixirs, durable goods like swords and shields, and even services such as skill training and repair of damaged equipment.

When Ozma was level 11, she resolved to reach level 20 as quickly as possible, since she was the last of my research assistants (prior to the Lich King expansion) and I hoped to complete her missions before the project concluded. Checking her preparedness, she saw that her skill in staves was 51 out of the 55 possible for a weapon at her level, but she had gained no skill in using a magic wand, and indeed did not possess one. Wands are extremely useful because they are the only ranged weapon that does not require any fuel, bullets, arrows, or mana, as in the case of killing spells. She told her friend Aristotle, who immediately sent her a "blazing wand" he happened to have, which could do 12.7 damage per second (DPS). Her current staff had a rating of only 8.8, and her previous one only 4.2, so this would be a great improvement. Unfortunately, the blazing wand required the user to reach level 12 of general experience.

She went to Stormwind City to see what kinds of wands she could buy, but wand vendor Ardwyn Cailen had none for any character lower than level 15. Ozma visited the auction house, where she immediately ran an auxiliary program called Auctioneer, one of the most popular "mods" or "ad-ons," which analyzed prices of all the items for sale and estimated average prices and several other statistics to guide buying and selling. It told her that the average immediate buyout price for a blazing wand was 1 gold, 11 silvers, and 69 coppers, approximately. At the time, there were 113 wands for sale. The cheapest was the lesser magic wand that low-level enchanters learn to make, going for just 30 silvers despite having a DPS of 11.3. The price for this wand was probably depressed precisely because they were in abundant supply, 10 of them for sale, 6 of which had been made by Zyyon. Two fire wands having DPS of only 8.7 were for sale at 1 gold coin each.

Five shadow wands with 10.4 DPS and requiring only experience level 9 were for sale. Most items at the auction house have two listed prices. The immediate buyout price is the cost of getting the item right now, without having to compete with others or wait until a set auction duration was over. When a seller places an item for sale, he or she sets a minimum bid, which is also displayed to buyers, and the highest bid from any potential buyer replaces the minimum bid as the auction progresses. Pez had placed a shadow wand for sale at a buyout price of three golds, seventeen silvers, and seventy-two coppers, and the current (or minimum) bid was two golds, fifty-four silvers, and seventeen coppers. Three sellers had posted buyout prices between 1 and 2 golds. Perhaps by mistake, Alidon was selling one with both minimum bid and buyout prices of only twenty-five silvers. Clearly, Pez is going to have trouble selling his wand, and failing to do so before the end of the auction duration would cost him the deposit he had to make to post the item for sale.

All other available wands required a higher experience level than Ozma possessed. Three blazing wands were for sale, but of course she already had one. Seventeen greater magic wands were for sale, at low prices, because this (like the lesser magic wand) is a common product of enchanting. Suddenly, eleven of these vanished from the auction house, perhaps because their duration had run out. Ozma immediately paid the buyout price for one made by Sancatherine, for just thirty-five silver coins. With a DPS of 17.5, it would be a great improvement once she could use it at experience level 13. She gazed longingly at three 112.4 DPS dragonscale wands of the spirit, selling for an average price of eleven golds. Aside from the fact that she possessed less than three golds at that point, this powerful weapon required level 69 in general experience, which would take her months to achieve. She felt better after running to the mailbox between the bank and the inn, and picking up her greater magic wand, which had been instantly delivered by reliable WoW mail.

Notice the importance of experience level in moderating the economy. Because Ozma cannot use a dragonscale wand of the spirit, no amount of money sent to her from Aristotle or a high-level alt will allow her to become vastly more powerful than other characters at her level, merely by spending money. Players often do use gold from high-level characters to strengthen low-level characters, especially for player-versus-player combat. Optimized low-level characters are disparagingly called *twinks*. The WoWWiki online encyclopedia notes that WoW has a number of mechanisms to limit the impact of twinking:

- Minimum level requirements to use or equip items.
- Minimum level requirements to do quests and thus receive quest reward items.
- Minimum level requirements for potions, buffs and healing spells.

- Minimum level requirements to advance in professions.
- Minimum level requirements on enchantments in the Burning Crusade . . . expansion (new enchants have an item level requirement of 35 . . .).
- Binding of items on pickup or use to prevent "hand-me-downs."[5]

This last point refers to a general limitation on a purely free market, apparently imposed to reduce the tendencies of any competitive system to exaggerate inequality. When a character uses many items, or even just picks up some items, they become *soulbound*, meaning that no other character can ever use them. They may be sold to a vendor, but not sold in an auction house or given to a twink.

At every level, a character must constantly pay money to upgrade skills, armor, weapons, and other attributes. When Maxrohn was at level 57, and taking a ship between Booty Bay and Ratchet, a level-65 Night Elf hunter named Missgoetz inspected him and was not impressed by what she saw. She commented, "Wow, Max, you need some new stuff." When he defensively asked what she meant, she replied, "Just trying to help you out. If your armor matched your level, you would be a lot more powerful. Your armor should often match your level or come like three levels close. And your weapons are beat." Taking her advice to heart, he bought better gloves, a belt, and headgear, as well as a good wand at the buyout price from an auction house. But improving his gear was not a simple matter, because even in Stormwind the vendors seldom had what he needed, and visits to the auction houses were often disappointing.

Given all the things one can buy in WoW, it is important to economize. I found this especially difficult because I wanted each of my twenty-two characters to explore all their possibilities, and thus I tended to overtrain them, giving them every possible skill at their general experience level. This meant I could not easily save up for big expenses, the most valuable of which for higher-level characters is a mount. When Maxrohn reached level 40, he was allowed to buy a horse, but he just could not afford the roughly one hundred gold pieces required until much later. He was never able to buy an epic mount for seven hundred golds, which he was permitted to do at level 60. Mounts are extremely valuable because a regular mount increases the character's speed across the ground by 60 percent, and an epic mount provides a 100 percent improvement. By aggressive herbalism and skinning, and by thrift, Catullus was able to buy his mounts as soon as his level permitted, but he was not able to afford a flying mount when he reached level 70, when he was allowed to buy one, because all his gold went to the scientific conference I organized in WoW.

Among the miscellaneous costs characters face is weapon or armor repair, because battle damages them to the point at which they cease to function. Careful planning of battles can reduce the damage, and thus the repair costs. Some long-distance travel is free, using the public ship, zeppelin, or teleportation systems. But much flight from point to point has moderate costs. Maxrohn found that a nonstop flight from Light's Hope Chapel in Eastern Plaguelands to Nethergarde Keep in the Blasted Lands cost thirty-one silvers and fifty-nine coppers (see figure 6.3). However, it is possible to fly from Light's Hope to Stormwind for nine silvers and sixty-three coppers, and from Stormwind to Nethergarde for seven silvers and forty-seven coppers. Thus, stopping at Stormwind saves fourteen silvers and forty-nine coppers, or slightly over 45 percent.

Every player sets his or her own personal goals, explicitly or implicitly, and these determine his or her preferences for one investment over another. For the May 2008 scientific conference, I instructed Computabull to make about 250 telescopes, officially called *ornate spyglasses*, which actually worked and allowed participants to view distant objects as if they were near. (Computabull was the same Tauren character as Minotaurus, but when I paid Blizzard twenty-five dollars to move him to the realm where I was holding the conference, I was forced to rename him.) Of course, Com-

**Figure 6.3**
Maxrohn flying over the Night Elf seaport of Auberdine, illustrating commercial air and sea travel in Azeroth.

putabull could not grind the lenses or mirrors, or do anything to change the design of this device, because in WoW one assembles units rather than creating things from scratch. But building a telescope was a very complex project. Before he could even begin, he needed to reach skill level 135 in engineering, and go to Nogg's Machine Shop, where he paid Roxxik, the Goblin engineering trainer, three silver and sixty copper coins for the training. For several steps in the process, he needed to work at an anvil, and the shop called the Burning Anvil in Orgrimmar's Valley of Honor took care of that necessity.

The materials for the components of the telescope were as follows. First, he needed two bronze tubes, each of which required two bronze bars and one unit of weak flux. For reasons unclear to him, a spyglass also required two whirring bronze gizmos, each requiring two bronze bars and one piece of wool cloth. One copper modulator also was required, made from one copper bar, one linen cloth, and two handfuls of copper bolts, each of which was made from one copper bar. He could buy the weak flux from Sumi, a blacksmith supplier in the anvil building, but all the rest had to be collected from the environment or bought from the auction house. The metal bars could come only from a miner, who had the skill to extract the raw metal from the rock and smelt the ore into bars. Relying heavily upon the auction house, as he was forced to do, Computabull invested the equivalent of about five gold pieces in each telescope. This does not count the value of his time doing all the work, and commuting back and forth between the auction house and the anvil, a distance that even in ghost-wolf form took him one minute and twenty-five seconds to run.

At only level 30, there is no way that Computabull could afford the roughly 1,250 gold pieces required for the materials to make the telescopes. Here he had to rely on Catullus, who could earn far more than he, because he was at level 70. For many days before the conference, Catullus performed a series of a dozen or more daily quests, in Outland and the newly opened Sunwell zone called Quel'Danas. In nearly five hours of work, he could earn two hundred gold pieces. Thus, adding together the time required by both Computabull and Catullus, the telescopes for the conference cost around a forty-hour workweek to produce. No dollars were invested, however, and it is hard to estimate the conversion rate between WoW gold and dollars.

Any complex economy offers a number of ways in which participants may economize and profit, including the opportunity for buying items and reselling them at a higher price either at a different location or a later time. Azeroth offers some but not all of the mechanisms one might expect in a free market. I did not in fact see players set themselves up as merchants, obtaining things in one area, and then standing at a crossroads in another area and selling them to passersby. For example, for the scientific conference, Lunette bought cats in Goldshire and rabbits at a location east of Ironforge, toted them to Booty Bay, and smuggled them to conference participants on the third day of the conference that was held in that pirate town, billing them as exotic laboratory animals. The participants were all members of the Horde, so they could not have bought the animals themselves. I could imagine one of the participants buying up all of them, going to Orgrimmar, and standing near the bank saying, "Cute kitties and bunnies for sale, two gold pieces each." Since the cost including the auction fee was well less than one gold piece, this could have been a profitable business, given that customers were willing to buy.

In general, the WoW economy operates through well-established institutions. Buying and selling is done through vendors, at auction houses, and to some extent, inside guilds. Occasionally, an enchanter sells enchants in public, but often at a loss, to build up enchanting skill. Rogues sometimes open lockboxes for other characters, accepting tips but not usually demanding set prices. Much of the complex economic behavior by players is not exchange, but production.

## Major Professions

When a character reaches experience level 5, he or she can begin to learn professional skills that produce wealth for the economy. Three of these are relatively minor and do not interfere with learning other skills: cooking, first aid, and fishing. The other ten (prior to the Lich King expansion) are more demanding, and any one character can practice only two: alchemy, blacksmithing, enchanting, engineering, herbalism, jewelcrafting, leatherworking, mining, skinning, and tailoring. My characters have practiced all these skills above level 100, in several cases all the way to 375, and in two cases to 450, but each profession involves so many bits of information, and often alternate learning tracks at the upper levels, that it is hard to master all the intricacies. Therefore, I decided to do a little statistical study, to give me a solid basis for explaining the professions, while reserving the mathematical details for some future academic journal article.

I tabulated the major professions for 1,096 characters in Alea Iacta Est, the guild in the Earthen Ring realm to which Catullus belongs. To do this, I looked up each member in the online Armory database provided by Blizzard, saved the first Web page as an XML file, and wrote a little computer program to parse the XML files, format the data for a spreadsheet, and port it over to SPSS (Statistical Package for the Social Sciences). None of my findings was a big surprise, but they provide a solid foundation for discussing the professions, based on the knowledge possessed by the AIE guild members as reflected in their own decisions in selecting professions. The fact that this guild is connected to the very popular long-running weekly WoW podcast *The Instance* means members of this group are among the most sophisticated players in the game.

First of all, as I had expected, the three gathering professions are most popular. Of the 1,096 characters, 40.6 percent practiced mining, 36.3 percent did skinning, and

23.4 percent did herbalism. Unlike the crafting professions, these three do not require raw materials, and they are widely reputed to be more profitable precisely because the only costs are in labor. I especially like skinning, because my characters inevitably must kill many skinnable animals anyway, whether as an explicit part of a quest, to clear an area of danger before doing something else there, or because one of them jumped out at my character without warning. Also, my characters often find recently killed and looted animal corpses lying on the ground, left behind by someone who lacked the skinning skill, and it takes just a few seconds to harvest them.

The fourth most popular major profession, enchanting, was practiced by 19.6 percent of the AIE members. This is just a hair below the 20 percent level of popularity it would have if people selected major professions entirely at random. There are ten professions, and one may learn two, so one practices two tenths or 20 percent. Enchanting has some qualities of both gathering and crafting. Chiefly, it is a crafting profession, in which one uses magical ingredients to enchant objects, adding, for example, to the strength of some armor, or turning wood into a magic wand. However, an enchanter can also disenchant objects, which means gathering the magical ingredients from objects that have already been enchanted. Occasionally, one picks up an enchanted item while looting a corpse, gets one in trade, or wants to recycle one after obtaining a similar item of better quality. Disenchanting an item destroys it, so it cannot be sold or used, but produces magical materials for future enchanting. Because it has aspects of both types, it makes sense that enchanting falls between the popular gathering professions and the less popular crafting professions.

The most popular pure crafting occupation is tailoring, and characters do commonly obtain the cloth that is the main raw material simply from the looted corpses of defeated enemies. Leatherworking and alchemy are close together in popularity at 15.0 percent and 14.3 percent. Engineering is at only 10.3 percent, blacksmithing at 7.6, and jewelcrafting at 6.4. The last of these was introduced in January 2007, so many characters had already adopted other professions. (The data do not include the most recent profession, inscription.) In addition, jewelcrafting trainers are found only in the Blood Elf and Draenei newbie zones, and in advanced zones of Outland and Northrend, so many characters are discouraged from learning it. Given the differences with jewelcrafting, I decided to do a statistical analysis of the nine traditional professions.

The next question to ask was how the professions fit together. Each character can have two professions, so I could analyze them statistically by means of correlation coefficients. I created a new set of variables, one for each profession, giving a character a 1 if he or she had the given profession, and a 0 if not. A correlation coefficient is a modest number, ranging from a possible low of −1.00 up through 0.00 to +1.00. Numbers far from zero tell us there is a relationship between two variables.

Consider enchanting. Characters who have enchanting for one of their two main professions tend to have tailoring for the other. There is a correlation of 0.54 between enchanting and tailoring, which is a very strong positive correlation, as correlation coefficients go. In contrast, there is a negative correlation of –0.28 between enchanting and skinning, meaning there is a somewhat weaker but still very significant tendency for characters who do enchanting *not* to do skinning. The strongest positive correlation for skinning is 0.55 with leatherworking, naturally enough because leatherworkers need the raw materials obtained through skinning. Indeed, a leatherworker has less need to have his or her armor strengthened through enchanting, because leatherworkers can make armor kits that have the same value as enchanting their armor. There are (9 × 8)/2, or 36, distinct pairs of these nine professions, and the highest correlation, 0.66, is between herbalism and alchemy. Alchemy uses some ingredients gathered by herbalism, just as leatherworking does with skinning.

The correlations between professions have a slight bias toward the negative side, because if you already have one, you have given up one of your two chances to obtain any of the others. Therefore, a statistical method that compensates for this bias is needed to be absolutely sure. One of the most traditional methods is factor analysis, which I have used in many previous studies. The input is the correlation matrix, and the computer fiddles iteratively to find some small number of abstract dimensions of variation that explain most of the meaningful connections in the data. For the technically minded, I did a principle-components analysis, identifying all factors with eigenvalues greater than 1, and applying varimax rotation, which converged immediately. Four factors resulted.

Each factor is a dimension, so imagine a 4-D map, with each of the nine traditional professions arrayed in space and time. The position of each point is measured in terms of its "loading" on a factor. The first dimension puts herbalism and alchemy way out in one direction, with loadings of 0.89 for herbalism and 0.87 for alchemy. Loadings are based ultimately on correlation coefficients, but tend to be much larger, while also not exceeding 1.00. Farthest away from the herbalism-alchemy pair is mining, which has a negative loading on the first factor of –0.56.

The second factor is dominated by skinning and leatherworking, which have loadings of –0.85 and –0.84 respectively. Although based on correlations, these negative loadings cannot be interpreted in the same way that negative correlations would be. Rather, the two professions stand together in space, far away from the others in a direction that happens to have a minus sign associated with it. If you were graphing the first two dimensions on paper, for example, a plus sign on factor one could mean graph the point far to the right, and a minus sign on factor two could mean graph the point far down (rather than up where positive points would be). The most distant profession again is mining, which has a loading on factor two of 0.48.

The third factor brings together enchanting and tailoring, with loadings of 0.84 and 0.85, respectively. Again, they are most distant from mining, which has a loading on factor three of −0.50.

The fourth factor is defined by two professions, blacksmithing and engineering, which have loadings with opposite signs. Blacksmithing has a loading on factor four of 0.74, and engineering has one of −0.72. The loadings of the other seven professions are all very small, all within 0.05 of zero. This may seem mysterious but it actually has a very clear explanation. Mining is the gathering profession that collects materials for both blacksmithing and engineering. It has a raw correlation of 0.31 with blacksmithing and 0.29 with engineering. But one character cannot practice all three; blacksmithing and engineering compete directly with each other for the materials gathered by mining. Alberich could do both professions only because Maxrohn sent him money to buy materials, and both Stephie and Etacarinae sent him the results of their mining.

Despite the importance of both market and reciprocity exchanges in the WoW economy, characters often gather materials and craft products for their own personal use. It is my impression that economists do not study the production and use of valuable things by individuals for their own use in the absence of trade, yet if economics includes the study of the production of value, this logically should be a subfield of economics. We can see evidence of this phenomenon in the fact that different classes of characters tend to practice different professions. While only 7.6 percent of all 1,096 AIE members are blacksmiths, 37 percent of warriors and 34 percent of paladins practice this craft. The reason is simple: these two classes, and no others, can wear the metal armor produced in blacksmithing. No other class has more than 3 percent who do blacksmithing. Leatherworking is popular among hunters (33%), rogues (33%), druids (31%), and shamans (20%), all of whom can wear leather armor. Tailoring is popular among priests (54%), warlocks (53%), and mages (46%), all of whom wear the cloth armor made by tailors. Similarly, enchanting is popular in these same three classes: priests (41%), warlocks (38%), and mages (46%). One reason is that enchanters can manufacture magic wands, and only these three classes can use wands. Thus, it is largely personal needs that brought together enchanting and tailoring in factor three.

People who take up manufacturing crafts hope to profit, but will they? Four of the first things Vadvaro learned to make in leathercrafting required obtaining pieces of light leather, which he could get from skinning. Each piece would sell to a vendor for fifteen copper coins, so although they cost him nothing but labor, this must be figured as part of his investment. A piece of coarse thread cost nine coppers, bought from a vendor. He could make a hand-stitched leather cloak out of two pieces of light leather and one of coarse thread, for an investment of thirty-nine coppers, and sell it to a vendor for thirty-four coppers, getting nothing for his labor and actually losing five coppers on the deal. To make wrist bracers took two pieces of light leather and three of coarse thread, for an investment of fifty-seven coppers, but sold for only twenty-eight, a loss of twenty-nine coppers! He could make a pair of boots out of the same material as a cloak, for an investment of thirty-nine coppers, but they sold to a vendor for only twenty-nine coppers. A vest took three pieces of leather and one of thread, for an investment of fifty-four coppers, but sold for only forty coppers.

Vadvaro's problem was partly a result of the fact he was a rank beginner. Products made by higher-level crafters can be sold at the auction house, sometimes for good prices, although the highest auction prices are for rare items not manufactured by characters but looted from high-level NPC corpses. Enchanting behaves more like a service occupation than a manufacturing one, because enchanters cannot sell their labor on the auction house and must find customers as best they can. The WoWWiki article for enchanting explains:

Low-level enchants (below skill 250) require rather large amounts of expensive components, but can hardly be sold. Even attempts to give them away for free can fail. Thus enchanters frequently end up re-enchanting the same item dozens of times just to increase their skill. Leveling enchanting is possible just with the materials gained from disenchanting items you find yourself and items from quests, but due to the slow rate, buying materials from the AH [auction house] or having friends or members of your guild supply you with items or materials can be quite a boost. Farming magic items for disenchanting is not recommended, thus enchanting is a profession for players with either backup from a guild, enough money to buy most of the materials, or a lot of patience.[6]

A fellow member of the Blood Ravens guild, Irilos, gave Catullus a newly enchanted magic wand at no charge, then said, "I may as well enchant your bracers with stamina. Even if you vendor them later, it'll help raise my skill, and otherwise I'd just enchant my own gear over and over." Catullus admitted he did not understand the process of disenchanting, so Irilos explained, "Whenever you loot an item that's green, enchanters like me take it and 'disenchant' it. That destroys the item, but it gives us things like greater magic essence or strange dust or small glimmering shard that we can use to enchant things." It was experiences like this that convinced Catullus to ignore the crafting professions, and take up herbalism and skinning, which could earn him much money at little effort as he was questing and exploring alone. Only when the May 2008 scientific convention required him to drop one of these and take up tailoring to make carrying bags for the participants did he learn how to make products.

Each crafting profession requires the character to learn skills, by buying them from trainers, while gathering professions gain experience for characters mainly in the doing of them, but they demand much knowledge of the player. For example, certain locations are especially favorable spots to kill large numbers of skinnable beasts safely. A great spot is in northern Barrens, where a hill overlooks a pair of gigantic skeletons. It is here that one of the quests requires killing Echyeakee, a white lion. Some hunters tame Echyeakee for a pet, as Sciencemag did, because he is one of only two white lions anywhere. But for a character in the midteen levels who wants to gain experience safely, and to collect valuable animal skins, this is a great location.

Minotaurus went there to kill Echyeakee, but then stayed for a long while because he found he could stand partway up the hill and lure lionesses to their deaths, or sally slightly away from the hill to kill higher-level male lions. He was overjoyed to discover these possibilities because he was just beginning to get serious about his leatherworking skills, had a supply of the course thread, and was able to manufacture goods to his heart's content. With the help of the thread, he made leather boots plus a vest and a cloak. Then he manufactured thirty-one light armor kits, leaving the area with a leatherworking skill level of 50, and a skinning level of 124. He happened to be impoverished at the time, so the six silver coins he sold his handiwork for were welcome.

Players often discuss economic issues. While he was killing giant crustaceans in Desolace, disappointed that their carcasses could not be skinned to make armor, Catullus overheard a debate among members of his guild, beginning when a level-22 Tauren druid named Cairubel said, "I wonder if I should pick up herbalism or mining."

Alisa, a level-54 Blood Elf warlock, opined, "Mining makes more money."

Shadowthief qualified that judgment, saying, "But both are good."

Cairubel explained, "Yeah, my only profession right now is skinning."

Halleigh interjected, "Herbalism can make a ton of money at higher levels."

Deaderin contributed, "I'd go with mining unless you are also an alchemist, because alchemists use the herbs that herbalism collects."

Faeline noted, "I've been making quite a bit selling herbs lately."

Amid the high expectation for the forthcoming Lich King WoW expansion, Cairubel replied, "I wish I could do all three. I think with the new expansion they should give us a third profession slot."

Alisa noted a problem with this idea, however, saying, "I don't recommend mining with herbalism, though. You can only track one at a time." She was referring to the fact that an herbalist can set the minimap in the user interface to show the locations of nearby herbs, and a miner can do the same for ore deposits, but somebody with both professions would need to switch back and forth constantly.

Thinking about Cairubel's current profession, skinning, Lukka said, "You could make a fortune following me around, because I've got tons of bears that need to be skinned." At that point, Lukka was working in the Hillsbrad Foothills, where bears and other skinnable animals abound.

Another character, who at that moment must have checked the mail, exclaimed, "Yay, my junk sold off the auction house!" One of the main ways to profit from high-level items obtained from any of the gathering professions is to put quantities of it up for auction.

Baniah joked, "We should be able to skin centaurs." Deer, cattle, and some other hoofed animals can be skinned, but humanoids cannot. Given that centaurs are a little of both, it seemed arbitrary to exclude them.

Diameduertos exclaimed, "And humans!"

It is, in fact, not possible to skin Humans in WoW, nor to cook them. The secondary cooking profession can be practiced in addition to any pair of primary professions, and any character can also learn first aid and fishing. Cooking does add value. For example, five chunks of uncooked boar meat sell to a vendor for fifteen coppers, whereas cooked they sell for thirty. Cooking can also be pleasant. When Aristotle completed his three murloc quests for Captain Grayson, the two of them celebrated. Despite the falling rain, Aristotle was able to light a small bonfire with his flint and tinder, upon which he cooked many kinds of meat he had recently killed. He roasted boar, grilled pork ribs, and baked vulture eggs in mild spices. His crowning achievement was two portions of Westfall stew consisting of stringy vulture meat boiled with goretusk snout and murloc eyes.

In first aid, a character creates bandages, using the same kinds of cloth as tailors do. The WoWWiki page on this secondary profession says: "First Aid is highly recommended to all classes as a way of reducing downtime between battles, by quickly restoring health after combat. Even classes with healing spells can benefit, since using a bandage after combat will conserve mana, saving the time otherwise spent drinking."[7] Note how this echoes the Goblin dictum, "Time is money." The ultimate coinage in WoW is not gold but labor, and in a virtual world where muscular effort is valueless, labor equals time spent.

Catullus took all three secondary professions to the maximum 375 skill level, and found fishing the most frustrating, precisely because of how much time it took. For hours he stood beside one or another pool of water, repeatedly using his fishing rod to cast his hook. He obtained many fish this way, sold some and cooked the others, but as he progressed, more and more fish were required to advance to the next skill level. He would daydream about slaying monsters, as he cast that accursed hook over and over and over.

**Property and Theft**

In a sense, the chief source of wealth in WoW is not practicing a gathering or crafting profession but murdering enemies to loot their corpses. One wonders what lesson about the real world this teaches. In his book *Crime as Work*, Peter Letkemann made a case for the proposition that we can understand the activities of professional criminals best if we realize they have jobs just like every other employed person, setting aside the small fact that their labor is illegal.[8]

Many people wonder what in the world Proudhon must have had in mind when he proclaimed, "Property is theft." Yet the concept of ownership, and thus of theft, does rest on a somewhat shaky foundation. Humans evolved on this planet as hunters, and hunting has much in common with robbery. Rights are defined by the legal system of a particular society, and societies often give their leaders special rights, often disguised by rhetoric about the needs of the community. For example, many people praise a leader who goes to war to promote the welfare of the nation, but consider an individual who kills for his family's welfare to be a murderer. In any case, when broad consensus about property rights does not exist, defining theft becomes subjective.

We see this in WoW in the case of the special professional skills gained by rogues. The quest Snatch and Grab, available only to Alliance rogues, trains them in the fundamentals of picking pockets. Arguably, the act of theft required was not really a crime because it consisted of picking the pocket of the dockmaster of the Defias bandits to obtain the schedule they use to ship contraband from Redridge to their outlaw bases in Westfall. When he learned it, Vadvaro first approached the small dock and house at Jerod's Landing, using the stealth mode, which only rogues have, so he would be invisible. The shipping master, who happened to be a greedy Goblin, did not notice him as he entered the building very slowly and crept behind him. A deft movement of his fingers, and Vadvaro had the Defias shipping schedule in his inventory. A few more moments walking silently and invisibly in stealth mode and he had escaped.

Knowing that there was a group of Defias bandits nearby at the Blackwell pumpkin patch, Vadvaro decided to try picking their pockets as well. Again in stealth mode, he entered the house where three of them stood, Erlan Drudgemoor, Surena Caledon, and Morgan, the Collector. From Drudgemoor's pocket, he quickly picked two copper coins. Unfortunately, when he slipped close to their leader, Morgan, the man sensed his presence, and he was forced to battle with the trio. Luckily, he was able to gut Morgan before the others had time to react, and even combined, at levels 8 and 9, the other two were quick work for his experience of level 16.

On the streets of Old Town in Stormwind, Osborne, the Night Man, taught Vadvaro how to pick locks, for the mere payment of sixteen silver and twenty copper coins. Later, on the Lakeshire docks, a local crook named Lucius told Vadvaro to practice at nearby Alther's Mill, giving him the necessary thief's tools. This training is available only to a rogue, and only to one who has reached level 16 and learned the basic skill from a rogue trainer. At the mill, several lockboxes of different levels of difficulty are scattered on the floor. Beginning at lock-picking skill level 1, Vadvaro opened the easiest box, and gained level 2. He opened the box again, and gained level 3. Again and again, he opened a box, switching to more difficult ones, until he reached level 51 and had obtained a token of thievery as his graduation diploma. Rather than celebrating, he continued to practice at Alther's Mill, all the way to level 80. His diploma read, "The bearer of this certificate is entitled to the respect and regard that any first rate pilferer and thief deserves."

Lock picking is a valuable skill, conferring social benefits. Often, players who are not rogues loot lockboxes and have no way to get their contents other than finding a friendly rogue. On weekends, rogues who want to earn a little money, or make friends, often station themselves at an economic center, and ply their trade. In Stormwind, the usual spot is at the fountain outside the bank, which happens also to be next to the inn with its mailbox, and just down the street from the auction house. One Sunday, a level-70 Human rogue announced on the Alliance-wide Trade channel, "Free lock picking in Iron Forge for the next 10 minutes. All boxes can be opened! On the bridge between the bank and the auction house. (Tips greatly appreciated.)"

If rogues are the class of players that most stretches the economic system in the direction of crime, one group of ubiquitous NPCs does the same: the Goblins. They are the capitalists of WoW, as well as rivaling the Gnomes in their mastery of technology. When they remark that time is money, as they often do, they append the word *friend* at the end of the sentence. However, it is not clear they have any friends, only customers and exploited workers. WoWWiki describes the Goblins thus:

Goblins are small humanoids, crafty and shrewd, bearing an overwhelming interest in commerce and a strong curiosity about mechanical things. Goblin society is fragmented, defined chiefly by commerce and trade. The ultimate schemers and con artists, goblins are always in search of a better deal. Other races universally view goblins as inventors, merchants and, without exception, maniacs. Goblins value technology as a useful aspect of commerce. Some say that their advantage—and their curse—is to be the primary users of technology in a world governed by magic. While dwarves and gnomes share a similar gift, goblin technology is more far-reaching and sinister and makes a larger impact on the natural world.[9]

Neutral between Horde and Alliance, Goblins run six towns: Ratchet, Booty Bay, Gadgetzan, Everlook, Area 52, and K3. Each of the first five has a bank, and both Horde and Alliance characters can access their personal storage through it. Both factions can ride the boat between Ratchet and Booty Bay. There also are offices of a neural auction house in Booty Bay, Gadgetzan, and Everlook, the latter two being difficult for low-level characters to visit. The fees of these neutral auction houses are much higher than in the faction-specific ones.

Prior to becoming neutral in recent years, the Goblins primarily did business with the Orcish Horde, and they still dominate intercontinental travel for the Horde. They run the zeppelin service linking Orgrimmar, Undercity, Grom'gol and two bases in Northrend, plus the shipping line between Ratchet and Booty Bay. For a time, the zeppelins had NPC crews of Goblins, and vending machines below decks, but now the only obvious presence are the Goblins occupying the tops of the zeppelin towers.

**Figure 6.4**
The colossal statue of Baron Revilgaz, capitalist redeemer, at Booty Bay.

On a small island in the entrance to Booty Bay harbor, rather like New York's Statue of Liberty, stands a heroic sculpture of a Goblin in what appears to be priestly attire with his arms outstretched in welcome. The pose also resembles the colossal statue of Jesus in Rio de Janeiro, Brazil, Christ the Redeemer, and this reference is made explicit by the fact that the location is called Janeiro's Point. Do you get the point? The only thing this messiah wants to redeem is your coupons, and only at a profit to himself. He is Baron Revilgaz, ruler of Booty Bay, a leading Goblin associated with the Steamwheedle Cartel (see figure 6.4). Gold is the Goblins' god, and money is their religion. They employ both technology and piracy to get it. Booty Bay bills itself as a seaside resort, but it is really a pirate town. Their advanced technology base is Area 52 in Outland's Netherstorm, where a smaller version of the baron's statue watches over the cemetery.

The centerpiece of Area 52 is a huge rocket, under construction and nearing completion. Periodically, a comparably huge robot invades the town and damages it, even as workers are repairing and completing it, and the local bartender is trying to produce more powerful rocket fuels. Named Boots, this "master mixologist" says, "I make a good living selling drinks to the boozehounds around here. But I want something more!" Actually, when he says rocket fuel, it is possible he means more potent booze, or the distinction may not be clear in his own mind. Anyway, he gives two quests, the second of which sends the character in search of nether ray stingers to get "that little extra kick." The nearest good place to find nether rays is the Crumbling Waste north of the town, where the edges of the world are crumbling into boulders and mountains that levitate away from solid land. A host of potent alien monsters attack, as the character is trying to catch up with wandering nether rays, in one of the most surreal environments imaginable. When Boots gets the needed stings, he takes bottles of two liquids, one light green and the other cream, and appears to shake them together. It is hard to resist the feeling he is mixing a "stinger" cocktail, rather than a rocket fuel. In either case, the mixture explodes! Fire marshal Bill and the doctor revive Boots, and he returns to his bartending chores. This incident exemplifies the Goblin orientation toward business and technology, which sometimes causes more harm than it does good.

Goblins are not a monolithic group, but are divided into competing organizations. For example, the Tinkers' Union, a consortium of Goblin engineers, is constantly trying to steal technology from the Venture Company. A Goblin in Ratchet named Sputtervalve, for example, has been assigned by the Tinkers' Union to develop shredders, advanced robotlike user-augmentation machines to facilitate clear-cutting forests. Sputtervalve then gave his colleague, Ziz Fizziks, the mission to steal shredder plans from the Venture Company. WoWWiki describes that group thus: "The Venture Company is the most notorious goblin organization, it deforests and plunders the world for its natural resources."[10] Ziz Fizziks lives in a small cabin in Windshear Crag, monitoring the technologies by which the Venture Company is despoiling the area. As WoWWiki says, "The Crag is now home to a massive logging expedition by the Venture Company. The once green landscape is now a barren area of tree stumps, polluted waters, and creaking machinery."[11] Ziz Fizziks has no intention to protect nature, but the unintended consequence of sending both Horde and Alliance characters in to steal shredder plans is indeed to slow down the ruin Goblins are inflicting on the environment.

### Gold Farming

Many virtual worlds have internal currencies, like the gold in WoW, but only some of them are convertible with dollars, euros, and other real-world currencies. Examples of virtual worlds where one can buy internal currencies are *Second Life*, *There*, *Entropia*, and some servers of *EverQuest II*. That is not supposed to be true for WoW, but some people do it nonetheless. On *The Instance* podcast about WoW, Andrew Konietzky referred to "a guy who pays his kids for doing chores around the house in WoW gold."[12] Rather more serious is organized *gold farming*, the business of collecting and selling virtual gold.

Gold farming is a business conducted in the real world that is legal there but illegal inside WoW.[13] Many players despise others who pay real-world money for in-game gold, or even buy developed characters, because the buyers have not paid their dues in terms of effort, learning, and helping out other players.[14] These practices have the effect of importing players' socioeconomic statuses from the surrounding society, rather than having each player start from scratch, gaining status on a level playing field.

On March 24, 2007, a character called Rfsdtgfg whispered to Maxrohn, "Hi, please visit http://www.wowforever. (om \\ We have gold available at rock bottom prices and are online 24/7 to fulfill your orders! You get the best price, and the fastest delivery of WOW GOLD." No such character was in fact in his vicinity, and the Armory did not list anybody by that name, so we must assume it was a spambot advertising a gold farming operation, using a randomly generated name. Note that the URL has "(" instead of "c" in ".com." to avoid a spam filter. WowForever.Com describes itself as an "online game shop" that takes credit cards, and describes its gold delivery methods thus:

After the process for the order and payment sent have been completed, your order will appear in our delivery queue. Our delivery team will log in the relevant game and contact the character specified on the order form. Some games currency can be mailed in the game, if we have made sure that your information is correct, we will tip your currency through game mail system when you are offline. If we can't make sure your information, we will send an email to confirm your information. For some game should do the trade face to face in game, you should tell us when you are online, then our team will login the game and do the trade with you face to face. If our delivery team is unable to make contact, an e-mail will be sent to the contact address provided. You may reply to this e-mail or log onto our live chat to verify the status of your delivery.[15]

Note that the author of this paragraph does not seem to be a native speaker of English. To see the current exchange rate, and start the order process, the player must say what server their character is on, and state whether it belongs to the Alliance or the Horde, because the WoW e-mail and economic trade systems are limited to the character's realm and faction. However, I could not seem to start the process for buying gold on that website. It was also interesting to discover that clicking on an unobtrusive blue square took me to a Chinese-language website.

On March 30, Maxrohn got the identical message from a "person" named Dtgdfg, except that the URL of the website was now www.wowjx.com. It said it took payment via PayPal, eCheck, JCB J/Secure, Amex, Discover, MasterCard, and Visa. I did not visit it until the next day, and again, I could not seem to make it work. I was however very quick to check out Dtgdfg. I shift-clicked on the name in the chat stream, to get information about the character, and got only "0 players total." I quickly used the "Who" search in the social utility, and found that no player by this name was actually online.

Some offers of WoW gold are simply credit card fraud, and no gold gets delivered to the player. But I have interacted with three players who successfully bought gold, one purchasing 5,000 gold pieces. This person is no longer in WoW, and he said he blasts from one game to another, finishing them as quickly as he can and then moving on to the next. Given that some gold really is delivered to buyers, we can ask where the gold farmers get it. I have heard two plausible stories, first that there are sweatshops in China where low-wage workers run high-level characters twenty-fours hours a day, and second that ordinary Chinese players sell whatever gold they normally collect to a company. In WoW mythology, the king of the Chinese gold farmers is named Ding Pong, who may also be a general in the Red Army. A third theory about the origin of the gold is that Ding Pong's minions steal it.

The message of the day of the Alea Iacta Est guild for December 28, 2007, said: "Maui was hacked, cleaned out on Dec, 27. Guild vault is completely empty!" That is, a thief had somehow hacked into the account of Maui, the master of Alea Iacta Est, the famous guild to which Catullus belonged. The thief must have obtained the account's password and mailed the loot to gold farmers. The thief also drained the guild bank account that Maui managed, stealing 1,000 gold pieces from the vault and about 4,000 from Maui and his alt characters.

An AIE member named Nural confirmed that the thief had somehow obtained Maui's password, logged in as him, and cleaned everything out. "I was on this morning at 6:30 AM when somebody logged into his account. I whispered him and got no reply. I whispered again, and then whoever logged off."

Aitherios observed, "Last year the Super Bowl site was hacked to put a key logger in specific to WoW . . . I found one on my system last year in February. The thing was persistent. I had to reformat and reinstall." *Key loggers* are malicious programs that monitor every key the user presses, intercepting the user's password and automatically sending it to the criminal who inserted the key logger on the user's computer surreptitiously.

Akkilla correctly noted, "I read that on the online black market WoW account info is worth more than real bank account info. They'll steal less, but no police are coming to look for them."

Others members expressed their horror: "Talk about terrible trouble!" "Indeed, it is alarming and a sad day for AIE." "May the blood of these gold sellers spill on Horde ground!" "I'm going to line me up some gold seller skulls on my mantle." "Got to love gold farmers . . . not!" "We shall play badminton with the souls of their firstborn!" "I'll make soulshards from them, then make them into healthstones that I'll let disintegrate by logging out!" "These gold farmers will be my pet's pet." "Is there any way for the guild to get all the stuff back?" Catullus himself commented, "Maybe we need to consider it part of the 'game'—a dastardly attack that will not deter us from victory."

Tarqq chimed in, "So, are we gathering the electronic posse to lay waste on some gold sellers?"

Maui himself told readers of the guild chat he intended to use his podcast to retaliate: "The question is, can I be stopped from using The Instance to verbally throttle everyone who has ever bought gold from a seller? It's going to take restraint."

Balerius commented, "The thing is, Maui, do they really deserve your restraint?"

Maui replied, "I like where your head's at, Balerius." On January 5, Maui's player reported to *The Instance* podcast: "We get e-mails every week from listeners who have had their account hacked—by 'hacked' I mean someone unauthorized logged into their account and took their stuff. All the time, we get these e-mails, and I really feel for these people. I feel particularly for them, since that happened on my personal account." Every one of his characters, on several realms, had lost everything except some soulbound items that could not be sold. He surmised that a key logger had captured his password when he accessed WoW on a machine belonging to an acquaintance. "It's sickening! Gold sellers cannot possibly go any lower in my esteem. They're the scum of the Earth! When you buy gold, you are supporting people that ruin the game for honest players. If you ever buy gold again, you're funding that entire process."[16]

After reflecting on the disaster, members began to worry about the wider implications. In the guild chat, Ionara said, "See you all later. I need to check on my other character and then change passwords. Paranoia is setting in."

Agnetha, who was an alt of Zewt, exclaimed, "I hear you," and proceeded to change her password to a random twelve-character string.

Moobie spoke for all the others, saying, "Yeah, I may do the same myself."

News of the burglary in Earthen Ring reached Maxrohn in the Shandris realm, who immediately contacted Aazenroth, the master of his own guild, Winged Ascension. Aazenroth assured him that Winged Ascension was okay, but sadly reported that a different guild, Absolution, had not only been looted but also disbanded by an intruder. With great difficulty, its members were reassembling under the new name of Merciless.

Blizzard does its best to warn subscribers about security threats. For example, on May 28, 2008, WoW placed this warning on the home page of its website:

A recent vulnerability has been discovered in popular web-content delivery program Adobe Flash, and it could potentially be used to target World of Warcraft players and accounts. The newest available version of Adobe Flash, version 9.0.124.0, does not contain this vulnerability, and we recommend that everyone upgrade their Flash player as soon as possible. . . . In addition, to avoid exploitation of this vulnerability, we have temporarily disabled the ability to post hyperlinks in our forums. Any links will need to be copied and pasted into a browser. We'll continue to evaluate any potential security threats and take any steps necessary to ensure a safe and fun environment.

Coincidentally, exactly a year after the great burglary of guild vaults, at the end of 2008, the message that greets a character upon entering WoW read:

We've recently seen a rise in the number of compromised accounts. To protect your security, we recommend that you keep your email address in Account Management up-to-date; scan your computer for viruses, Trojans, and key loggers; update your OS [operating system] and web browsers; and change your password to something new and unique. Please remember to keep account information private, and consider using the optional Blizzard Authenticator for additional protection.

I was able to avoid falling into a gold farmer trap myself, on June 4, 2008, when the following convincing e-mail arrived at my Gmail account:

Greetings!

You are receiving this email to notify you that you are eligible to sign up for World of Warcraft beta testing of the new expansion pack, Wrath of the Lich King!

The beta testing will run through summer of 2008 until December 31, 2008! The opening day of the beta testing has not been released yet. However, you will be notified via email after you sign up the day it is opened.

During the beta testing you will be able to copy up to three(3) characters and/or automatically create one(1) of the new classes in Wrath of the Lich King expansion, the Death Knight! We are seeking loyal customers, previous beta testers, and end game players to beta test for us.

You have received this email for one of the following reasons:

- You beta tested The Burning Crusade expansion during its testing cycle previously.
- You have been a subscriber since the very early stages of the launch of World of Warcraft.
- You are the guild leader of an endgame progression raiding guild.
- You have previously signed up for Wrath of The Lich King beta testing.
- You are one of the lucky few randomly chosen to test.

You will need to sign up at www.worldofwarcraft.com/wotlkbeta/id+327924 to become a member of this exciting process. If you wish not to sign up, Please disregard this email in its entirety.

Thank you for your time and on behalf of Blizzard Entertainment, we hope to see you enjoying the testing period of our exciting new expansion, Wrath of the Lich King!

Regards,

The World of Warcraft Team

Blizzard Entertainment

For many months, players had anxiously awaited the next WoW expansion that would add an entire continent to the geography and ten more levels to the experience ladder. Everybody knew that a few lucky players would be invited to try the expansion before it was sold to the public, to fine-tune its parameters and identify bugs in the programming. This message seemed very plausible, but there were some problems with it. I had not in fact used my Gmail account to communicate with Blizzard, but one of my many other e-mail accounts. Although the message seemed to come from noreply@blizzard.com, I could not verify this. As a matter of general caution, I do not click on a URL in suspicious e-mail messages, but paste the URL into a plain text editor to strip off any hidden code, then copy it into my browser. When I did that, I got a "file not found" message from Blizzard's website. Gritting my teeth and trusting my firewall, I clicked on the URL in the message, figuring that if something disastrous did happen, the result at least would be a valuable research result!

I found myself at a website that looked like the standard Blizzard account management sign-in screen, in beautiful colors and shading, with text indicating that this indeed was the Lich King beta test sign-in site. However, when I checked the URL, it was not a Blizzard address but h1.ripway.com/VerifyLichKing. I refrained from logging in, and when I returned to the site three days later, I found the message "account terminated." Clearly, it was a scam, attempting to get my password to loot my account.

Of course, I am not sure why I was targeted. If you google "Warcraft gemail.com," you get nearly a half million websites that carry somebody's Gmail address plus something about World of Warcraft. My Gmail address was in fact on the website I used for the May 2008 scientific conference, although happily I had not posted any other participants' e-mail addresses there. It is possible that being a guild master could have been a factor, because, as in Maui's case, access to one of my accounts would have also been access to a guild vault. WoW's account security Web page says, "The vast majority of account compromises originate from one of three sources: 1. 'Spoof' websites and emails; 2. Downloading hacks, cheats, or other executable content; 3. Sharing account information and/or using power-leveling services."[17] The e-mail message I had received was an example of spoofing. The two other categories of vulnerability Blizzard mentioned are examples of using what they consider illegitimate means to advance in WoW, with the chance that the player as well as the game would fall victim.

## Epilogue: Becoming Urban

When Alberich and Stephie reached level 20 and achieved master status in their professions, they decided to settle down in Ironforge to work at their blacksmithing, engineering, and tailoring. While Stephie had enjoyed questing, she was somewhat dismayed by the third minion she acquired, a succubus named Disona: an oversexed winged woman wearing a sadomasochistic leather G-string, cracking a whip, and towering high over Stephie herself. For Alberich, the decision reflected his fascination with technology, rather than any dissatisfaction with hunting. Indeed, he had become quite attached to Pardner, his snow leopard pet, who would be out-of-place in the city. After some debate, they decided to return Pardner to the area where he had been tamed, and hope he could re-adapt to the wild. The only way they knew to wean Pardner from the relationship was to stop feeding him, and this raised the very real prospect that a hungry Pardner might eat Alberich. So, as Pardner got hungrier and hungrier, Alberich dismissed him and called him back repeatedly, standing near a tunnel entrance to escape if attacked. As he warily watched Pardner come and go, Alberich thought about their good times together, then recalled he had never really given the animal all the training he required. When Alberich returned to Stephie that night, he was forced to admit he was so attached to Pardner that he had fed him handsomely, begun training him properly, and housed him temporarily with stable master Shelby Stone at Kharanos. There was no escaping the fact that the emotional tie between Dwarf and beast was stronger than the efficiency of economic exchange.

# 7 Identity

My name, Papadoc, is said to hold magical meaning, but I do not know its significance. To me, this uncertainty is emblematic of the dubious status of the race to which I belong, the Trolls. Our tragic history has splintered us into innumerable isolated groups that suffer hostility from all their neighbors. Perhaps my group, the Darkspear Trolls, is most fortunate, because we belong to a much larger coalition of five races, called the Horde. Originally an Orc army assembled by sinister forces and sent to war against the Humans, the Horde has grown under the leadership of Thrall, an Orc who was raised by Humans, and now includes the Tauren, Undead, and Blood Elves, as well as ourselves. Some Trolls may derive a sense of identity through our membership in the Horde, but for me this diverse amalgamation only underscores the painful question: Who are we?

The standard description of Trolls, seen just before one of us enters Kalimdor, says we are "fierce," originated in the jungles, and have a "shadowy heritage." Yet level-1 Trolls find themselves mixed in with Orcs of a similar status in the Valley of Trials. I am a priest, and was pleased to discover my first priest trainer was a fellow Troll who had heard from our spirits about me, and of course the Orcs lack priests. The trainer, whose name was Ken'jai, gave me a hallowed tablet to read, which he had written in our dialect: "Ah hope da spirits have protected ya thus far, mon. Ya have many tests ahead of ya, and ah be willin' to share me experiences witcha when yer ready. It be up to ya to decide how quickly and how powerful ya become. Ah can only guide ya once yer ready."

A little while later, Ken'jai explained to me that the Orcs do not approve of all our traditions, so we keep some of them secret. He then referred me to Tai'jin in the Razor Hill fort in Durotar for further particulars. She said the Horde had taught us to adapt and to gain strength in order to defeat our enemies, gave me my first lesson in spiritual healing, and sent me to treat Kor'ja, a wounded warrior. To my surprise, Kor'ja was a wounded Orc female. I suppose I have nothing against women playing the role of priest or warrior, nor against having Orcs for allies, yet these encounters were deeply disorienting. Restored by my healing power, Kor'ja returned to duty with these words of thanks: "May our ancestors be with you always!" Whose ancestors, hers or mine? Surely our departed ancestors have not joined into a supernatural Horde! When the departed ancestors abandon the ancient traditions, then you know their tribe is lost.

When I returned to Tai'jin, having performed successfully my first healing, she bestowed upon me a Troll priest's garments of spirituality, which are juju hex robes. Shortly thereafter I happened to overhear several Orcs chatting. One casually asked, "What race makes the best hunter for Horde?" An Orc hunter replied that Orcs made the best hunters, and the first Orc asked why. "Trolls are slow," the Orc hunter replied, "the Orcs are way better, and they look better too. Trolls are gay!" I looked at my juju hex robes and had to admit that they might look like a feminine gown to trouser-wearing barbarians such as the Orcs. A third Orc mimicked our accent, saying, "You get to say 'mon' and such." A fourth exclaimed, "Trolls are sexy beasts!" A fifth reminded the group of Orcish rowdies, "According to our good friend, however, Trolls are flaming homosexuals."

When I left the Valley of Trials, on my way to find Tai'jin, I stopped at the first settlement I encountered, a Troll village called Sen'jin. There I encountered a student witch doctor named Bom'bay, was trained in herbalism by a Troll woman named Mishiki, and beheld many Human skulls decorating the huts. A trade supply seller named Tai'tasi launched into a lusty and sinuous dance when I approached her, quite unlike the stodgy Orc women. Although a little primitive for my tastes, this lively village charmed me, and I looked forward with great anticipation to the Troll towns and cities that I imagined lay beyond.

Missions to save the village from a dire threat sent me across a narrow span of water to the Echo Isles, inhabited by a renegade group of Voodoo Trolls and Hexed Trolls led by a sorcerer named Zalazane. I was actually required to kill seventeen of my fellow Trolls, males and females alike, tasks I found quite abhorrent despite the good justification. Some consolation came from liberating the spirit of Minshina, a Darkspear Troll imprisoned in a Voodoo pentagram of torches.

Razor Hill was an Orc outpost, and just north of it lay Orgrimmar, the Orc capital. There I actually met the great Thrall himself, who told me, "All members of the Horde are equal in my eyes, Papadoc. We have all suffered many burdens, and if it were not for wisdom and honor, then we would be no better than the Scourge."

Inspired by Thrall's broad-minded welcome, I began thinking about joining a Horde guild, even though it would not be a Troll organization. Before long, I saw the following on the guild recruitment channel: "The Scions of the Darkmoon seek to find others who bear the mark of the Darkmoon. (This no-pressure, casual guild welcomes all levels, classes, races.)" I asked the leader, Kushkura, to explain the name. He replied, "The Scions of the Darkmoon are those people born under a rare event called the Darkmoon, something akin to a lunar eclipse. Those people are all blessed by Cenarius and chosen to defend the fragile balance of nature."

I learned that each member had a personal focus on some facet of nature. After a few moments of thought, I told Kushkura, "My own focus is the far-flung tribes of Trolls living in nature and despised and exploited by 'civilized races.' I hope to visit my people in their native lands." Encouraged by Kushkura's reaction, I decided it would be possible to commit myself both to Scions of the Darkmoon and to the Horde, without relinquishing my Troll identity.

Conscripted into the Horde army, I hiked across Durotar to Crossroads in the Barrens to get orders from Serga Darkthorn. She is a shaman, the Orc equivalent of a priest, and one of the most aggressive women I had ever met. "Alright, Papadoc," she snarled. "Thrall himself has declared the Horde's females to be on equal footing with you men. Disrespect me in the slightest, and you will know true pain."

I saw an occasional Troll, Undead, and Blood Elf at Crossroads, but lying as it does roughly halfway between Orgrimmar and the Tauren capital of Thunder Bluff, it is primarily a settlement of two races. Speaking with Kushkura again, I said, "I am saddened to see the Barrens are Orc and Tauren, with only a small Troll contingent."

In an exceedingly friendly manner, he replied, "I long to see the return of their numbers."

I thanked him for these kinds words, and said, "Nothing against Orcs and Tauren, but we Trolls are so scattered and fragmented."

Minotaurus told me he had overheard a mixed group of Horde members at Thunder Bluff debating the status of the Trolls. An Undead warlock commented, "Who was saying Orgrimmar was an Orc and Troll City?" One of the group affirmed that it was, and the Undead replied, "But it's even named after an Orc leader, and all the guards are Orcs, and there are barely any Trolls in the city."

A Troll rogue asserted, "The Trolls got their city wiped out, so they moved in with the Orcs."

The Undead would not give ground: "Trolls are just welcome in Orgrimmar, doesn't mean it's Orc and Troll."

The Troll rogue replied, "They live together as one now."

A Troll shaman added, "No Trolls? The mage trainers, priests trainers . . . oh that boss in Thrall's building."

The Undead warlock responded, "I said there are hardly any Trolls; didn't say there weren't any."

Minotaurus contributed his own two cents: "The Orcs have no priests or mages; that's why the ones in Orgrimmar are Trolls."

I knew that only one of Thrall's chief advisers was a Troll, and I doubted that the Trolls had recently lost their city, as had happened to the Gnomes who had moved in with the Dwarves. However, as I gained experience questing across Durotar, Mulgore, and the Barrens, I learned that the other two Horde races, the Undead and the Blood Elves, did indeed have their own cities, both far away across the sea. Only we Trolls seemed to be homeless.

One day, while I was doing business at the Crossroads, a Blood Elf woman named Sins-baby offered me some clothing. They were not rags, such as one gives to a beggar, but well-made gear with a higher armor rating than the things I was wearing. Somewhat frazzled, noting that my very limited carrying bags were full, I told her I had no place to put them, and she went away. Thinking to myself that I had been impolite, I tried to put her gesture of kindness out of my mind. The next day, however, I received them in the mail from her. I sent her a note, expressing profuse thanks, and she replied, "Awww shucks lol . . . You're too kind. Maybe you can come hang out some time with this lil ol Blood Elf and do a bit of questing. Hope you enjoy the gear." We never did go questing, but the episode endeared the Blood Elves to me.

Upon reaching level 16, I resolved to go in search of other Troll communities. Maxrohn said he had encountered many Trolls in Stranglethorn Vale and the Hinterlands, but these zones were far beyond a mere level 16. Catullus suggested I visit Ghostlands, the second zone for Blood Elves, although he gently suggested I should be prepared for the worst. Recalling Sinsbaby's kindness as evidence that the Blood Elves would be hospitable, I followed his suggestion. A zeppelin flight took me from Orgrimmar to Undercity, the capital of the Undead, and a teleportation link conveyed me from there to Silvermoon City, the Blood Elf capital. But I discovered that the Ghostlands Trolls were under constant attack from the Horde, and they assaulted me on first sight.

In my depths of despair, I happened to hear a rumor that a Troll religious center existed on faraway Yojamba Isle, in the sea between Westfall and Stranglethorn Vale. I resolved to make one final effort to find my people, and go there. However, Westfall was dominated by the Alliance, and Stranglethorn held ferocious beasts far above my level. A crazy idea entered my head. I took the zeppelin from Undercity toward Grom'gol Base Camp in Stranglethorn, but just as it came out over the sea, I leaped from the airship.

Amazingly, I dove into the water unhurt and was able to swim the short distance to Yojamba, where miraculously the Zandalar Trolls invited me to join their religious retreat. You will find me there today, studying the secret doctrines we do not share with our Horde allies, sitting at the feet of Al'tabim the All-Seeing, beside his magical map (see figure 7.1). I suppose you could call it a "virtual world," because we can look down upon any region, from Kalimdor to Yojamba itself, and see tiny versions of the people and nations going about their chaotic business, just as we go about ours. I study hard, so that someday I can learn what everything means, and how I fit into the wider reality.

### Theory of Identity

Many people today naturally think of psychoanalysis when the question of a person's identity comes up. Erik Erickson's widely read book *Identity, Youth and Crisis* popularized the concept of "identity crisis," with the implication that this uncomfortable episode of confusion about oneself was especially common in adolescence.[1] Perhaps Papadoc's problem was exactly this, an identity crisis in which race, gender, and social status became problematic. Unfortunately, psychoanalytic theory was very simplistic in asserting that a very small number of well-defined psychological conflicts were the

**Figure 7.1**
Papadoc, a Troll, leaping to express his excitement at becoming a disciple of Al'tabim the All-Seeing, who is gazing at the world map, while a Zandar headshrinker looks on, at Yojamba Isle.

universal sources of human problems. Authoritarianism helped psychoanalysts appear authoritative when they were promoting their dubious treatments in the middle of the twentieth century, so the simplicity and rigidity of their ideas were competitive advantages. This does not mean these ideas were true, and a much less dogmatic school of thought in the same period was probably much closer to the truth, but made no claim to be able to cure anybody of identity problems.

I refer to what sociologists call *symbolic interactionism*. A diluted version of this perspective permeates modern thought, as several intellectual branches have flourished inside sociology, and in the mid-1990s even a computer simulation approach emerged.[2] Among the classics of this tradition is *Human Nature and the Social Order*, by Charles Horton Cooley, published in 1922.[3] Cooley emphasized the way that sociability creates ideas in our minds that represent other individuals, and the way that others give us impressions of ourselves. A friend exists in our mind as a system of thoughts and symbols, representing how that person acts, sounds, looks, and responds to us. Society exists in our mind as the collection of ideas we have about specific other individuals. Cooley stresses that the solid facts of sociology are the imaginations that individuals have of one another.

Cooley acknowledged that part of an individual's sense of self is biological, but not all of it. The *social self* is the set of ideas individuals have about themselves, which are derived from communication with other people. An important part of the social self is our impression of how other people view us. Since we cannot see into others' minds directly, we learn about their picture of us by observing how they respond to us, almost as a mirror might reflect our image back to us. Cooley called this the "looking-glass self," a term widely quoted by later sociologists. It has three main parts: (1) how we imagine we appear to the other person, (2) how we think the other person judges us, and (3) how we react to that judgment, whether with pride or shame. If Cooley were alive today, he might add other mirrors to the optics of his metaphor, representing the characters that stand between us and other people in World of Warcraft. In the real world, humans try to manage the impression they give others, and in WoW they can do so possibly even more powerfully by selecting particular kinds of characters to represent them.

Fifty years ago, *The Presentation of Self in Everyday Life* by Erving Goffman marked a watershed in the development of symbolic interactionism, and this work has become especially influential on contemporary thinking about avatars and virtual worlds.[4] Sociologists had long spoken of the role that people play, but Goffman shifted the emphasis in sociological understanding of role-playing in two ways. First, he described people as very active shapers of their own roles, rather than merely accepting the roles society scripted for them. Second, he developed a language for talking about roles, partly derived from the theater, that he called the "dramaturgical" approach.

In the theater, some people called the "actors" play roles on stage that fit together into a particular drama. Other people play a very different role and belong to a group called the "audience," which exists only in relationship to the actors but is excluded from much inside information that the actors possess. The actors on stage impose a definition of the situation on the audience, for example, asserting that this is not a stage filled with actors but the castle of Macbeth populated with Scottish nobles and servants. Similarly, in the "real world" outside the theater, people attempt to impose upon others a definition of the situation that attributes to them characteristics that they may or may not possess.

Performances vary in the degree of sincerity with which the actors play them, but insincerity is not necessarily undesirable. A shoe clerk sells a customer a shoe that fits well, and lies when saying it is the size the customer requested. Carried off well, this performance satisfies the customer not only with physically comfortable feet but also with the pride that his or her feet are not too fat. Little white lies commonly serve the needs of the audience as well as those of the actors, but often it is possible to use innuendo, strategic ambiguity, and crucial omissions to achieve a successful performance without actually lying. Goffman asserts that all legitimate vocations and relationships require the performer to conceal something, and thus all everyday performances are precarious. Social life is possible only because all ordinary human beings have some skill as actors.

A decade after Goffman wrote, Herbert Blumer summed up symbolic interactionism in three principles: (1) humans act in terms of the meanings things have for them, not the objective nature of the things themselves; (2) meanings are created and sustained largely through social interaction, and (3) the person actively modifies and applies meanings.[5] These principles strongly shape the individual's own identity, what a person means to himself. When Vivian Chen and Henry Duh applied Blumer's perspective to World of Warcraft, the key principle was that "social interaction in MMORPGs is viewed as a dynamic process of meaning-making occurring within a historical context and examinable through the analysis of in-game language and in-game joint actions of players."[6]

Blumer and many of his fellow symbolic interactionists were quite contemptuous of schools of social science that believe research can find objective truths, and Blumer himself rejected research methods such as statistical analysis that mimic the physical sciences. However, modern symbolic interactionists differ among themselves in their feelings about "objectivity" and "scientific methodology," while many other social scientists draw occasionally on the ideas of symbolic interactionism. The key point is that Goffman's tradition speaks directly to the problem of understanding identity in virtual worlds, and it does so in terms of role-playing.

Consider the point mentioned in chapter 1 that Undead characters could have come from one of the three movies based on a science fiction novel by Richard Matheson: *The Last Man on Earth* (1964), *The Omega Man* (1971), and *I Am Legend* (2007).[7] The star of the first of these versions was the veteran actor, Vincent Price. The premise of the novel and all three movie versions is that a plague kills most humans and transforms nearly all the survivors into leprous zombies or vampires. This, of course, is the story of the Undead in WoW, as well. Vincent Price plays a man who is immune to the plague, and who took it upon himself to try to kill the zombies, even as he defends himself from them. His character is named Robert Morgan, whereas the one in the novel and the other films was Robert Neville. Charlton Heston played Robert Neville in *The Omega Man*, and Will Smith did so in *I Am Legend*. Each story is somewhat different from the others, and each protagonist also is somewhat different. Different individuals can play the same role, but they do it differently.

It is also true that every person can play many roles, and a skilled performer merely does it to a greater extent than the average person. Vincent Price encountered the dead and undead in many other films. In Roger Corman's 1964 film *The Tomb of Ligeia*, Price played Verden Fell, whose second marriage is threatened by the ghost of his first wife. In the 1971 film *The Abominable Dr. Phibes*, he destroys the medical personnel who failed to save his wife by inflicting upon them the Biblical plagues described in Exodus 7–12.[8] In the pioneering 1953 3-D movie *House of Wax*, he played Professor Henry Jarrod, who operated a wax museum and made especially lifelike sculptures by killing suitable people and coating their corpses with wax. Outside his film career, Vincent Price also impersonated the playwright Oscar Wilde, in the one-man stage performance, "Diversions and Delights."[9] In that, he served as Wilde's posthumous avatar, bringing a dead man back to life.

### Race, Gender, and Status

People often conceptualize themselves, and are identified by others, as members of groups. In WoW, as outside it, these include racial categories, genders, and social strata, which in WoW generally mean experience levels.[10] The races in World of Warcraft not only have a number of distinctive characteristics but they also are attributed characteristics by the stereotype held by players of other races. Thus, racial identity is as complex a mixture of truth and prejudice in WoW as in the real world.[11] Within a race and class, the capabilities of male and female characters are identical, but players nonetheless hold gender stereotypes as well.[12] Especially problematic are the issues of attributing a character's qualities to the player, and interpreting the meaning those qualities have to the player.

Taurens, for example, have a reputation for being placid and reliable. The graphic novel *Shadows of Ice* gives a central role to Trag Highmountain, who proves to have great wisdom and dedication to truth, without being crafty or intellectual. In the end, this noble Tauren sacrifices himself for a band of Humans, Elves, and dragons in their battle against the Scourge.[13] Minotaurus (later renamed Computabull), my level-30 Tauren, is indeed placid and reliable.

This does not mean that members of other races respect Taurens. Visiting the Darkmoon Faire in June when it was held at Goldshire, Vadvaro noticed a Tauren attending in this Alliance zone. He then overheard the following conversation among a group including Humans plus a Night Elf and a Draenei.

First, Phelps commented, "They speak of the Tauren . . . Why they use the term 'man,' I do not know."

"More of a steak than a man," Omeria observed.

"Heh," interjected Laroque, "If he behaves, who cares? I've gone to the faire in Mulgore before."

Sevatoo agreed with Omeria: "Isn't the term 'cow' or 'steak' a bit more fitting? Or 'dinner?'"

Feloistine supported their logic, saying, "They are just a few fireballs away from being a gourmet meal."

Sevatoo added, "Alright, why did I just rush over to skin a cow? The critter, not the player."

"Heh, skinning a Tauren," Feloistine observed. "I don't see why it shouldn't work."

Laroque asked scornfully, "Leather fetish?"

Examples of racial prejudice abound in the Warcraft literature, as well as in the virtual world, notably the belief that Elves are superior to all the other groups. Having transformed herself magically into an Elf, the haughty dragon Tyrygosa was unwilling to descend further when she entered Tarren Mill, a Human settlement: "I'll not demean myself by taking human form. At least elves are aesthetically pleasing."[14]

In Richard Knaak's novel *Day of the Dragon*, a Night Elf named Vareesa Windrunner meets a Human named Rhonin and thinks to herself, "Like most humans, this one cared nothing for anyone but himself."[15] The distance between these two races sets up a nice tension in the novel, resolved at the conclusion when the two marry.

Both NPCs and players in the world itself comment on racial tensions. Kum'isha the Collector, at the Rise of the Defiler, says, "I have heard orcs proclaim the odor of humans to be sickening and I have heard humans proclaim the odor of orcs to be wretched; yet, to me, all of the races give off the same odor: The foul, dizzying scent of greed."

When Papadoc was questing in the Barrens, he overheard Bedemere say, "The Orc means well, if he is a bit stupid."

Navahr responded, "Why do my clothes smell of Orc? By the Sunwell, that man needs to be flung in the river!"

*Cycle of Hatred* by Keith R. A. DeCandido deals with escalating tension between Orcs and Humans, stimulated covertly by the evil Shadow Council. Humans commonly refer to Orcs as "greenskin devils," "filthy greenskins," or even "greenskinned bastards."[16] At one point, DeCandido tells us what an Orc named Byrok thinks about Humans: "Humans were monsters, and Byrok wanted nothing to do with such uncivilized creatures."[17]

A Human character in Aaron Rosenberg's novel *Tides of Darkness* learns that the Orc are gaining allies, and exclaims in horror, "They've teamed with the trolls then, greenskin and greenskin!"[18]

In *Cycle of Hatred*, Jaina Proudmoore said to Thrall, "Is not what separates us from animals that we can change our nature? After all, there are those who would argue that an orc's nature was to be a slave."[19]

Thrall's own doctrine of cooperation across races is occasionally repeated by lesser Horde functionaries. When Catullus entered Tranquillien, the village at the center of the Ghostlands, he was surprised to see members of the Forsaken mingling with the Blood Elves. As a splinter group from their dire enemy, the Scourge, members of the Forsaken are not warmly accepted by young Blood Elves. Arcanist Vandril explained to him, "These Forsaken are here to help" and told him to see their leader, High Executioner Mavren.

"I assure you we mean your people no harm," Mavren said. "We are here because of a common enemy."

Although the two genders are of equal power and opportunity in WoW, gender remains as powerful a marker of identity in WoW as it is in the surrounding world. While walking in the ruins of Old Silvermoon, Catullus overheard a debate among Blood Elves about the "real" gender of female characters. Hayami started the discussion, asking, "Is it just me, or are all the 'girls' really guys?"

"About 80% are guys," Luthin responded.

Alleinia said, "I've seen a few girls. I'm a guy myself."

Amye, a friend of Catullus, announced, "I am a gal."

Charrae said, "I'm a girl."

Luthin told Charrae, "Sucks to be you then."

She frowned at him, then said, "Be quiet Luthin."

Alleinia interjected, "Sucks to be you due to the WoW rule, guy until proven girl."

Theleion asserted, "MMORPGs draw more women players than any other genre."

Hayami complained, "It's just a lot of the guys make girl characters and pretend to be girls."

Luthin figured, "But the odds of a girl playing WoW are about 40-1, the odds of a guy being a lonely pathetic freak is about 4-1."

Charrae concluded, "Well, then they are gay."

Alleinia disagreed, saying, "I usually play male characters, but this one goes into my main's role playing."

Theleion scornfully exclaimed, "Role playing! Nooo!"

Hayami asked, "Like the park?"

Theleion continued, "Someone is an Alliance refugee."

Alleinia admitted, "That's pretty much the area."

Luthin, thinking of the view a player usually has of his character, said, "I hate it when they pull that 'I play a girl because I don't want to look at a guy's ass' bullshit excuse."

Alleinia further acknowledged, "I did come from the Alliance, but that was on a PvP server."

Once, in the Shandris realm, Lockness and Sathura bantered about their genders. Lockness couldn't decide what pronoun to use for Sathura, who asserted "She!" Lockness replied, "Yah, thought 'she.' Did I say 'he?' Or is it 'she?'"

Sathura responded, "That's okay. I called you 'she' earlier. But I am definitely female."

Lockness laughed. "Oh that is a relief. I am definitely male."

Another time, a player logged in using his wife's feminine character, and a guildie joked, "Ooooh! Okay. Felt like a little crossdressing today, did you?"

My census of 1,096 characters belonging to the Alea Iacta Est guild found that 298 of them, or 27.2 percent, were female. Given how well established this guild was, with many players who were clearly mature adults, it was certainly not dominated by early-adolescent boys, and it thus conceivably could have had this high a proportion of females. However, we just don't know. When I compared the classes of these female characters against the males, I found a mixture of similarities and differences that suggested standard sex roles. The most popular class was hunters, 20.1 percent of females and 21.7 percent of males. Both priests and warlocks were chosen more often for female characters. Priests constituted 17.4 percent of female characters, and 8.3 percent of males. Since priests are the quintessential healers, this fits the stereotype that women are supposed to be more nurturant. The gender difference was weaker among warlocks, 17.4 percent of female characters belonging to this magical class, versus 11.5 percent of males.

Druids were favored more by males, taken by 10.4 of them compared to only 5.4 percent of females. The chapter on religion noted that druid and priest NPCs were strictly segregated by gender among the Night Elves, all druid trainers being male, and all priest trainers, female. However, AIE is a Horde guild, so this gender assumption about druids may not apply. The class with the most males was warriors, which constituted 12.2 percent of the male characters, versus only 2.3 percent of females. This difference in the most aggressive class also fits gender stereotypes,[20] although the fact does not prove the characters have the same genders as their players. It could be that when players create a character of the opposite gender they are especially likely to make that character play the role dictated by common gender stereotypes (see figure 7.2).

Playing the opposite gender became somewhat more difficult in mid-2007, when WoW added private voice channels to its array of chat options. For some time, ambitious players had used voice communications to improve the efficiency of raids, employing TeamSpeak or Ventrillo that were designed for this purpose, or conference calls over Skype. One's natural voice may not suit the character one is playing. Warriors should have deep, commanding voices, not the squeaky little voices possessed by many of the youngest players. Female characters should have the melodious voices of women, not the rough sounds that men make when they speak. Age, ethnicity, and some traits of personality express themselves in people's voices, perhaps incongruously with the given game character.

The sound effects in WoW sometimes give the character a voice. For example, if Etacarinae attempts to cast a magic spell prematurely, a feminine voice with a slight

**Figure 7.2**
A Draenei woman and a Human woman, whose players' identities are not in fact both female, dancing on a tabletop at the Stormwind bank, without attracting much attention.

foreign accent says, "That spell isn't ready yet," or "I can't cast that yet." Presumably, that is her voice, and the accent is logical given that she is a Draenei and the Human language, Common, is not her native tongue. Dwarf NPCs speak with a Scottish accent, and Troll NPCs with a Caribbean one. For players to stay entirely in role while speaking, they would need to adopt such accents.

Within each racial or gender group, and cutting across them, is the social status represented by the levels 1 through 80. Gaining levels of experience does not merely have instrumental value, because it gives you the power to do things you could not do before. It also has expressive or symbolic value, increasing self-esteem. It is the custom for someone who advances a level to proclaim in the guild chat: "Ding!" The typical response is, "Gratz!" or "Grats!" This is a colloquial way of saying, "Congratulations!"

Players joke about status all the time. Doma, a level-29 Draenei warrior, exclaimed to fellow members of Winged Ascension, "Oh, what the hell. 44,299/44,300 and nothing to kill by me!" This meant Doma had only one more experience point to gain out of 44,300 to reach level 30.

Lilmalius joked, "So kill yourself. Does that give credit?"

Other measures of advancement, such as learning new skills, also enhance self-esteem and a feeling of being formidable in a competitive society. A level-54 Night Elf rogue excitedly told a friend of hers, "I just learned shadowstep!" When the friend asked what that does, she replied, "Makes me magically pop up behind somebody. Say I'm dueling you, and you get close enough to see me, I use that and I'm magically behind you."

During the period of most of this study, no player could rise above level 70. When Maxrohn reached level 70, a fellow member of his guild joked, "Welcome to the World of Warcraft job."

Another explained, "Now be ready to quest for money, run instances for reputation and gear, and farming—and I mean a lot of farming."

A player who is online almost daily said, "You're going to scare him. It's still fun once or twice per month."

The same guild's chat carried dubious news. "I'm killing Hogger!" exclaimed Evelexan. "It was a tough fight, but we prevailed." This caused Aazenroth, the guild master, to roll on the floor laughing. Hogger is famous as the very first elite NPC a Human is likely to encounter. Nominally level 11, Hogger has the endurance of about a level-15 character. But Evelexan was a level-70 priest, probably capable of killing Hogger by casting a single spell, or simply punching him a few times with his fists.

Status comparison may be more of an issue for sociable players who develop ties to others they play with. For example, a level-65 Night Elf priest exclaimed on a guild channel, "Sigh! I need to level faster. All the people I was doing instances with not long ago are now all level 70. I need to make new friends. All my friends on my list are level 70. Sigh! Since they hit level 70, they don't want to play with lobies like me." A level-64 Human mage in the same guild would seem an ideal playmate for the Night Elf, and the two compared their situations. The Human mentioned he had reached his level in fourteen days and ten hours, and the Night Elf admitted he was only one level higher after a total of twenty-eight days and five hours. Thus, leveling slowly was a source of shame, even at a very high level.

Status competition between people is a zero-sum game; for some people to win, others must lose. However, as Edward Castronova notes, in a game like WoW this is not entirely true, because people can defeat endless numbers of NPCs, thereby in a sense allowing a majority of people to score above average.[21] He suggests further that many people like virtual worlds because the real world is not sufficiently satisfying. They lack social connections, have no sense that their actions have significance, and feel that the "game" of pursuing wealth does not provide happiness.[22] Castronova has also argued that people come to identify with their avatars, perceiving them as extensions of themselves.[23] By my observation, players do take their status level very seriously, and take great pride in advancing. In the summer of 2008, I happened to lecture about virtual worlds to a business group, and I found myself pridefully boasting that I had two level-70 WoW characters. It does give me pride to say I have taken two of them through tough battles all the way to the top, and by early December 2008, one of them had achieved the new ceiling of level 80.

It is not at all clear, however, that many players allow their characters' races or genders to define their own personal identity. The fact that one of my characters, Adalgisa, is a female Tauren, does not seem to define my identity at all. Experiencing WoW as Adalgisa does not make me feel female or bovine. In short—in case you were wondering—I am not a cow.

**Names**

In World of Warcraft, as in the larger surrounding society, the fundamental atom of individuality is the person's name, distinguishing him or her from all other people.[24] When creating a new character, a player is expected to type a name in a box, or to let the system suggest a name at random. The system proposes pronounceable words that lack obvious meaning, and thus look like names. For example, when I asked the system to suggest names for a Human male, the first five it suggested were Danos, Jaceda, Waya, Samaris, and Mandes. The first five for a Human female were Tandra, Willa, Ciandra, Marly, and Averiarcy. Trying this same little experiment again gave me new choices, but one of the female names was actually the word *Hope*. I suspect that most players who create their own names follow their subconscious notions of what syllables make acceptable but meaningless names for the given gender. However, many others seek to inject meaning into their names.

I often found that my first choices were unavailable. When I was creating a female Tauren druid, I thought of Bellini's opera *Norma*—named after the high druid priestess character—but the name Norma was already taken, so I settled for a lesser soprano priestess in the opera, Adalgisa. Sometimes, I would labor long and hard to find a suitable name, struggling against not only other people's prior choices but also WoW censorship. Blizzard Entertainment seeks to prevent names that would have an unfair or unpleasant impact on other players, or that might in some way violate law. Here is the list of prohibitions published in the game's terms of use agreement:[25]

(i) Belonging to another person with the intent to impersonate that person, including without limitation a "Game Master" or any other employee or agent of Blizzard;

(ii) That incorporates vulgar language or which are otherwise offensive, defamatory, obscene, hateful, or racially, ethnically or otherwise objectionable;

(iii) Subject to the rights of any other person or entity without written authorization from that person or entity;

(iv) That belongs to a popular culture figure, celebrity, or media personality;

(v) That is, contains, or is substantially similar to a trademark or service mark, whether registered or not;

(vi) Belonging to any religious figure or deity;

(vii) Taken from Blizzard's Warcraft products, including character names from the Warcraft series of novels;

(viii) Related to drugs, sex, alcohol, or criminal activity;

(ix) Comprised of partial or complete sentence (e.g., "Inyourface", "Welovebeef", etc);

(x) Comprised of gibberish (e.g., "Asdfasdf", "Jjxccm", "Hvlldrm");

(xi) Referring to pop culture icons or personas (e.g. "Britneyspears", "Austinpowers", "Batman")

(xii) That utilizes "Leet" or "Dudespeak" (e.g., "Roflcopter", "xxnewbxx", "Roxxoryou")

(xiii) That incorporates titles. For purposes of this subsection, "titles" shall include without limitation 'rank' titles (e.g. , "CorporalTed," or "GeneralVlad"), monarchistic or fantasy titles (e.g., "KingMike", "LordSanchez"), and religious titles (e.g., "ThePope," or "Reverend Al").

Some players select the names of favorite characters from culturally related fantasy worlds, implying that for them World of Warcraft is merely the current step on a long journey through vicarious identities. To explore this possibility, I used the online Armory database of the official WoW website, entering the names of characters. Recognizing the close cultural connection to Tolkien's work, I checked for names from *The Lord of the Rings*. Apparently, the system prevents a player from selecting the best-known versions of the names of the two heroes, Frodo and Bilbo, but thirty-eight characters were called Frodobaggins, and fifty were called Bibbobaggins. There were also forty-two characters named Frodoo and eight named Bilboo. Bilbo was the hero of *The Hobbit*, the short novel that preceded *The Lord of the Rings*, and 240 WoW characters were named simply Hobbit. In the trilogy of long novels, Frodo led the Fellowship of the Ring, so I checked the Armory for guilds with this name.

Eighteen realms had guilds named Fellowship of the Ring, but seven of these were abandoned guilds, each with only a single member. Inspecting the memberships of these guilds revealed the ingenuity with which Tolkien fans circumvented the game's attempt to exclude Tolkienesque names. Tolkien's fellowship is comprised of nine characters, starting with four hobbits, led by Frodo Baggins, who is followed by Meriadoc Brandybuck (Merry), Peregrin Took (Pippin), and Samwise Gamgee (Sam). Two humans also belong, Aragorn and Boromir. Especially relevant to the races of Azeroth, there is also a Dwarf named Gimli, and an Elf, Legolas. Finally, all are guided by a mage, Gandalf.

In *The Lord of the Rings*, Aragorn first cloaks himself under the pseudonym Strider. No WoW character was called Strider, but 276 had names I could locate in the Armory like Striders, Striderr, or Striderx that begin with "Strider." No WoW characters were named Gimli, but there were 66 called Gimly, 79 Gimmly, and 167 Gimmli. Similarly, none was named Boromir, but 60 names began with "Boromir." Among the most popular characters is the elf Legolas. An astonishing 448 characters had names beginning "Legolas" followed by other letters, plus an additional 43 called Llegolas, and usually they were Elves. There were 228 characters whose names begin with "Aragorn," plus an additional 26 named Araggorn.

There were no Gandalfs, but 27 Gandaalfs, 35 Gaandalfs, and two Gaandaalfs. Apparently the censors missed the names of some popular Tolkien characters. The name of Frodo's stalwart companion, Samwise, was carried by 128 characters. Fifty-two characters were named Meriadoc, and 227 Peregrin. A murloclike creature is called Gollum in *The Hobbit*, and Gollum/Sméagol in *The Lord of the Rings*. There are no Gollums, but 54 characters had names beginning with these letters. Apparently, Sméagol was not an illegal name, because 11 characters were called this. Another 61 add extra letters. Female versions of this male character were Gollumina, Gollumena, and Smeagolina.

For a statistical study intended for a later journal article, I ran the CensusPlus character tabulation program on two computers, tallying all 22,851 characters who appeared online in the Emerald Dream and Scarlet Crusade realms during a twenty-four-hour period. Unsystematically, I scanned through the list of names, looking for interesting examples. Some names implied feminine gender, including Hearthwoman, Tinwoman, Fireprincess, Darkprincess, Killerqueenn, Bluegirl, Dixiegirl, Sweetgirl, Priestgirl, Babygurl, Qsbabygurl, Baddgurl, and an Undead priest called Dedgurl. Others implied masculine gender: Wickedman, Machohunter, Manuelmacho, Hockeydude, Boymajesty, Bugboy, Bergerboy, Yorkshireboy, Evilboy, Bubbleboy, Mommysboy, Theboy, Sunnyboy, Superguy, and a Gnome called Lilbaldguy.

I can easily understand why a fantasy character in a role-playing realm might be called something romantic like Mindfire or Heartsfire. I am less clear why someone would call their character Bigdummy, Deceitfulbob, Baddesires, Baddream, Badrat, Badreaction, Spiritless, Dontbotherme, Thedivineone, Myangelface, or Milksgonebad. Occasionally I found names that were meaningful words, such as the following Blood Elves: Amiable, Angelic, Arbitrator, Ascendancy, and Therapy. A hunter was named Beasttamer. A rare name circumvents the rules against obscenity, notably Badmutafuca. Eighty-one of the 22,851 names contained the word *death*, including Deathbearer, Deathflayer, Deathblood, Deathsentenz, Dreamofdeath, Fearnotdeath, Kissofdeathh, Deathawaitsu, Deathblossm, Oldmandeath, Soulessdeath, Deathlust, Deathweaver, Deatthdealer, and Ragingdeath. Some players whimsically employ accent marks to give their characters' names an exotic or European flavor, including Androníc, Calåmity, Énigmus, Rëd, Uñmërcyfül, Zòrrò, Çhãøs, Çqueer, and Ææñ.

Some characters are named for their class. *Lock* is slang for "warlock," and the following characters were indeed all warlocks: Lockcraft, Locksomess, Psylocke, Legendlock, Lockafeller, Lockedup, Magiclock, Padlock, Lockdown, Beerlock, Coolwarlock,

Warwarlock, Whoalock, and Wiilock. Orclock is an Orc warlock, and Lockmidget is, not surprisingly, a Gnome warlock. *Pally* is slang for "paladin," and *shammy* for "shaman." The following are indeed paladins: Pallyelve, Pallypoon, Pallyer, Reddypally, Palydin, Palydon, Palisade, Principally, and Wannabmypaly. And these are shamans, just among the Draenei: Shamidraenei, Shamajestic, Shamikaze, Shamanater, Shamara, Shamatha, Shamyofdeath, and Shamyrocks. A Night Elf druid was actually named Drudnightelf. Other druids use equally descriptive names: Albinodruid, Druiddude, Druidlover, Omegadruid, Deaddruid, and Samthedruid. Rogues can escape detection through stealth, especially if they are small, and three Gnome rogues are Sneakpants, Sneakygnome, and Sneeker.

Some names identify the character's race. The slang word for "character" is *toon*. Bloodtoon is a Blood Elf, whereas Animaltoon is a Tauren. Disrespectful Tauren names include Cowpancake, Cowsgomoo, Momocow, Moobell, Moodusa, Moohoof, Moomanchu, Moomoocow, Moopheus, Mootilator, Moozzarella, and Udderevil. Druimoo is a Tauren druid. Three of the Undead were Undeadchar, Undeadone, and Undeadsoul. In WoW chat slang, a Blood Elf is often called a *belf*, and one of them called himself Belfpunn. Other Blood Elves called themselves Anotherelf, Boyabloodelf, Elfalpha, Elfling, Exiledelf, and Testyelf. Among the Night Elves were Darkelfs, Devilelf, Elflord, Elfstalker, Elfstar, Elfstyle, Sinisterelf, Superelf, Thaelfkilla, and Wiccanelf, whose name refers to the Wicca (witchcraft) religious tradition.

By name, Alistomper must be someone who stomps on members of the Alliance, and two Undead characters were Gnomeater and Sliceagnome. Mygnome is indeed a Gnome. Both Trollslayer and Killerdwarf are dwarves. Gnomes are small, so it is not surprising one Gnome warrior was called Minitanker, and another, Smalltank. However, the Gnome warriors, Supertank and Biggylittle, seemed misnamed. Other diminutive Gnomes were Littlebitty, Littlepete, Minikiller, Minimite, Smallbit, Smallipops, Teeni, Tinyblade, Tinyshadow, Tinyterrer, and Tinytraitor. Two Gnome warlocks in the Scarlet Crusade realm were named Evillmidget and Evilmidgget. Ironically, one Dwarf was called Thebigguy.

Twenty-three level-1 characters had "bank" in their names, such as Banktoon, Ourbank, Iamabanker, and Justabank. These are what are known as *bank alts*, characters that exist only to give the player more space to store things. Scott Johnson, host of *The Instance* podcast, once remarked, "I keep a level-8 warrior just sitting in Orgrimmar, waiting to cash in my stuff, and send my money to me, and put stuff on the auction block. I'm constantly mailing back and forth with that poor guy. He's just sitting out there in lagville, going, 'Oh man, I want to fight.' And I made him a banker!"[26]

Once in Mulgore chat, Keepitreal asked, "Do I need a better fishing skill to get better fish?" Of course, the correct answer was yes, but Anderisa joked, "Nope, just a better name." As it happens, "Keep it real!" is one of the expressions Goblins like to say when doing business with their customers, but the phrase raises the question of just what *real* means in a virtual world.

Some character names are imported from the external world. Geztrezz once commented about Everton's name, "Isn't that a football club in the Liverpool area?"

Everton, who was a level-70 Tauren druid, replied, "Yes, but it is also my name in real life."

Grundomango interjected, "He's also a mint," referring to the traditional British sweet, Everton mints.[27] Everton, the Tauren druid, explained the origin of his name this way: "It was my crazy father's idea. He used to work for Unilever, a UK company, and he heard someone talking about it and he liked the sound of it."

Everton was a member of the Alea Iacta Est guild in the Earthen Ring realm. AIE can remind us that most character names are not jokes but display a wide range of qualities. When Catullus joined AIE in September 2007, the Caesar of the guild was Maui. The next rank, Imperator, was held by Dreadspine, Wiiremotus, Milliway, Imriela, and Imriela's alt Winema. Praetorian rank was held by Gerp (alt of Dreadspine), Lanctharus , Stigg, and Worradius (alt of Wiiremotus). Below that stood the Centurions: Ahrian, Alisandele, Ashayo, Astuss, Boboshanti, Cloudhoof, Frostybites, Kalisynth, Mynydd (alt of Stigg), Oottoo, Palatinus, Secondaid, Tamuk (alt of Stigg), Tearic (alt of Astuss), Thyatira, and Xanar (alt of Frostybites).

Guild names are important expressions of identity, as well. Alea Iacta Est repeats the proclamation Julius Caesar made when he crossed the Rubicon, "The die is cast!" An offshoot of the popular podcast *The Instance*, AIE was originally named I Eat Babies, but one player protested to Blizzard and forced the guild to change. For a brief period, Maxrohn belonged to a new guild named Mister Nasty Time, but Blizzard forced a name change, and Sythyn, the guild master, renamed it simply Sythyns Guild.

In my sample of 22,851 characters, the largest guild in the Emerald Dream realm was E B O L A, with 168 members logging in the day of my sample, and the largest in the Scarlet Crusade realm was Axiom, with 134 members. Note that there are spaces between the capital letters of E B O L A, and this may have prevented the guild from being forced to change its name, because Blizzard might have the deadly disease Ebola listed among the forbidden words that an automatic name-screening program would look for. Among the much smaller guilds that also use separated capital letters for their names were Y A T T A, G O D L Y, V A S H, and B A N A N A S.

My census counted at least 75 members for these additional guilds: Honor The Fallen, The Order of Mjolnir, Myrmidon Council, Ashes of the Phoenix, Saçrosançt, Legion, Angst, House of the Phoenix, Legio Fidelis, Sneaky Snakes, The Phoenix Rebellion, No Mercy Mafia, The Warsong Clan, and Clan Red Hand. While the styles of these names vary, most seem dignified, if a little dramatic, with the exception of the Sneaky Snakes, which frankly sounds like a children's guild, although I have no direct evidence it is.

Given the vast number of character and guild names in WoW, one could imagine equally vast research projects to analyze the many dimensions of identity they express. For now it is worth noting that a significant minority of players choose names that say something meaningful. Many others select names that lack obvious meaning, unless it is to express the fact that it denotes a person, and one who is not simply an ordinary William, John, Mary, or Sue.

## Shards of Self

One of the more dubious advantages of participant observation is that it lets you talk about yourself. With more than a little shyness, I do conclude it is worth explaining how I constructed the personalities of my twenty-two WoW characters, beginning with the ones I lavished the most time on. To some extent, Maxrohn and I are the same person, but we also have our differences. He is a little more pessimistic than I, although both of us are rather old and worn out. He is able to cast a protective spell around himself, kill monsters with a magic wand, and resurrect deceased members of his team without help from any deity. I lack all those abilities. He lacks my abilities in social science and computer programming. His name actually derives from my uncle, Max Rohn, an Episcopal priest who died a number of years ago, and who had some of the qualities of an adventurer. So, to some small degree, he reflects my uncle as well as myself.

Perhaps my most fully developed WoW character is Catullus, a Blood Elf priest. I named him after the ancient Roman poet Catullus, whose works I read in the original Latin half a century ago. My image of Catullus was shaped not only by his writings but also by my Latin teacher Charles P. Twichell and by the cantata *Catulli Carmina*, by the German composer Carl Orff, which portrays Catullus as a disillusioned romantic. I think of Blood Elves very much in terms of ancient Rome, a society very proud of its technology and organization, but corrupt on many levels, intellectually brilliant and intensely hedonistic. In other ways, Catullus is a younger version of Maxrohn and me, more vigorous, more aggressive, and very quick witted. Yes, he is a reflection of me, but also of these other influences as channeled through my perception of them.

Some writers about avatars assume that users consider them to be very direct representatives of themselves in a virtual world, but my observation suggests the widest possible range of connections between the biological person and the electronic person, only occasionally fulfilling the definition of second self.[28] For example, throughout years of watching my two daughters play Nintendo games, I never saw them conceptualize themselves as fat Italian plumbers with blue pants and black mustaches. No, Mario was their friend, toy, pet, or puppet, not their selves.

A good case is my Night Elf priestess, Lunette. Many players, and some social scientists, assume that creating an avatar belonging to the opposite gender is tremendously significant, almost certainly expressing gender ambivalence if not full-blown gender reassignment wishes.[29] Anything may be true in particular examples, but these assumptions are false much of the time. My daughters were not male when they played Mario, and I am not female when I play Lunette. She is female, and I have that in mind when working with her, but that is only one part of her identity. Other parts are probably more important in marking differences between us.

Lunette is a devout believer in the Moon goddess, Elune, whereas I am not religious at all. As it happens, one of my first cousins, Donate Pahnke, is an actual believer in the lunar goddess, whom she calls Selene, thereby verifying that Lunette's beliefs are credible to sophisticated human beings—even if I myself do not believe in them.[30] Lunette's personality overlaps mine in some respects, but both Maxrohn and Catullus are closer to me. She's a little crabbier than I am. She is not as even-tempered, a little bit solemn, and—so I imagine—a little bit more obsessed with order and clarity.

My two other level-30 characters, Minotaurus (also called Computabull) and Etacarinae, express highly focused but powerful images of personalities that are not mine, but are to some extent ideals. Neither broods constantly about the meaning of life, as Maxrohn, Catullus, and I do. Lunette broods, too, but despite her emotional volatility and social isolation, she imagines she possesses the final answers to all questions. Both Minotaurus and Etacarinae are serene. He trusts his traditional Tauren culture completely, whereas she has great confidence in her own technical competence. The Tauren's name, of course, refers to the classical minotaur, half man and half bull. When I moved him over to the server holding the May 9–11, 2008, scientific conference, I was forced to rename him, and this seemed a good time to take advantage of the pun Computabull. For the conference, he exhibited great competence, manufacturing and distributing many of the needed resources. The name Etacarinae was suggested by my younger daughter, Constance, after the remarkable, luminous star, Eta Carinae. Constance is a star, too, so I naturally think of the character as one, in the metaphoric sense.

Three of my more incidental characters are named after characters from the Mars novels of Edgar Rice Burroughs, which deeply impressed me when I was a boy. When it was time to create an Orc character, I naturally thought of Tars Tarkas, Jeddak of Thark, the leader of the nomadic Thark tribe that cruised the deserts of the red planet. Searching the online WoW database on April 27, 2007, I discovered that thirty-two characters were named Tarstarkas, and forty-seven Tarkas. Tars Tarkas is arguably the first well-developed extraterrestrial character in literature, introduced in Burroughs's 1911 novel, *A Princess of Mars*.[31] An anonymous Wikipedia author described Burroughs's character thus: "Though a great warrior and leader among his people, the brutal and mirthless Tharks, he possesses a sense of compassion and empathy uncharacteristic of his race."[32] Tharks are huge, green, tusked, and possess four arms. All but the last of these characteristics defined the typical male Orc.

The hero of most of the ten novels was John Carter, an Earthman transported mystically to Mars, called Barsoom by its inhabitants, where he fell in love with a humanoid Red Martian woman, Dejah Thoris. Despite the fact that in the novels Martians lay eggs and thus must have rather different biology from that of Earthlings, they were able to produce a son, given the name Carthoris, combining their own names to express their interplanetary union. Nineteen WoW characters had the name Johncarter, seventeen Dejahthoris, and seventeen Carthoris. One of the most interesting characters in Burroughs's Mars novels is the brilliant but unprincipled scientist Ras Thavas. Only two WoW characters were called Rasthavas, but one of them was a member of Warlords of Barsoom, an Alliance guild in the Sentinels realm, eleven of whose dozen characters have Barsoomian names.

To investigate this guild, I created a new character in their realm, a rogue known as Vadvaro, named after the nemesis of Ras Thavas, Vad Varo, from the novel *The Master Mind of Mars*.[33] Like John Carter, this character was originally a fictional American, named Ulysses Paxton. Remarkably, the novel is in the form of a long letter to Edgar Rice Burroughs from Paxton, who was a fan of the writer. Paxton read *A Princess of Mars* while in training to become a U.S. Army officer in 1917, and became obsessed with the martial symbolism of the planet Mars, and the idea of possibly traveling there by astral projection, as John Carter had done. On one level, he knew the novel was fantastic fiction, but on another level, it seemed to communicate a deeper truth. Later, on a French battlefield, Paxton received a mortal wound and lay dying, legless, alone, and in darkness. Burroughs writes that Paxton recalled:

Then my eyes suddenly focused upon the bright red eye of Mars and there surged through me a sudden wave of hope. I stretched out my arms towards Mars, I did not seem to question or to doubt for an instant as I prayed to the god of my vocation to reach forth and succour me. I knew that he would do it, my faith was complete, and yet so great was the mental effort that I made to throw off the hideous bonds of my mutilated flesh that I felt a momentary qualm of nausea and then a sharp click as of the snapping of a steel wire, and suddenly I stood naked upon two good legs looking down upon the bloody, distorted thing that had been I. Just for an instant did I stand thus before I turned my eyes aloft again to my star of destiny and with outstretched arms stand there in the cold of that French night—waiting.[34]

In a moment, he was transported at "the speed of thought" to Mars. Equally swiftly, my Vadvaro character entered the Sentinels realm as a level-1 character, and on my second visit I was able to chat with the master of Warlords of Barsoom, who called himself Morskajak, after Mors Kajak, king of the second city of the Red Martian nation of Helium. He explained:

As originally conceived the guild was limited only to those who were willing to start a new character named from the ERB novels. But we recently changed that rule. To gain rank in the guild, however, a person needs to have a main in the guild with a Barsoomian name. All alts and new members who come without Barsoomian names are stuck at the lowest guild rank of Panthan . . . Our backstory in this light role playing guild is that Azeroth is the afterlife or Valhalla for the most valiant fighters on Barsoom that have died in battle.

*Panthan*, I recognized, is the Barsoomian term for "soldier of fortune," one who may be valiant but lacks loyalty.

In addition to their son, John Carter and Dejah Thoris had a daughter, Tara, whose name was not distinctive enough to tabulate, and a granddaughter, Llana, after whom I named my third Burroughs character. On May 25, 2008, there were 68 other characters named Llana in WoW.

Adalgisa and Alberich are both characters from grand opera, she from Bellini's *Norma*, and he from Wagner's *Das Rheingold*. Folwell was named after my great-grandfather, William Folwell Bainbridge, and Lusea after my great-grandmother, Lucy Seaman Bainbridge. My wife, Marcia, created Stephie, naming her after a younger sister; I named another character Marcya. Aristotle was specifically intended to be the reincarnation of the ancient Greek philosopher by that name, and Price is the deceased actor, Vincent Price. Papadoc, my Troll priest, was named after the late dictator of Haiti, Duvalier, whose nickname was Papa Doc, in recognition of the fact that Trolls speak with a Caribbean accent. Zodia, the Draenei priest, is named after the zodiac. Sciencemag was created to head the Science guild for the May 2008 conference, so named because the journal *Science* publicized it on its website, www.sciencemag.org.

Incognita was the first of my female characters, and the name implied the gender deception; only later did I get fully comfortable having female characters. My last character, Annihila, is an Undead female death knight, expressing complete annihilation of my own identity. When I decided to create my penultimate character, a Human mage who would be Aristotle's apprentice, I selected the name Ozma from L. Frank Baum's Oz books, in full awareness of her dubious history. When princess Ozma first appears in the Oz books, she is a boy!

### Second-Order Role-Playing

Any mentally competent human being can play the role of another, but it takes some intellectual maturity to play the role of a person who is playing a role. Second-order role-playing is like the play within a play that adds additional depth to several of Shakespeare's dramas. The most notable example is *Hamlet*. An actor plays Hamlet, the prince of Denmark. The backstory says that Hamlet's father was killed by his uncle, Claudius, who then married Hamlet's mother and took control of the kingdom. Hamlet learns about this from the ghost of his father, which one would think is not a very reliable way of getting information on which to take extreme action. Hamlet hesitates and behaves in a distracted fashion, either because he is under too much psychological stress, or because he needs to hide his suspicions until he can confirm what the ghost said and assassinate Claudius. This aspect of the drama has been an endless source of scholarly and psychoanalytic speculation by many writers, but the important point to note here is that Hamlet, the character, is *not entirely himself*.[35] There is a distance between the character's inner self and his superficial behavior. This takes the behavior further from the inner self of the actor, and thus represents something like a second step in role-playing.

Sociologists have noted that real people in real settings often exhibit *role distance* in behavior that acknowledges that the person is somewhat separate from the role he or she is playing.[36] A prime example is medical personnel who may use humor not only to distance themselves from the horrors of disease but also to tell their associates that behind the white mask there is the human face of a friend who is not merely a surgeon. Hamlet's erratic behavior, thus, may be a mixture of dissembling, role confusion, and neurosis, but whatever combination of these factors is at work, it demands an extra measure of skill from the performer.

Hamlet resolves his uncertainty through the play within a play. This point was raised by a character named Melyanna in World of Warcraft as part of a game within a game. Melyanna was a level-70 Blood Elf female priest. We can safely assume that the player behind this mask is not a Blood Elf; it seems unlikely that she is a priest, and we have no clue whether she is female. A leading member of the Alea Iacta Est guild, she is known for her wit and breadth of knowledge. Melyanna is a top-skill tailor, thus able to make capacious carrying bags she can give away as prizes in a trivia contest she often stages in the guild chat. It is called "Who Wants to be a Melyann-aire?" in imitation of the popular television program *Who Wants to be a Millionaire*. The game consists of about five trivia questions, often requiring the contestants to identify a quote, and the person who gives the correct answer first is the winner. One time Melyanna said, "The play's the thing wherein I'll catch the conscience of the King." Catullus immediately responded, "Hamlet," and won a sixteen-slot netherweave bag. Hamlet's play within a play mirrors the murder from the real world, triggering a reaction from Claudius that lets Hamlet know that Claudius was indeed his father's murderer, even as Claudius realizes that Hamlet knows.

Among the most common examples of second-order role-playing in WoW are disguise quests. Two series in Blade's Edge Mountains illustrate the range. Both Maxrohn and Catullus did these quests, and they do not involve a member of one faction pretending to be a member of the other. Rather, in one the questor must obtain materials by killing scouts of the Blackwing Coven, then enter its cavern disguised as a particular NPC, Overseer Nuaar. While wearing the disguise, the character may walk past other coven members without causing any reaction. The other quest series is directed against a different group of NPC enemies, the Burning Legion, and one of them is called Deceive Thy Enemy. In this case, the character does not take on a particular false identity, but merely dons a gas mask. This does not deceive the various low-level enemies in the camp, but only a distant Legion communicator with whom the character converses by means of a holographic teleconference device.

A series of quests in one of the higher Outland zones, Shadowmoon Valley, required Catullus to obtain the three lost fragments of the Cipher of Damnation, the magic words spoken by Archmage Gul'dan to sever the connection between the Orcs and their original home. The location of the third fragment was unknown, so Catullus was forced to rely on a ruse. Disguising himself as a messenger of the Eclipsion Blood Elves, he authoritatively ordered Grand Commander Ruusk to transport the cipher along a particular route, so he could intercept the shipment. Note that Catullus really was a Blood Elf, so he did not need to change his race as others doing the quest would generally need to do. But he disguised his character and his purpose. If he had asked Ruusk where the cipher was hidden, his real purpose would have been revealed immediately, and he would have been killed on the spot. But by pretending merely to deliver an order to move the cipher, he concealed his real motive, learning the location not by asking for it but by prescribing it.

Disguise quests abound in Northrend. A comic quest in the Borean Tundra has one dress up in a foolish murloc suit. Especially notable is a double series of quests around Voltarus in the Zul'Drak zone that require the character to be disguised as a ghoul of the Scourge and to do a number of quests for the Scourge overlord Drakuru in order to gain a position with him from which to carry out quests of sabotage and espionage against him. Another series of quests centers on the town of Valkyrion in the Storm Peaks zone—named for the female Valkyries of Norse and Wagnerian legend who rescue the spirits of dead warriors from the battlefield—requiring disguise as a Norse woman. After completing a few of these quests in disguise, the character can return at any time to use that town's facilities in the alternate female identity, even if the character is usually male.

## Two Weddings, Multiple Identities

On April 12, 2008, rumors buzzed through the chat channel of the Alea Iacta Est guild that there was going to be a wedding in the Zangarmarsh zone of Outland, in a swamp dominated by giant mushrooms. The bride was to be Letholas, a level-64 Undead rogue, and the groom, Cairubel, a level-58 Tauren druid. According to the observation of Catullus, and confirmed by the Armory online database, both characters were male. Fellow AIE members, however, referred to Letholas with female pronouns, and I do not know what the biological genders of the players are IRL (in real life). Presiding over the ceremony would be a Blood Elf mage named Mandlexan.

As people were just beginning to assemble, a guild member asked, perhaps naively, "Is this a real wedding?"

The bride responded shyly, "No . . . I wish!"

The groom blushed, smiled, and agreed, "Me too."

The presiding mage admitted, "No it's not legally binding. Sorry guys."

Indeed, the seriousness of this wedding was rather ambiguous. There was an element of parody to the affair, and yet it was more than a joke. When the wedding was originally announced in the AIE online forum in early February, there was a contest to see who could write the best script for it. As Cairubel put it, "The person who writes the vows we like the best will be our minister." He also revealed something about the human beings behind the characters: "Please keep in mind that we both enjoy lyrics and poetry."

Another member posted a critical comment, saying, "Seems wrong to have other people write your vows. For my real wedding we wrote our own vows. Seems like something only you can put to paper." This comment expresses one view of personal identity and what it means to be genuine.

Cairubel took a different perspective, arguing in the forum, "Well, to me the best person to perform the ceremony for me, would be the person who knows me the best so much so that they are able to write my vows and do a darn good job doing it. The people who know me enough to know my thoughts and put them on paper are the people who care enough to know those things about me, and a true test of friendship. Anybody can say that they are my friend, but only the real ones pay attention to me."

The exchange in the forum became rather angry, and Cairubel revealed more: "Honestly, this in game wedding is to show our (RL) love for each other, as we are a couple IRL. To me, some of my most important friends are in game, and some of them I've been playing games with for 6 or 7 years. This isn't about two tweens in their parents basement giggling over 'in game relationships.'" Before long, the critic of the wedding had left the guild.

On the appointed day, AIE guildies struggled to find their way to the site against a host of technical problems, including a server crash. Thirty-eight characters assembled, the three principals standing on a tall rock surmounted by mushrooms, and the congregation standing up to their knees in the swamp water (see figure 7.3). The bride wore a pinkish dress, and the groom insisted on wearing his AIE tabard over a somewhat overstuffed tuxedo. Mandlexan proclaimed, "Greetings my brothers and sisters, this is a joyous day. One of the few things we Sin'Dorei revel almost as much as the Arcane ability, is the union between two souls, forever intertwined, a destiny of ethereal bliss. Welcome, and we shall now proceed."

Under the broad bells of the gigantic mushrooms, he began,

Dearly beloved, we are gathered here today in the sight of the Goddess Elune to join this Tauren, and this Undead in Unholy matrimony. Not to be entered into lightly, unholy matrimony should

**Figure 7.3**
The wedding of Letholas and Cairubel in the Zangarmarsh mushroom swamp of Outland.

be entered into solemnly and with reverence and full buffs. Into this Unholy agreement these two mischief makers come together to be joined. If any person here can show just cause, why these two should not be joined in Unholy matrimony, speak now or /IgNoRe. We are all here today to witness the matrimonial Bind-On-Pickup of Cairubel and Letholas. This joyous day celebrates the commitment and love with which Cairubel and Letholas start their Epic-Quest-Chain together. Through the Goddess Elune, you are joined together in the most holy of bonds.

The climax of the ceremony began. Mandlexan asked the groom, "Do you, Cairubel take Letholas to be your lawfully wedded wife and live together forever in the Inn of Unholy Matrimony? To love, honor, and keep her, in rez-sickness and in full bars of health, for richer or poorer (mostly poorer), for better or for worse for as long as ye both shall remain un-deleted?"

Enthusiastically, Cairubel exclaimed, "I do!"

Mandlexan turned to the bride: "And do you, Letholas, take Cairubel to be your lawfully wedded husband, to live together forever in the Inn of Unholy Matrimony?"

Letholas likewise exclaimed, "I do!"

At this point, a bedlam of weeping and cheering broke out among the audience. One latecomer exclaimed, "Oh, damn, I must have missed the wedding!" Mandlexan instructed the couple to say their vows.

Cairubel began: "Letholas, from the first time we met, I have known that we should be together. Through all we have been through, and all we shall be through, I want you by my side. I love you. Cairubel: With this epic ring, I thee wed."

While the bedlam of weeping and cheering increased, the groom said as an aside to the latecomer, "Yeah, sorry mate, we had to go on with it." Kezz cried on Rajaah's shoulder, Ionara wept with joy for the bride and groom, and an Undead warlock annoyed by the clamor admonished people to be quiet.

Letholas spoke next, "From the first instance I ran you through, to all the days we have grouped together, I have come to love you and know I will as long as my foul blood beats in my body, and until time immortal past that. With this epic ring I thee wed."

Mandlexan then enunciated the fateful words: "What the Goddess Elune has joined together let no Alliance spam sunder armor. With the power invested in me by The Sunwell, the Holy Light, The states of Orgrimmar and the Undercity, I now pronounce you Husband and Wife. You may kiss the bride."

Bedlam surged. Mandlexan addressed the throng, "I present to you the new Horde couple of Cairubel and Letholas . . . ALL HAIL! May you and yours kill Many Many Gnomes." Letholas and Cairubel blew kisses to each other, and members of the crowd began setting off fireworks. Kezz danced with Moobie, and others commented what a beautiful ceremony it had been. Letholas tossed her bouquet to one of the other ladies. And there was a cheer for the glorious guild and the glamorous couple. Things spiraled down from here, as grilled picnic treat and cake were passed around. Brewfest Brew soon turned more than a few of the revelers tipsy, while Moreyn and Avadakedavra got somewhat drunk, and soon Moreyn and Kezz were completely smashed.

On May 11, 2008, to conclude the three-day scientific conference on convergence of the real and the virtual, a mock wedding was held in the old fort at Booty Bay, yet with the solemn tone of a serious ritual. The bride was to be a level-30 Troll hunter named Gonzorina, and the groom, Optimoose, a level-49 Tauren shaman. As characters, the bride was clearly female, and the groom male. In this case, we know the genders of the actual players, which were male and female, but reversed from the genders of their characters. This might pose a conundrum for anyone who would complain about the Cairubel-Letholas marriage of two male characters. In that case, possibly only one of the parties was of the "wrong" gender. Here, in the marriage of a male playing a female with a female playing a male, both genders are wrong. At the very least, this situation gives the term *heterosexual* a new twist.

The mock wedding began when Catullus proclaimed,

We gather together in the Holy Light, on land blessed by the Earthmother, and in knowledge that beyond this world of illusion exist many mysterious levels of reality. We have gathered to celebrate the marriage of Gonzorina and Optimoose, the union of a duality that links not merely two individuals and two genders, but two races. Tauren are the original inhabitants of Mulgore, rare among races in still dwelling on the same land as their ancestors. Now, as members of the Horde, they possess powerful allies in preserving that heritage.

At this point, Optimoose blushed. Catullus continued,

Trolls are descendants of a great but fallen civilization. During the disintegration of the Gurubashi Empire, the Darkspear Tribe became refugees, but now they have found a home with us, in the Horde.

Having established the couple's ethnic identities, he then considered their cultural heritages:

Tauren know well that the universe is a fabric of many dualities, beginning with the four primary elements. In nature, forces oppose one another, but at the same time, one cannot exist without the other. Earth is the essential foundation, providing strength, stamina and patience. Fire is the principle of destruction and chaos, whereas Water means rebirth. Air represents spiritual freedom. Trolls know well that morality must rely upon the wisdom of the three cardinal virtues: Tenacity, Respect, and Compassion. All creatures and some objects have souls or spirits. Some, unfortunately are malign, greedy, hostile and dangerous, so at times we must rely upon spiritual healing to support our tenacity.

Preambles completed, Catullus finally got to the business at hand:

Now, Gonzorina and Optimoose have come together to heal each other, to respect each other, and to share compassion for each other. Let us show them our respect and compassion!

The congregation knelt, leaving only the wedding couple standing, as they made their pledges to each other.

The female Troll hunter spoke: "I have prepared a vow. First, I want to thank you all for coming. Now, let me gather myself . . ." She let out a hacking cough, and her husband-to-be smiled at her. Then Gonzorina recited a stanza of poetry she had prepared: "Optimoose, I pledge to be as true as a troll can be . . . To love you in every season, across land or sea . . . I pledge to stand by your side for every battle . . . And to kill anyone who says I married cattle!" She ended with a smile, many participants laughed, and Optimoose grinned wickedly at Gonzorina.

The Tauren proclaimed, "I pledge to protect, honor and defend you. I promise to fight at your side and heal your wounds. I understand the sacrifice you are making to live with me and my people."

Gonzorina then exclaimed, "Now kiss me you big stud!"

Catullus brought the ritual to an end: "Then let us raise a shout of joy for Gonzorina and Optimoose! LOK'TAR!" Wild dancing of a hundred characters in a small space, interspersed with blazing fireworks, unleashed an enjoyable form of chaos.

These two mock weddings, with their rather different relationships between character and player, illustrate the ambiguities of identity in WoW, and the fact that here as elsewhere relations between people are a prime determinant of self. The character of a person, like those avatars WoW calls characters, is a social construction. From the dramaturgical perspective, and perhaps in truth, everybody is always a fictional character.

### Epilogue: The Price of Individuality

I, Price, Undead warlock, am the reincarnation of Professor Henry Jarrod, Dr. Anton Phibes, the playwright Oscar Wilde, and the Hollywood actor Vincent Price (see figure 7.4). Of my past lives, I especially remember being the last man on Earth, Dr. Robert Morgan, whose

**Figure 7.4**
Price, an Undead warlock (named for the deceased horror movie actor Vincent Price), with his succubus, standing on either side of Sylvanas, the banshee queen of the Undead.

sorry task it was to kill Undead Scourge, day after day until he kills himself. But I get con-fused easily, because sometimes I think the legendary omega man was really named Robert Neville, or Charlton Heston, or Will Smith, or possibly even Richard Matheson. I suppose in some way I possess all these identities. At times, when I half-kill the half dead, I feel I am cannibalizing their souls, as if enough soulshards would bring me fully back to life. As it is, so be it. Scourge of the Scourge, I shuttled back and forth between the sewers of Undercity and the Scar burned south from the Sunwell, dispatching rotting corpses to their final rest. Deatholme, the Scourge citadel in southern Ghostlands, has air as thick as soup, or better said, like the contents of a bedpan. Beating my way past minions there, I slew Mirdoran the Fallen, Borgoth the Bloodletter, Jurion the Deceiver, and Masophet the Black. Thereby, I won the right to summon a bride from the beyond, a beautiful succubus named Heltai, with a sexy squeal and crack of whip. For her I developed a new goal, to slay Dar'Khan, ruler of the citadel, not to complete a Horde quest of purification, but so Heltai and I could rule as Duchess and Duke of Deathholme.

# 8   Transcendence

I, the Player, decided to conclude this saga in a chamber deep beneath the Stormrage Barrow Dens in Moonglade. There, I commanded Maxrohn and Catullus to fight a duel to the death. Thus would I determine which was better: Human or Elf, Alliance or Horde, old or young. The loser would die without hope of resurrection. The winner would go free.

A barrow, like those I have seen in England, is an ancient burial mound, often containing the tombs of many members of a single tribe. In the barrows of Moonglade, one may find sleeping Elven druids whose spirits are walking another plane of existence called the Emerald Dream. According to legend, Archdruid Malfurion Stormrage, hero of the battle for the Well of Eternity thousands of years ago, still wanders here, unable to find the route to reality. The Emerald Dream is a replica of World of Warcraft, but without any intelligent creatures to make war or serve as vehicles for players. It is beautiful, verdant, and peaceful, reminding us what we lose when we despoil nature. It is like the Garden of Eden, but without Adam, Eve, or a talking serpent. Elves, Humans, and the other races believe in a second transcendent plane of existence as well, the Twisting Nether. It contains many worlds, and many demons who both create and destroy them. Among them are the Titans who created Azeroth.

I have my own view of what these two planes of existence represent. The Emerald Dream is the computer hardware, the processing chips and other equipment that sustain Azeroth. The Twisting Nether is my own world, and the Titans are the people of Blizzard Entertainment who created World of Warcraft. From the standpoint of my twenty-two characters, I am a demon who, unbeknownst to them, has guided their lives and now demands the death of one of them.

I told Catullus and his spiritual love, Lunette, that if they did exactly as I commanded, I would make it possible for them to meet, marry, and build a life together. Lunette quickly recovered from her bout of madness, came down from the rigging of the Night Elf ship docked at Shalandis Isle, where she had been dancing half naked for months, and set about to do my work. I told her to quest upward from level 20 to 30, while gaining more experience with enchanting, because she was the only character possessing that skill. When the Lunar Festival for 2008 began, she visited twenty of the elders stationed around the world, including four standing dangerously deep inside Horde outposts. She believed that her piety would strengthen Catullus.

To prepare for a domestic life, she used the ancient coins given her by the elders to buy a black pants suit and three formal dresses, one pink, one purple, and one green. She sold all her armor and weapons, keeping only a set of work clothes and a magic wand she had made herself. Her one souvenir of questing was the statuette of a cat she had found in the ruins of Mathystra. By great good fortune, she discovered that a white wedding dress was for sale on the Alliance auction system, and she bought it for two gold coins. She dressed in it and went to the moonwell in the northern part of Moonglade to pray and await Catullus.

When Maxrohn arrived on the Earthen Ring realm, he quickly realized he had lost all his connections with other people, including not only family members like Alberich and Stephie but also fellow members of his beloved Winged Ascension guild, and even his respected old friends in the Shadow Clan. The only names he knew were Lunette and Catullus, because I had told them to him, so he wrote his last will and testament in the form of a letter to the Night Elf priestess: "Dear Lunette: I do not know you, but I imagine you are an honorable person. Having been taken from my own realm, there is no one to whom I can bequeath my few possessions. Therefore, I send them to you, in hopes you will return them if I survive, or make good use of them if I do not. Sincerely, Maxrohn." He placed forty gold coins, thirty-five levitation feathers, and an arcane book called *The Libram of Constitution* into a package and mailed it to her.

Just then, a low-level person in Stormwind named Multiply yelled, "The guild twinks are looking for members to sign its charter. Any twink any level, please come and sign. Thanks!"

Maxrohn deduced that a very young person was trying to create a guild of well-equipped, subsidized characters called *twinks*. Having lost his Winged Ascension guild affiliation when he was torn from the Shandris realm, he decided to help the fellow out. Multiply turned out to be a wizened old Gnome with a fluff of gray hair around a bald pate, and his partner, Lagato, was a red-bearded Dwarf. However mature they appeared, both behaved rather young and inexperienced. When he signed the charter, Maxrohn saw that the name of the guild, twinks, was not even capitalized. He told them, "I just transferred to this realm to duel my arch-enemy, and there is a good chance I will die without resurrection this week. In any case, good luck to you!"

Maxrohn then took stock of his situation, noticing that his armor was 3,037. Only then did it occur to him that he had never upgraded his priestly abilities when he reached level 70, so he walked to the Stormwind to see High Priestess Laurena. She wanted nearly eleven gold coins to increase his favorite lingering spell, Shadow Word: Pain, to its maximum strength. But having sent most of his money to Lunette, he could not afford it. Stupidity can be fatal, he thought, but then realized his problem was not stupidity but resignation. He told the twinks, "This priest is near the end of his life. In a few days, he will face another level 70 priest, and only one will survive." The twinks were discussing the creation of a tabard, the guild-specific garment that carries an emblem of its fundamental concept. "I belonged to Winged Ascension on the Shandris realm, which had a flying dragon on it. Today, I moved to this realm, so my tabard is blank."

The lunar festival had begun, and a shaft of light stood like a triumphal pillar in the Stormwind trade district. Maxrohn stood in it for a moment, letting the light bathe him, meditating, and purifying his thoughts. He remembered the lunar festival from the year before, when he had visited Moonglade. It had been a joyous place, but now it signified doom. Such is life. If death is part of life, then life is death and deserves to be feared. Maxrohn emptied his quest log. No more seeking for him, no more goals, and no more stories.

A couple of people who had signed the twinks charter merely to help Multiply start it left, and he asked Maxrohn, "Do you want to leave too?"

Maxrohn replied, "No need, I'll be dead by the weekend." Ignoring the import of what Maxrohn had said, Multiply selfishly begged him to run him through the Deadmines instance for low-level gear and experience. "No, I did not finish all quests in the world, just the hundreds I needed to do."

He could have used the Lunar Festival teleport to get to Moonglade, but his mood was hardly festive. He flew to Menethil in the far north and took a ship for Auberdine on the other continent. There he paid seven silvers and forty-seven coppers for a flight to Moonglade, possibly his last economic exchange.

Catullus responded very differently to the challenge I set him. The first thing he did, after realizing the remarkable position I had placed him in, was to reread his favorite story. Yes, scholars habitually read, and Catullus was a scholar. But for him, reading was not merely a passive pastime but an active quest for inspiration. Thus, while others might have rushed around in a frenzy, sharpening their swords, Catullus did something far more effective. He sat down to read "Of Blood and Honor" by Chris Metzen, the man primarily responsible for the lore and storyline in World of Warcraft.[1]

This is the story of the terrible dilemma that faced Tirion Fordring, paladin of the Order of the Silver Hand and governor of Mardenholde, one day a dozen years after the Alliance defeated the Orcish Horde in the Second War (see figure 8.1). Alone, without his guards, he was exploring the hill country when he discovered tracks left by an Orc in the vicinity of an abandoned tower. Most of their race had been captives for years in Alliance concentration camps, and evidence that at least one of these monsters still roamed free was an ominous sign. Tirion drew his sword as he saw an elderly but fierce-looking Orc step out from the trees and unsling his axe. They traded blows for a few moments, then the old Orc slipped and fell. Rather than take advantage of this accident, Tirion chivalrously motioned for the Orc to rise before resuming their battle. Thinking that Orcs could not understand honor, he was astonished when the Orc saluted him. Again they fought, until the collapse of a wall rendered Tirion unconscious.

**Figure 8.1**
Tirion Fordring, in his happier days before disgrace and war, in the Southshore inn, as seen in the Caverns of Time.

When he awoke, four days later back in Mardenholde, he was surprised to discover that he still lived. His wife, Karandra, explained that he had been found tied to his horse, wounded but safe. Tirion realized that the Orc must have spared his life, and he quietly swore to himself not to betray this trust. This is the dilemma of blood and honor. Blood means the family ties that bind a person to his or her group. An ethic based on blood ties sets no limits on what may be done against members of other groups, so long as one's own group benefits. In this case, by keeping silent about the old Orc in the hills, Tirion hoped he was not endangering his family, but it was possible that he was. Honor refers to an objective code of ethics, based in obligations incurred through respect and principles of fairness to individuals. Honor demanded that he spare the Orc's life, just as the Orc had spared his. For a second time, Tirion rode into the hills. He and the Orc talked, rather than fighting, and he learned his elderly enemy's name was Eitrigg. They agreed, honorably, to leave each other in peace.

Back in Mardenholde, Tirion refused to tell Karandra anything about what happened on his two lonely rides into the hills. She revealed her hatred of the Orcs, and the fear that some of them may still be at large. Their son, Taelan, wondered if some Orcs might not be so cruel as Human prejudice imagined them to be. In his son, Tirion saw the possibility of hope for the future:

"I think so," Tirion replied. "Sometimes we need to be careful of how quickly we judge people, son."

The boy seemed pleased with the answer. Karandra was not. Despite everything else, she would be damned if she let Tirion fill the boy's head with such nonsense.

"Don't tell him that!" she hissed. "Orcs are mindless beasts who should all be hunted down and killed!"[2]

Who was right? Political opponents discovered Tirion's secret, forced him into exile, and cast his family into disgrace. The story ends when Tirion's son, Taelan Fordring, earns knighthood in the Order of the Silver Hand because of his own valor, not by family inheritance. Catullus actually met Eitrigg years later because the white-haired old Orc had become one of Thrall's trusted advisers. He also met Tirion, who was living alone in a ramshackle cabin in the Eastern Plaguelands, bitter and resigned to his fate. Tirion made Catullus do a series of trivial quests, killing plaguebats, plaguehounds, and carrion worms. Catullus assumed these quests were feeble attempts to cleanse the area of the biowarfare disaster from the Third War.

We cannot know whether Tirion might have been able to prevent the release of the plague in the Third War, but it seems unlikely that one more paladin would have made a difference. Although I have no proof, I imagine that Karandra died from the disease, because her son, Taelan, joined the radical Scarlet Crusade sect that set extermination of all the Undead as its holy mission. She had told him years before that his father had died, and she had actually taken the boy to a false grave where he had innocently buried the toy warhammer his father had given him. Now, he was an officer in the dangerous conspiracy that ranged across the Plaguelands and surrounded Undercity.

After Catullus had completed seemingly meaningless tasks for Tirion, the exiled knight asked him to undertake a powerful series of quests called Redemption. First, Catullus went in search of Taelan's toy warhammer, then retrieved the banner Taelon had cast down when he abandoned the Order of the Silver Hand. The third stage of the quest series required speaking with an artist who had painted a picture of the happy family before the tragedies had begun, but she was only a departed spirit in a ruined village. The next stage was too difficult for Catullus at first, but he returned to it when he reached level 68, entering the Scourge-infested city Stratholme to find the painting, titled *Of Love and Family*, a clear parallel to "Of Blood and Honor."

Then, Tirion asked Catullus to deliver gifts to his son. From a witch named Myranda, who had defended Tirion before his exile, Catullus obtained a disguise that allowed him to enter the Scarlet Crusade stronghold at Hearthglen. Upon viewing the gift from his father, Taelan exclaimed, "I have dreams, stranger. In these dreams my father is with me. He stands proudly at my side as I am inducted into the Order. We battle legion of Scourge, side by side. We bring honor to the Alliance, to Lordaeron. I want not to dream anymore." Seized by a frenzy of rage, Taelan battled his way out of Hearthglen, killing one after another of the minions of the Scarlet Crusade.

Despite all his effort, Catullus could not prevent Taelan's death at the hands of the final band of guards, just at the moment his father reunited with him. Tirion did not react with grief or shame but with resolution. He resolved then and there to revive the Order of the Silver Hand. His parting words to Catullus united both the past and the future: "May we meet again, in better times, and reminisce of days long past . . . battles hard fought . . . dreams redeemed." Whether they would meet again depended on the fate of Catullus, because Tirion went on to become a leader of the invasion of Northrend, and the giver of many more quests.

Now, on the threshold of his own battle of love and family, of blood and honor, Catullus resolved to meet his fate with tenacity, compassion, and respect. Hatred is said to be a great motivator, and fear is another. However, reading this story again, Catullus sought within himself the energy to fight his final battle, without hating Maxrohn or being fearful of him.

## A Game of Games

Of course, some people will say that none of this is real. It is only a game! As we noted in chapter 1, many social scientists have analyzed the "real world" in terms of games, and this metaphor seems most apt in the realms of economics and politics, where competition between winners and losers is most explicit. Shakespeare wrote, "All the world's a stage," but he could just as well have written, "All the world's a playing field." Yet World of Warcraft is not the same environment most people live in every day. It provides some degree of transcendence from the cares and concerns of everyday life, at the same time it is dependent upon the surrounding economy. Here we will consider a variety of ways in which WoW relates to the society that created it, beginning with the implications of the fact that it began as a game but became a virtual world.

As a mere game, WoW has its own heritage and heroes. World of Warcraft is the crowning accomplishment of a decade of creation of multiplayer online games, but it was built on an ancient basis. Setting aside physical sports that are often called games, we must say that the culturally most significant traditional game is chess. As the preeminent strategy game, chess is the direct but remote ancestor of Warcraft I: Orcs and Humans. Two armies composed of units with diverse abilities face each other across a battlefield. They struggle for position in the combat territory and to kill units on the opposing side, until one has triumphed over the other. Each army is commanded by a single player, and a player does not experience the battle from the vantage point of a lone avatar or character.

Jetan, the strategy game devised by Edgar Rice Burroughs for his Barsoom novels about a dying civilization on the planet Mars, is a variant of chess, what is often called *fairy chess*. In the appendix to his 1922 novel, *The Chessmen of Mars*, Burroughs explains:

The game is played with twenty black pieces by one player and twenty orange by his opponent, and is presumed to have originally represented a battle between the Black race of the south and the Yellow race of the north. On Mars the board is usually arranged so that the Black pieces are played from the south and the Orange from the north.[3]

Notice how Burroughs explicitly connects his game to the fantasy world in which it is played, both as a reflection of historic interracial conflict, and in terms of geographic orientation. Warcraft: Orcs and Humans also involves combat between two different races, but the board, pieces, and moves are vastly more complex than in either chess or jetan.

World of Warcraft is a role-playing game, not a strategy game. However, as we see in chapter 2, it is built upon the earlier trilogy of Warcraft strategy games. Its role-playing heritage has two branches, the tabletop game *Dungeons and Dragons* (D&D), and the online games known as multiuser dungeons (MUDs). On March 5, 2008, immediately after the death of D&D creator Gary Gygax, WoW posted this memorial at the head of its website:

Many of us here at Blizzard got our start in gaming with Dungeons & Dragons or one of its computer adaptations and have fond memories of rolling dice, pouring over rulebooks, braving dark caverns and castle keeps, battling kobolds and hill giants. Gary Gygax's work on D&D was an inspiration to us and in many ways helped spark our passion for creating games of our own.[4]

The reference to kobolds suggests just one of many close linkages. In Germanic traditions, kobolds are house spirits or miners—after whom the chemical element cobalt is named—but in D&D they are ratlike miners, just as in WoW. Gygax himself was heavily influenced by varieties of fantasy closely related to science fiction, including authors like Edgar Rice Burroughs, L. Sprague de Camp, Fletcher Pratt, Fritz Leiber, Jack Vance, and indeed J. R. R. Tolkien.[5] Although played on a tabletop, with cards and polyhedral dice, the structure of D&D is very similar to WoW. Players "roll" avatarlike characters they then role-play, engaging in RPG-style individual combat and collecting information, treasures, and experience. Although dice are not rolled when a WoW player creates a character, the term used for creating a character in World of Warcraft is exactly *roll*.

D&D was first published in 1974, and four years later the first online MUD was created by Roy Trubshaw and Richard Bartle, at least partly inspired by D&D and by Tolkien.[6] This was a text-based game, so players imagined their avatars rather than seeing them on the computer screen. By 1998, much of the cultural and technical basis for a graphic MMORPG version had been developed, as documented by Bruce Damer's book *Avatars! Exploring and Building Virtual Worlds on the Internet*.[7] This wide-ranging publication included a CD-ROM that let users experience the potential of avatars and virtual worlds, and it was comparable to a textbook introducing the field. Among other early efforts introduced on the CD was the virtual world system Active Worlds, which still exists a decade later.[8] A brief section of the book referred to two Internet-based action-adventure games, Ultima Online and Diablo, both of which are direct predecessors of WoW. Ultima Online is generally considered the first really successful example of the genre, and Diablo was created by Blizzard Entertainment, the same company that produces WoW.

Fantasy video games, like most novels, tend to be consumed by users, in the sense that they have a brief period of popularity, then are dropped from notice. Few players return repeatedly to experience them again and again after killing the final boss once. Chess, of course, does not follow this pattern at all. Once a person learns the rules of chess, he or she tends to play it periodically throughout life. It is possible that World of Warcraft is so complex, so culturally rich, and so expansive, that it will become a permanent part of our civilization. By early 2007, when I first entered Azeroth, observers of the online gaming community were already speculating about what game would replace WoW at the top of the charts, after it faded. But it did not fade throughout 2007 or 2008. Consider the board game *Monopoly*. It was issued more than seven decades ago during the Great Depression, and seemed tailored to the psychological needs of that difficult decade, but it has persisted through massive economic and cultural changes. To be sure, some competitor will someday garner more subscribers than WoW, but WoW may never die.

Technological change could conceivably render any computer game obsolete, but Internet-connected home computers are already a rather mature technology, so we cannot assume this will happen to WoW anytime soon. Full, comfortable, compelling 3-D virtual reality has not yet been achieved in the laboratory, let alone with sufficiently cheap equipment to be purchased for the home. The current generations of console games—Nintendo Wii, PlayStation 3, and Xbox 360—all support online gaming, but every middle-class household already has one or more computers, so it is unlikely that PC-based games will be killed off easily. Today, there is much talk about pervasive or ubiquitous networked computing, but we can safely assume that something like a desktop computer will remain a key element in domestic computing for the foreseeable future.

The one sociotechnical breakthrough that seems poised to happen, and that could take gaming to an entirely new level, is pervasive live-action gaming. In particular, researchers have been prototyping *pervasive LARPs*—pervasive live-action role-playing games. Such games would be played out both online and in the real world, so they would not really be virtual worlds. Computer scientists use the term *virtual reality* to refer to fully immersive substitutes for the normal world, and *augmented reality* to refer to mixtures of the real and the virtual. Thus, these might be *augmented world systems*, even if they were also MMORPGs. However, they may not involve full role-playing or anything like an avatar, and the playing field would be a real city or section of countryside, rather than a desktop computer.

I like to imagine my own city, Washington, DC, as the setting for a LARP that takes place in 1944, and is played between teams of tourists who come to Washington for a ten-day intense experience learning the history of World War II. A player would sign up as a member of either a team of Nazi spies and saboteurs, or a team of American OSS agents defending against them. The two sides would conduct a number of missions against each other, played out on the actual streets of the city, by use of portable computers or souped-up cell phones. For example, a Nazi spy player might be given the mission of picking up the plans for the atom bomb at one location, and delivering them to another, each location being an actual building that existed already in 1944. Of course, the plans would be entirely virtual, existing only electronically, and virtual assassinations and shoot-outs also could be part of the game.

Rumors exist in the WoW-player community that some kind of limited mobile game might be added in a future expansion of WoW.[9] Consider the range of possibilities. A simple cell phone–based game comparable to a very small instance, perhaps involving just pairs of dueling players, could earn virtual gold that could be spent by the player's character in WoW itself. That could be added today, but full LARP activity might take a decade of concerted effort to develop. At huge investment, a real-world theme park could be created, simulating part of the world of WoW, where players cast spells on their enemies using wearable computers. In WoW itself, one relatively underdeveloped area is the Human city Theramore, which in the mythology is a major center of government, but actually has few interesting quests and few players at any given time. I can imagine a real Theramore replacing the virtual one, set in an appropriate area of swampy territory representing the surrounding Dustwallow Marsh. However, it is not clear where the investment capital for any major online LARP would come from at the present time, doubtful whether the tourism market is ready for one, and unclear how much technical research and development is needed before a new industry of this kind could be launched successfully. Then there is the issue of legal liability if the Washington police arrest one of the "Nazi spies," or somebody actually drowns in Dustwallow Marsh!

In his second book, Edward Castronova argued that gamelike virtual worlds could influence the surrounding socioeconomics in powerful ways, starting even today.[10] As millions of people experience games like WoW, they will come to expect the economy in the outside world to function in a manner similar to WoW's. Notably, WoW characters all start life with equal resources, not having special advantages if their parents happen to be wealthy or well educated. Also, there are no unemployed people in WoW, and all players can reach the top levels if they work hard enough. Players may come to expect equality of opportunity, full employment, and even equality of outcome in the real world. This could tip the current political balance in favor of greater state intervention in the economy.

As an economist, Castronova naturally thinks of economy-related changes that virtual worlds might stimulate. Yet it is also possible that virtual worlds will have impacts on governance and foreign policy. In his first book, he did express some skepticism that MMORPGs could be model utopias for remaking the political systems of nations: "The typical governance model in synthetic worlds consists of isolated moments of oppressive tyranny embedded in widespread anarchy. Basically, the state of nature is never allowed to occur. There is a tyrant in place from the beginning, but an extraordinarily inactive one."[11] However, as we have seen, WoW offers a multiplex model of relations between nations, tribes, and races—harsh in many respects but also allegorically critical of real-world defense politics.

Consider dispassionately—as difficult as this may be—the Iraq War, also called Gulf War II and the Second Persian Gulf War, which began with the American-led invasion of the country in 2003. Over the more than six years of this conflict to date, justifications for it, critiques against it, and the actual facts on the ground have constantly changed. Any well-meaning person has every right to be confused about key factual questions as well as the fundamental morality of the invasion itself or the more recent strategies for dealing with the resulting situation. In this discussion, I cite no sources, precisely because I want us to think about principles that might relate to WoW and the long-term future strategies of nations, and I do not intend to claim I have a correct analysis of the Iraq War itself.

One theory is that the war was a defensive action, responding to the attacks of September 11, 2001. Much of the criticism has focused on the early debate of whether Iraq was directly involved in the September 11 attacks, which would have justified the war morally in most people's minds. Consider this the first of three hierarchically arranged self-defense arguments for the war. An aggressor deserves to be retaliated against in punishment for crimes, as well as destroyed in order to prevent further aggression.

The second level of defense justification is the claim that Iraq was preparing weapons of mass destruction, and had used such weapons before, so it must be anticipated that Iraq will use the weapons in the near future. Setting aside the factual basis of this justification for the war, it asserts that lethal action can be morally appropriate to prevent a potential enemy from attacking us or our interests, so long as the danger is determined to be rather probable.

The third level of defense justification is more abstract, and almost sociological in its conceptualization of world politics. An aggressive war is justifiable if it is based on a solid analysis that the long-term consequences are likely to be less rather than more death and destruction. In this view, the Middle East is one of the world's few regions that directly or indirectly endanger world peace and the stability of the global economic order. Decades of effort have failed to solve the region's problems, and given the danger of local wars escalating at any time into wider conflicts, waiting more decades is more dangerous than taking decisive action. Iraq may not have been responsible for the attacks of September 11, 2001, and Iraq might in the future use weapons of mass destruction only in the way other nations do, as a factor in national prestige and deterrence of attacks from its enemies, rather than as a tool of aggression. The point is that this justification requires analysis on a much higher level than individual nations and their leaders, looking for opportunities to turn history in a positive direction even if a few thousand innocent individuals will die in the process.

At this point in the discussion, critics of the war may find themselves exclaiming, "But this line of analysis would justify what Hitler did! By the middle of the twentieth century, civilization had decided that preemptive military attacks were immoral, equivalent to mass murder!" However, much of the justification for World War II on the side of the Axis was access to natural resources, with national defense only a background justification, because Germany, Italy, and Japan needed resources in order to be strong. Critics of the Iraq War mutter that oil must somehow have been involved in the invasion, because both President George W. Bush and Vice President Dick Cheney came from the oil industry, whereas supporters of the war often refer somewhat vaguely to American interests that are at stake. Perhaps wars really are extreme examples of gamelike competition for resources, as in WoW.

In a lecture I gave in 2008 at Yale University, I compared the resource competitions in World of Warcraft with those of World War II, commenting that the postwar economic success of Germany, Japan, and even Italy suggested those nations were wrong to think they needed to conquer resource-rich territories in order to survive. A member of the audience immediately contradicted me, saying it was not nations that were competing for natural resources, but entire economic systems, and World War II really was a conflict over resources. So, I agree it is hard to be sure about either World War II or Iraq War II, but it would be nice if civilization could figure this out before the Roman numerals reach III or IV.

Compare the morality of the wars between the Horde and Alliance in WoW. In the First War, the Orcs were surreptitiously seized by malevolent forces that sent them rushing into Azeroth to seize the wealthy territory of the Humans. This was aggressive war, but the general population of the Orcs had not made an informed, ethically considered decision to do this. Conspiracies among their leaders had sent them on the warpath. Later, the Orcs came into resource conflict with the Night Elves, over the wood in the forests the Night Elves held sacred, and they formed a marriage of convenience with the Tauren in their conflict against the Centaurs, who were seizing

Tauren territory. But today in WoW, when I think about the leaderships of the ten races, it is not a Human leader who appears especially ethical, but Thrall, the chief of the Orcs. Until the return of his father in late 2008, the king in Stormwind was a mere child, and the Human power elite was hopelessly corrupt.

To quote the language translation example from chapter 5 on cooperation: "The Horde is a mass of contradictions, and the Alliance is a marriage of convenience." WoW's view of its world, and by implication of our own, is that self-interest will establish alliances between groups that have little in common. All-out war between factions would be so destructive that great effort must be expended to avoid it. However, too many people and groups are competing for scarce and declining natural resources, so local conflict is absolutely essential for the survival of one's own group. It is morally appropriate to kill people merely to obtain their natural resources, so long as three conditions are observed: (1) the conflict does not escalate to catastrophic scale, (2) the people you kill are not members of your own group, and (3) you kill them with full respect, acknowledging that they do not deserve to die.

Is morality a social contract among members of a bound society? If so, is it possible for that society to encompass the entire world? Or is morality a property of a relatively small "nation" or "ethnicity" or "religion" in competition with others to which it cannot extend its moral principles? Sociologists call this latter ethical perspective *amoral familialism*, loyalty to the welfare of one's own extended family or clan, and pure expediency in dealings with others.[12] The great world religions, and academic philosophers of ethics, have sought to transcend amoral familialism and establish a universal morality, and this is fundamentally what Tirion Fordring struggled with in Chris Metzen's story "Of Blood and Honor." Thoughtful players of WoW, especially those with Human or Blood Elf characters who see the corruption of their own race's leadership, might ask themselves a profound question about human life: "Are there really any rules to this game?"

## Virtual Passions

WoW has implications for not only the public sphere of life, represented by politics and the economy, but also the intimate sphere. Often players discuss their personal lives, and here is an unedited example from March 24, 2007, in a conversation among members of a guild, using pseudonyms to protect anonymity:

[Alpha]:   ahhhh, i just got roses delivered to my door . . .
[Able]:   awww :) how nice
[Baker]:   WhoA!
[Alpha]:   take note guys, my hubby in iraq and i still get flowers
[Able]:   wow, he's a keeper :)
[Charlie]:   man making us look bad :(

[Dog]:  lol
[Alpha]:  that's why we have been married 6 years today
[Able]:  sweet . . . how's he doing over there?
[Alpha]:  i got flowers and pearls, he got a coffee grinder and an office chair, lol
[Baker]:  Aww
[Alpha]:  he is good
[Able]:  lol
[Able]:  well, we see who the romantic one is
[Alpha]:  don't blame he, that is what he wanted, lol
[Alpha]:  don't blame me, that is
[Able]:  that makes sense, what would he do with flowers?
[Alpha]:  lol, true, being in the desert and all
[Able]:  lol, yeah
[Alpha]:  can't even plant them

This example testifies to the more exalted aspect of a marriage, but virtual worlds offer the potential for raw eroticism as well. World of Warcraft is a game for all ages, and players typically guess that the youngest ones are eleven. "Adult content" is thus out of place. However, male players may find female characters sexually alluring, and a certain amount of sexual banter takes place between players. I have no evidence that significant numbers of people find real-life erotic partners, but it is possible that they do so in a range of private places within this virtual world. In my 2,300 hours inside WoW, I recall seeing only two clear examples of erotic behavior between players. By accident, my character embarrassed a man and woman in an upstairs room at an inn, by entering when they were apparently about to begin a passionate moment. Another time, a character came upon a couple embracing amid the trees behind the Goldshire Inn. In both cases, the couples were Human.

None of the thousands of quests I have undertaken was primarily sexual, but a number had a certain tinge to them, notably those that involved killing female NPCs. Very early in his career, Maxrohn found himself pitted against Defias bandits, many of whom appeared to be young women. Although dressed from head to toe, and even wearing bandannas over their faces, these NPCs were clearly female, and they emitted feminine cries when they were wounded or killed. The most extreme examples he encountered were vampirelike female NPCs in Outland, who wore scanty black leather straps and carried whips, following the sadomasochistic fashion. The third minion any warlock can obtain is a succubus, who looks exactly like these Outland NPCs. In the European Middle Ages, a succubus was a legendary demon who came to monks in their sleep and seduced them into unwilling sexual intercourse. When otherwise inactive, a succubus may admire her fingernails or emit a sound like a spank and the exclamation, "Oooh!" In action, she says things that can be interpreted in erotic terms: "Couldn't resist, could you?" "Hmmm, you're in trouble now." "Don't touch what you can't afford." "Being bad never felt so good." "Let's get this party started." "As the master wishes." "Next time I'll be the master." "Don't do anything I wouldn't do." "Try not to miss me too much." "I hope it was good for you."

Lunette's first experience with erotic female NPCs was when she had to kill a number of winged harpies, whose clothing consists of bikinis and whose flying bounces them up and down in a provocative manner. Indeed, Lunette noticed that, like other Night Elf females, she herself had a habit of occasionally bouncing on her toes, which had the effect of waving her ample breasts at anybody in the neighborhood. She found that no amount of self-control could break this habit, as though it were programmed into her.

At level 7, while he was still in the Blood Elf newbie zone, Catullus overheard a raucous argument about what we can delicately call courtship. In the general chat, a brash fellow calling himself Themystic exclaimed, "Hey cutie!"

A maiden named Iwingedangel responded, "Who's cutie?"

"You," he replied.

At this point, Kantharina interrupted, "Stop hitting on her. Where are you two?"

Themystic laughed, and Endlessmike supported him, telling Kantharina, "You're just jealous."

Themystic apologized, saying he had not intended to flirt with Iwingedangel on the general channel, but to whisper to her.

Kantharina asserted, "Please! If I wanted a guy, I could get one."

"Riiight," Themystic said sarcastically.

"No you couldn't," Iwingedangel told Kantharina. "You're probably a fat one who's stuffing her face with smarties."

Laughing uncontrollably, Themystic corrected, "No, twinkies!"

"Whatever," responded Kantharina dismissively.

Endlessmike laughed. "I'm happy guyless, because I'm a dude! I pity the fool."

Scarletlight joined the conversation, complaining, "What sickens me is people who have cyber sex on WoW. There's kids that play this perversion."

"That's gay," asserted Endlessmike.

Iwingedangel wryly inquired, "Like your father when him and your mother split up?"

The conversation then drifted to drug use, and it is worth noting that conversations on either topic are actually quite rare on public chat channels, and I saw only a modest amount on the more private guild channels. However, any two players may whisper to each other, and a group of as many as five can create a party, ostensibly to go questing but actually to chat privately. Scarletlight suggested, "Ok, if you all want to talk about sex and stuff, just go to a private channel or a raid chat group."

Dancing often has erotic connotations, and dances often play a role in courtship. One Saturday, Maxrohn came upon a group of about eight people dancing in the trade district of Stormwind, after having stripped off their outer clothing. This is a simple matter of putting each piece of armor into one's backpack, which leaves each male clothed in trunks, and each female clothed in panties and a bra that might be dignified with the name *bikini*.

On Sunday, a Night Elf woman named Diliailind yelled in Stormwind, "Whisper for invite to my dance party!" When Maxrohn whispered his interest to her, she said the party would be in Ironforge. They met at the Stormwind station of the Deeprun Tram, bowed to each other, then sat waiting for the subway train. She created a party, using the software routine for questing parties, whereupon Maxrohn exclaimed, "This gives new meaning to 'party'!" She suddenly disappeared, and he asked, "Are you okay, or is this a practical joke." Returning, she said she had gotten disconnected, but when they reached Ironforge, she lay down, fell asleep, awoke, then muttered she had to go, and disappeared again. Maxrohn commented to himself that his feeble attempt at flirting had not gone well, consoling himself with the fact that he is a priest.

Incognita once happened to walk through an area in the trade quarter of Undercity where people were dancing, and she experienced an irresistible urge to dance herself. Apparently somebody had a powerful macro program that made other characters dance.

When Etacarinae was sightseeing in Stormwind, Tisiphoneire yelled, "Come see the gnome and the woman dancing! Tips accepted, at SW bank." Naturally, she ran to the bank, where she discovered two male Gnomes dancing on tabletops, who were towered over by a Human woman named Tisiphoneire, who was a level-19 mage, dancing in her bra and panties. Seeing that the woman was indeed receiving tips from customers of the bank, and not to be outdone, Etacarinae stripped to her own underwear and began dancing on the same table. With her high Draenei hoofs, she now towered over the Human towering over the Gnomes, and their sinuous movements caused quite a spectacle. To her great satisfaction, Etacarinae received two tips, one of twenty-five silver coins, and the other consisting of one gold coin, worth four times as much. Checking the online database, I found that Tisiphoneire had reached level 33 a little over two months later, but it seemed she was not really such a hot number as she had seemed, because her talent specialization was 100 percent "frost," implying she had the ability to produce intense cold.

The truth is if people are looking for sexual experiences, WoW is not the right place for them. A better choice would be the nongame virtual world Second Life, which has an extensive red-light district and where players may actually buy script programs from other players that allow their characters to go through a wide range of sexual motions and positions. In this area, at least, WoW transcends the carnality of the real world by permitting friendly communications between players, but inhibiting more physical interactions. Even this requires a good deal of role-playing, as in the two weddings described in chapter 7. Near Lake Elrendar, Catullus found an example of the limits of erotic role-playing. He heard Ophirria ask someone to serve as priest for her virtual marriage with her real-world boyfriend. Then Cyntine reminisced, "My last game my character became obsessed with an NPC, brought him flowers and everything. He was lovely, but he ignored me."

## Technical Intrusions

In many ways the visual beauty of the WoW landscape transcends the real world in the way that art has always done, by representing ideas that exist only in the human mind. But this beauty has technological roots. One of the most impressive features of the display is the fact that the environment is rendered correctly in high detail when you fly over it. In many older games, rides on trains or aircraft are often depicted as inflexible movies, always the same. It is true that the flights in the original zones of World of Warcraft always follow a set course. However, high-level characters can buy flying mounts that allow them to zoom anywhere in Outland and Northrend, and the same technically could be true in many of the earlier zones if extra effort were invested to fill in the graphics for the places characters cannot walk, such as high in mountain ranges.

Maxrohn saw several examples in which something he saw while aloft correctly depicted changing conditions in the area. Once while flying across Eastern Plaguelands, he saw a speck in the sky ahead of him, clicked on it, and learned it was another character flying in the same direction. When he landed at his destination, he indeed found the character to be there. Another time, when his guild was massing to attack the Orc capital, Orgrimmar, several members flew almost in formation from Rut'theran Village across Kalimdor to Ratchet. Yet another time, flying across Winterspring, he looked down to see the temporary bonfire from the Fire Festival, looking just as it did when he visited it on foot.

Nothing disrupts the willing suspension of disbelief so much as technical problems that forcibly demonstrate the utter dependency of a virtual world upon the real one. For example, in two separate incidents, both Maxrohn and Vadvaro were completely paralyzed when thunderstorms suddenly knocked out power to my computer during action. A more common real-world disruption is an emergency shutdown of the server that sustains the virtual world. For example, on July 5, 2007, "urgent database maintenance" rendered a dozen realms unavailable, including two of ours, Hydraxis and Shandris. Starting August 14, several realms were down for forty-eight hours for "infrastructure optimizations," which sounds like a fancy way of saying new hardware. Similar problems arose for a few hours at the time of the Lich King expansion.

On August 7, 2007, Minotaurus was flying across the Barrens, in a terrible hurry to complete a quest that had a time limit, when he suddenly noticed the message "[SERVER] Restart in 14:00." This meant he had to go to a safe place and log out before his realm shut down, but he resolved to finish the quest despite the added time pressure. As he scrambled, the server counted down one minute every sixty seconds. When there were just nine minutes to go, a level-70 Tauren shaman in Thunder Bluff quipped over the server channel, "It's the end of the world as we know it . . . it's the end of the world as we know it . . . and I feel fine."

A level-70 Orc warlock in Shattrath City added, "Yipes! At least it's only 15 minutes at most." With five minutes to go, the countdown began updating every fifteen seconds. By this time Minotaurus had reached the inn at Crossroads and was selling looted junk to the innkeeper. With three minutes and fifteen seconds to go before the end of the world, he logged off.

User errors also can interrupt the sense of reality. Many Windows computers have a special key that exits the game to the desktop, sitting just to the left of the Alt key at the left end of the space bar. When in the midst of a battle, the Alt key is used to heal or shield one's character without losing focus on the enemy character. Thus it is an important key for emergency use at dangerous moments. Unfortunately, I would sometimes hit the exit key by mistake, losing control over my character while the game kept running and the enemy proceeded to kill him. I found it awkward to use the other Alt key to the right of the space bar, because that forced me to place the keyboard where I liked to keep a guidebook or notes I had made about my quests. Eventually, I developed the habit of extending my left little finger and catching the left edge of the keyboard, so my left index finger would be positioned properly over the Alt key. The fact that authors seldom have occasion to discuss the positions of their pinkies emphasizes what insignificant factors in the real world can be crucial for today's virtual worlds.

Errors in the game itself, often called *glitches*, can be disturbing as well. A major subset of glitches is *bugs*, errors in the programming itself. Other glitches may be caused by hardware problems or by data corruption when packets are traveling over the Internet. World of Warcraft is so complex that it would be quite impossible for Blizzard to offer it entirely error-free, and error fixes have been a constant part of the Tuesday-morning updates.

Stephie ran into two programming bugs one day in late December 2007. In southeastern Darkshore, she found a quest giver named Aynasha, who asked her to guard her while she healed herself from a recent poisoning attack. As soon as Stephie agreed, Aynasha warned that something was approaching. What was supposed to happen was that Furbolgs would attack, and Stephie would need to hold them at bay while Aynasha healed. However, nothing in fact happened. According to messages posted by players on Thottbot, in late 2005, three waves of Furbolgs would attack, but by mid-November 2007, this part of the program had ceased to work. Note that the people posting in the online databases are not limited to one server, and several similar reports were entered at Wowhead and Allakhazam, so this was probably a programming error rather than data corruption. This bug appeared about the time of the major software update version 2.3, and some users logically assumed that an intended change to the quest introduced the bug.

Update 2.3 was largely intended to help characters level up more rapidly between levels 20 and 60, presumably so experienced players could get their secondary alt characters more quickly up to the levels of major instances and battlefields. This was accomplished partly by requiring fewer experience points for each level in this range, partly by providing more tools for finding quest givers and other resources, and partly by changing some of the quests themselves.

The second bug Stephie encountered was a simple bookkeeping error that rendered one of the instructions to the player incorrect. This case started in Menethil on the west coast of the Eastern Kingdoms, when Red Jack Flint told Stephie to go across the ocean to Theramore to start her adventures in the western continent, Kalimdor, by speaking with Fiora Longears. Stephie took the boat to Theramore and found it to be a major Human town, almost a city, not so large as Stormwind, but constructed of the same light gray stone and boasting several major buildings. However, she could not find Fiora, because update 2.3 had moved her to Auberdine, a Night Elf town on the opposite, western coast of Kalimdor. Apparently a bookkeeping error prevented Red Jack Flint's instructions from being updated, which would have solved the problem completely, because from Menethil boats go to both Theramore and Auberdine.

Theramore plays a big role in WoW lore, and is ruled by Jaina Proudmoore, perhaps the most distinctive Alliance leader and the heroine of Keith DeCandido's novel *Cycle of Hatred*.[13] However, Theramore has not loomed large in the experience of players. For Stephie, it could not because the surrounding zone, Dustwallow Marsh, was designed for players at levels 35 to 45, whereas she was only 19. The game designers themselves must have felt that Dustwallow Marsh was poor in quests, because update 2.3 added a number of them to this zone. Prior to patch 2.3, however, characters level 25 and above would have received from Fiora a quest called Highperch Venom, to be done in yet another zone, Thousand Needles. I surmise that the WoW design team decided that getting low-level players quickly to the Night Elf end of the continent was more important than moving higher-level players to Thousand Needles, but one would have thought the solution was to leave Fiora where she was, and have Red Jack Flint give a quest to speak with somebody who was already in Auberdine. So this bug seems to be the result of a hasty attempt to make many small changes to speed up character leveling, which is a quality of a design flaw rather than just a failure to update one short string of text.

One category of glitch probably caused by data corruption rather than programming error concerns discrepancies in the location, orientation, and condition of an NPC. This happens only very rarely, perhaps less than 1 percent of the time, but given thousands of battles with NPCs, every player encounters many examples. On June 11,

2007, Catullus encountered three within the span of just a few minutes at Durnholde Keep, during which the connectivity meter stayed green, so the Internet connection was generally good. He killed a Syndicate Watchman, then tried to loot the corpse. Although he stood directly on top of the corpse, he got the message, "You are too far away to loot that corpse." Moving short distances in different directions seldom solves this problem when it arises, and it did not in this case. Less than a minute later, he attacked another Syndicate Watchman from a distance using a spell. Rather than rushing toward him, the NPC faced sideways, beating the air with her weapon. Despite the fact that she was facing the wrong way, and at far too great a distance, her blows connected with him, one of them drawing blood. His attack spells failed to diminish her health bar, although after a while she fell dead without warning.

Seven minutes later, in a different part of Durnholde Keep, he attacked a third Syndicate Watchman while he was standing high above her on a wall. I believe that this relationship—being within striking distance but high above the NPC—may occasionally trigger a glitch, but these glitches are so difficult to reproduce intentionally that I have not carried out systematic experiments to test this hypothesis. When Catullus hit her with his first spell, she stood unresponsive, and "Evade" appeared over her head. NPCs have some chance of resisting or evading any one hit, especially if they are a much higher level than the character attacking them. However, she was level 21 while Catullus was level 22, and she evaded spell after spell consistently. Catullus broke off the attack, moved, restored his mana, then tried again. This time his spell hit home, and she rushed to the top of the wall to engage him. However, she stopped a medium distance away from him, inside a large block of stone, with only her head showing, while their battle proceeded normally in other respects. When she neared death, the usual message appeared on the screen: "Syndicate Watchman attempts to run away in fear," but she did not run.

This set of examples suggests why I think data corruption is primarily responsible for these glitches, especially because somewhat different variables seem to have been corrupted in different cases. I speculate this could be from dropped packets over the Internet, even when the connection seemed good. The most visible feature is a discrepancy between the location of the NPCs in the game's display model (what one sees on the screen) from the world model (implied by physical interactions within the game). In a significant fraction of these rare glitches, the NPC's health bar does not update, but the health is being damaged, although in a very few cases that did not seem to happen either, leading to my character's death.

A very different technical situation that relates to WoW's realism is the fact that players run multiple characters, even two or more at once if they are willing to invest in multiple computers and accounts. My chief aim in having two accounts was to be able to explore methodically the systems of communication and economic interaction between characters. I experienced my own technical limits when I tried with only partial success to run two characters simultaneously on two computers set side by side.

Alberich, the Dwarf hunter, and Stephie, the Gnome warlock, undertook several very low level quests together in Dun Morogh, the snowy zone where their careers both began. He would run toward a beast and halt just outside its aggro range. Using Alberich's computer, I would right-click on the beast, preparing him to hack at it with his axe, but since it was outside his striking radius, he would take a battle stance and just wait. Stephie would stand just behind him. Using her computer, I would left-click on the beast, then click on her attack spell and blast it. The beast would run toward the couple, and as soon as it came near Alberich, he would automatically clobber it, as she cast more killing spells.

I found it extremely difficult to use two characters simultaneously when I was not entirely in control of how the events would play out. Adapting to problems in real time was almost impossible. Thus I was quite impressed when I discovered that some players could do it far better than I. As Sciencemag and her compatriots were organizing the May 2008 scientific conference in WoW, a player joined their guild to demonstrate his technique at *multiboxing*, the formal term for running multiple characters simultaneously on multiple boxes (computers) and accounts. Just outside the Orgrimmar bank, he had four of his characters dancing together, three Undead mages—Ealphaba, Teriely, and Bevicenth—and Vertheamp, the Undead priest.

**Convergence of the Real and the Virtual**

In his report to *Science*, the respected journal and Web publication belonging to the American Association for the Advancement of Science, John Bohannon wrote: "The first scientific conference held in Azeroth, the online universe of the role-playing game World of Warcraft, went off virtually without a hitch. Although the participants all died during the final day's social event—a massive raid on an enemy fort—they agree that this event is a glimpse at the future of scientific exchange."[14] At Bohannon's encouragement I had organized this conference to explore the potential of virtual worlds as meeting places for scientists as well as laboratories for doing scientific research. Naturally, there had been many meetings already in nongame virtual worlds such as Second Life, but I thought there was no reason we could not do one in WoW, and that it could trigger fresh thinking about twenty-first-century scientific collaboration. The organization mechanism we used was establishing a guild named Science, using the guild chat for conference communications, and employing the "/chatlog" command to save a transcript. Its guild tabard showed a red infinity symbol against an orange background with yellow trim (see figure 8.2).

Starting half an hour before the first session, people took advantage of a photo-op with Thrall in Grommash Hold, getting their pictures taken with the chief of

**Figure 8.2**
Catullus, wearing the infinity-symbol tabard of the Science guild, flying around the world to gather resources for the conference on Convergence of the Real and the Virtual.

the Horde. They then walked a short distance east from Orgrimmar's main gate, past the zeppelin tower to Bladefist Bay on the sea, where they swam a short distance north to a span of costal hills where there were no hostile beasts, the site for the first formal academic discussion. The two session organizers, Bonnie Nardi of the University of California at Irvine and Hilde G. Corneliussen of the University of Bergen in Norway, took a highly visible position on a ridge. Two panelists moved near them: Celia Pearce of Georgia Institute of Technology and Nicolas Ducheneaut of Palo Alto Research Center in California (see figure 8.3). A third, T. L. Taylor at the IT University of Copenhagen in Denmark had contributed before the meeting. Most of the other participants spread out across the opposite ridge, although others ranged themselves across a wide area, even in the water. Because the whole session was being conducted in guild text chat, it did not really matter where everybody was, but being able to see about a hundred avatars in one general location was a tremendously impressive sight.

**Figure 8.3**
The first panel of leading virtual world researchers of the May 2008 conference: Maggiemae (Bonnie Nardi, University of California, Irvine), Kultura (Hilde G. Corneliussen, University of Bergen, Norway), Dyonesia (Celia Pearce, Georgia Institute of Technology), and Kartuni (Nicolas Ducheneaut, Palo Alto Research Center).

The first issue concerning the relationship between virtual worlds and the surrounding "real world" came up when Clarion said, "I would love to get a log of folks introducing themselves—names and where they are from." The issue is that some participants might want either to remain anonymous, preventing any repercussion from WoW to their real-world lives, or that a few might momentarily conceptualize their identities in term of their characters, rather than any player behind the character. Clarion identified herself and her institution, and many others immediately did the same. Apparently the great majority were happy to think of the conference as a place for real-world people to meet, only incidentally through their avatars.

After a while, Computabull parodied this attitude, by proclaiming, "I am Catullus, Blood Elf priest." Three more characters identified themselves with their players, then Computabull interjected, "Just kidding, I'm really Computabull, Tauren shaman."

Catullus himself responded, "And I am Catullus, Contemptabull!" Most of the remaining participants gave names, a few described themselves in general terms, and one also gave her Second Life avatar's name.

The topic of this first session was research and World of Warcraft. The five organizers and panelists had all already published research done in WoW. Maggiemae, Bonnie Nardi's character, called the meeting to order: "The panelists will answer questions. If you have a brief comment, whisper me and we will call on you. Near the end of the session we will have questions and comments from the audience. And then researchers can mention their work. Alrighty, Question One coming up! QUESTION: Some researchers have claimed that WoW (and other MMOGs) can be used as a laboratory for studying human behavior. What do you think about this?"

The panelists had prepared answers, and Kartuni, Nicolas Ducheneaut's character, replied first:

In my own work for instance I'm interested in the dynamics of social networks, and guilds are a perfectly valid laboratory to observe these networks—they are not that different from groups in the physical world like clubs, sports teams, or even workgroups in organizations with fairly well-defined goals. Generalizing a bit, anything that has to do with collaboration and group organization can probably be studied with high validity in WoW. The economy is another interesting domain, as I'm sure Ted Castronova would tell you if he were here. For that WoW is interesting less because of its similarities with the physical world and more for its differences—it lets economists put some long-held assumptions to the test.

Subsequent questions covered methodological issues, comparing quantitative with qualitative approaches, or asking how the multicultural playerbase affects WoW play and how WoW culture affects off-line culture. Jana Diesner, a student at Carnegie Mellon University, had her character Teilnehmer ask a very interesting question that was not on the prepared list of topics for the session: "How can people access or legally collect data on WoW? Especially for analyzing language one would need some actual logs, which are technically easy to collect, but that's not kosher with respect to Blizzard's guidelines."

As I read Blizzard's guidelines, there is in fact no prohibition against chatlogging, and the "/chatlog" macro is built in to the user interface for anybody to use. Blizzard explicitly says it reserves the right to record chat for its own purposes, which clearly announces there is no presumption of privacy. One clause in the WoW terms of service does say one must not "communicate or post any user's personal information in the Program, or on websites or forums related to the Program, except that a user may communicate his or her own personal information in a private message directed to a single user."[15] This appears to me to defend Blizzard against liability in any case in which the distribution of personal information caused material harm to anyone. It does not refer to publication in academic journals or books, and indeed people fairly often do communicate their real-world identities and other personal information, especially in guild chat. Sometimes they refer to a friend or family member by name, as well. But personal information would not be pertinent to most scientific studies, anyway.

Hilde Corneliussen's character, Kultura, asked one of the most interesting prepared questions: "How do you separate yourself as a player vs a researcher? Or do you?"

Again, Kartuni, had a clear answer ready, "I don't—any time spent in the game can be an opportunity to observe something new and worthy of further study."

This naturally fed into Kultura's next question: "Is 'the magic circle' a suitable concept for understanding *World of Warcraft*, or are there better ways of describing the relation between game and non-game?" The concept of a "magic circle" is a very old one, referring in one traditional meaning to a protective circle drawn on the ground by someone practicing natural magic, sometimes drawn as a pentagram rather than a circle. In his influential 1938 book, *Homo Ludens*, Johan Huizinga referred to the conceptual and normative boundaries of a game as a magic circle.[16] Inside the circle, the rules of the game apply and its premises define what is important, but outside this is not true.

The rules of traditional games exist only in the mind, or in a social consensus, so the concept of a magic circle may apply especially well to them. If you want, you can use a chess set to play checkers, merely agreeing to stay on the black squares and ignoring the difference between a knight and a rook. You cannot do the same with WoW, playing it as if it were Star Wars Galaxies, for example. The rules of the game are built in to the universe, just as they are in the real world, rather than being consensual. I cannot, for example, redefine a tennis court as a swimming pool, and cross from one end to the other doing the backstroke. The universe won't let me! WoW is not a game; it is a virtual world, with its own inexorable natural laws.

As before, Kartuni had an excellent answer to Kultura's question:

I think the boundary between the game world and the rest of a player's life is way too porous for a circle to exist or, if it did, to persist over the long run. Another way to look at it would be to say that it takes a lot of work, probably too much work, to try and maintain a clean separation between the two: play takes place in an environment (the home, most often) that places its own demands on the player and affects their experience ("gtg [got to go] , dinner time!", "AFK [away from keyboard], kid needs attention").

Thinking of the diversity of consensual realms outside WoW, such as church services and musical performances, Computabull commented, "The real world is divided into many different subcultures and settings with different rules. It has its own magic circles—a froth of magic bubbles more like, with few rules between."

The magic circle of the first academic session soon gave way to the very different reality of the expedition that followed it, a hike from Orgrimmar to Thunder Bluff, stopping halfway at the Shrine of the Fallen Warrior, and at a number of sites along the way. Led by Catullus on his purple bird, a mass of guildies rushed into the main gate of Orgrimmar, then became confused when some ran too far ahead. The main group exited the West Gate, crossed the bridge over the Southfury River, and headed down into the Barrens. The leaders cleared a path for the lower-level members through a population of giraffes, lions, hyenas, and crocolisks, then ran west, taking occasional potshots at plainsriders and zebralike zhevras. Most were able to reach Crossroads, where they picked up the local flight path, then ran toward the Goblin port town Ratchet. On the way, they paused to inspect the Tauren rock painting just south of the road, reflecting on the fact that these bovine humanoids were the original inhabitants of this region.

At Ratchet, some visited the gallows, right beside the cemetery, contemplating mortality, justice, and injustice. At Broken Keel Tavern, some low-level members set their hearthstone with the innkeeper, so they could easily return on Sunday and take a ship from Ratchet to Booty Bay, for the third session. The mass of Science guildies surrounded the flight master, waiting for a signal. As soon as all were ready, they flew back to Crossroads in a flock. There they ran southwest, over rocks beside a tower, passed the cemetery, and started up the mountain before them.

After a difficult climb to Falla Sagewind, they completed the short ascent to the peak, contemplating the struggle that is life. Directly north of the peak they saw a lower mountain, on which stood the Shrine of the Fallen Warrior. Knowing that this remarkable virtual place memorialized Michel Koiter, who died at age nineteen while helping to create World of Warcraft, they knelt in silent tribute.[17] Then, they danced in joyous celebration of the human creativity that Koiter's life had represented.

Next, they headed back through Crossroads and south down the Gold Road. This was the most dangerous section, and higher-level people protected lower-level people from beasts that strayed near the road. Catullus asked the group to pause and pay respects at the monumental Tauren totem poll, and to notice that west of there an oasis had been seized by their enemies, the Centaurs. When they crossed a bridge over a dry gully, Catullus hoped they would realize that the nearby house held the earthly remains of the wife of Mankrik, a guard at Crossroads. At Camp Taurajo, they picked up the flight path, headed into Mulgore, and broke into a wild stampede. Catullus had intended them to admire the indigenous Tauren architecture at Bloodhoof Village, and annihilate the vile Dwarven archaeologists at Bael'Dun, but they refused to delay in their mad rush to Thunder Bluff. As he sat with a half dozen others, cooling off in the pond on the city's lower rise, Catullus vaguely wondered if any would follow his suggestion to read the mysterious Tauren books in the Hall of Elders on Elder Rise. Oh well, he thought, the second day's academic session would give their intellects something to contemplate.

The topic of the second session, on Saturday, was relationships between WoW and the "real world." This session included contributions on such topics as the relationship of the WoW economic system to the economy of the surrounding world; interesting comparisons between WoW and other games or virtual worlds; allegorical features of WoW in such areas as colonialism and state corruption; the importation of real-world social movements into WoW, such as environmentalism; this virtual world as an arena for players who want to explore alternative personalities and roles; and the impact of WoW on players, whether educational or possibly harmful. Dmitri Williams, of the University of Southern California, was the session chair, and the panelists were Timothy Burke of Swarthmore College, Constance Steinkuehler of the University of Wisconsin, Nick Yee of the Palo Alto Research Center, and Julian Dibbell, who has published extensively on virtual worlds.

The site of the second session was a cavern in the sewers near Undercity, metropolis of the Undead. Each of the three sessions brought together slightly over one hundred conference participants, but this one had the largest number. One hundred nineteen Science guild members sat around a green pool of putrefying pus, lit by a torch, with giant windrider bats flying overhead. Some of the participants swam in the putrefaction, and others fished in it, as the session proceeded. The locale perfectly expressed the theme, because the pus was just a pretty green light on the computer screen; it did not stink, nor did it pollute, in the real world. The session ended with a Leap of Faithlessness—"To the pure, all things are pure"—as all the participants jumped from the city end of the sewer into the Canals of Corruption.

The postsession expedition began with a visit to the scientific laboratory called the Apocatharium, modeled on the laboratory of Dr. Frankenstein. In the throne room, the academics heard the beautiful aria of Sylvanas, sung three times because three of my characters were prepared to deliver to her the locket that made her sing this lament for the lost loves and glories of the past:

Anar'alah, Anar'alah belore
Sin'dorei
Shindu fallah na.

By the light, by the light of the sun
Children of the blood
Our enemies are breaking through.[18]

From the throne room, the group visited Jeremiah Payson, the cockroach vendor on the lowest level of the trade district. An honorable profession, perhaps, but they asked themselves how his life compares with that of the banshee queen they just visited. Is his sorrow any less deep? Royal Overseer Bauhaus says, "I've always been of the opinion that it takes a special gift to sell . . . cockroaches."

In one quest, Payson himself says, "Every time someone steps on a cockroach, I cry. Please don't make me cry." Some conference participants bought one of his pets, whether from pity or because they thought it was cute. The group assembled at the Undercity zeppelin station, just outside the main gate, and headed for Grom'gol Base Camp, far south in Stranglethorn Vale. There, some swam around the two sunken ships just off the beach, whereas others ran in a mob down the long and dangerous road to Booty Bay, slaying raptors, tigers, and gorillas as they went.

The third session was held on Sunday at the Old Fort at Booty Bay. Called The Future of Virtual Worlds, it was chaired by me in the guise of Catullus, and the three panelists were Diana Rhoten and Wayne Lutters of the National Science Foundation, and Henry Lowood from Stanford University. The goal was to analyze the future course of development of WoW and other virtual worlds, at a time when many highly involved observers had expressed concern that progress is stalling, even as other observers imagined we are passing a breakthrough threshold, after which virtual worlds will become central to society. Participants recognized that rapid future progress could actually depend on them, because the success of a virtual world will depend on the sociocultural design qualities that make it serve human needs, and their research will contribute to the fund of knowledge supporting innovative design.

Before the third session, participants could experiment with smuggling. At the neutral auction house, many bought moths from the Exodar and owls from Darnassus, Alliance areas the Horde members could not visit, for fifty silver coins each. The session ended with the wedding of Gonzorina and Optimoose, described in chapter 7. The climax of the conference was an attack on Sentinel Hill, in the Westfall zone belonging to the Alliance. The newbie scientists and scholars were able to seize the tower briefly, but soon were wiped out by higher-level Alliance members who came to the defense of their territory.

In a short article about the conference published in the print edition of *Science*, John Bohannon said, "After conducting over 2000 hours of ethnographic research in this world, Bainbridge knows it better than anyone."[19] In the online version of *Science*, he remarked upon my multiple high-level characters, as well as sheer hours of experience, while also saying something about how WoW had become central to his own family life:

It was with equal parts shock and awe that I realized Bainbridge has spent more time in Azeroth than my entire family combined—and trust me, that's a lot. (Level 70 is the highest possible and typically requires 300 to 400 hours of play, just for one character.) To spend more time together, my family has been meeting regularly in Azeroth for a year now—me from Austria, my father from Indiana, and my sister from New York—talking via Skype while we slay monsters. Our characters are night elves, the sworn enemies of the blood elves. Bainbridge chuckled and said, "I took part in a massive raid on night elf territory. I managed to sneak my 70th-level blood elf priest, Catullus, into the Temple of the Moon. I'll send you the screenshot [see figure 8.4]."

**Figure 8.4**
The famous screenshot of Catullus, a Blood Elf priest of the Horde, inside the Temple of the Moon, holy to the hostile Night Elves of the Alliance.

There was a pause as I took this in. Pulling off that feat is the equivalent of a Soviet spy snapping a picture of himself grinning in the U.S. president's Oval Office at the height of the Cold War.[20]

In truth, I think several people know WoW better than I do, starting with Chris Metzen. But I have examined it through the eyes of a social scientist, and I have reflected that vision back toward the surrounding world, seeing much about the modern human condition in the fires of Ironforge and the wreckage of the Exodar. World of Warcraft is no more a game than the surrounding world is; both have qualities of game, and of drama, and of many other metaphors. Precisely because it provides a different environment, it can teach us things about people we might not notice in their home environment, and it poses possible alternatives for the future of the world at large. In virtual worlds, human beings can partly transcend the limitations of daily life, and gain new perspectives on the challenges and choices we face.

## Epilogue

Lunette, waiting at the moonwell north of Nighthaven, felt not surprise but confirmation of her faith when she saw Catullus rushing toward her on his swift mount. As soon as they had greeted each other, and prayed to Elune for their future, Catullus spoke directly to me: "Oh, God, whose name is Player, please be witness. I have killed Maxrohn with respect, not because he deserved to die, but because you commanded his death. As I give him my respect, I beg you to give him resurrection, in the name of the Holy Light that he has served more faithfully than I." He then said farewell to his guild, believing that the end of his service to the Horde had come. (Months later he would rejoin Alea Iacta Est and be part of a spearhead of a hundred members invading Northrend as he zoomed to level 80 and triumphed over the minions of the Lich King.) I logged off Catullus first, and expected to see his image vanish from Lunette's computer screen. Remarkably, it remained. Perhaps hers will remain as well, after I log her off. Perhaps they both are real after all, living on a different plane of existence from our own.

# Notes

## Chapter 1

1. Tanya Krzywinska and Henry Lockwood, "Guest Editors' Introduction," *Games and Culture* 1 (2006): 280.

2. http://www.classicshorts.com/stories/danger.html. Accessed June 24, 2007.

3. Jill Walker Rettberg, "Quests in *World of Warcraft*: Deferral and Repetition," in *Digital Culture, Play, and Identity: A World of Warcraft Reader*, edited by Hilde G. Corneliussen and Jill Walker Rettberg (Cambridge, Mass.: The MIT Press, 2008), pp. 167–184.

4. Cory Ondrejka, "Finding Common Ground in New Worlds," *Games and Culture* 1 (2006): 112.

5. Esther MacCallum-Stewart and Justin Parsler, "Role-Play vs. Gameplay: The Difficulties of Playing a Role in *World of Warcraft*," in *Digital Culture, Play, and Identity: A World of Warcraft Reader*, edited by Hilde G. Corneliussen and Jill Walker Rettberg (Cambridge, Mass.: The MIT Press, 2008), pp. 225–246.

6. http://www.worldofwarcraft.com/info/basics/realmtypes.html.

7. Richard Rouse III, *Game Design: Theory and Practice* (Plano, Tex.: Woodware, 2001), p. 556.

8. As of late December 2008, the popular wowhead.com database listed 5,526 ordinary quests, although some of these are near duplicate pairs for the two factions, and this total does not include special festival quests, quests inside instances, or quests available to only a given profession or other category of character.

9. Michael Rymaszewski, Wagner James Au, Cory Ondrejka, Richard Platel, Sara Van Gorden, Jeannette Cézanne, Paul Cézanne, Benjamin Batstone-Cunningham, Aleks Krotoski, Celebrity Trollop, and Jim Rossignol, *Second Life: The Official Guide* (Hoboken, N.J.: Wiley, 2008).

10. John von Neumann and Oskar Morgenstern, *Theory of Games and Economic Behavior* (Princeton: Princeton University Press, 1944).

11. Johan Huizinga, *Homo Ludens* (London: Routledge & K. Paul, 1949).

12. Geoffrey Austrian, *Herman Hollerith* (New York: Columbia University Press, 1982).

13. Nigel Gilbert and Klaus G. Troitzsch, *Simulation for the Social Scientist* (Maidenhead, Berkshire, England: Open University Press, 2005).

14. William Sims Bainbridge, *Sociology Laboratory* (Belmont, Calif.: Wadsworth, 1987).

15. William Sims Bainbridge, "Neural Network Models of Religious Belief," *Sociological Perspectives* 38 (1995): 483–495; "Minimum Intelligent Neural Device: A Tool for Social Simulation," *Mathematical Sociology* 20 (1995): 179–192; *God from the Machine* (Walnut Grove, Calif.: AltaMira, 2006).

16. Peter L. Berger and Thomas Luckmann, *The Social Construction of Reality: A Treatise in the Sociology of Knowledge* (Garden City, N.Y.: Anchor, 1966).

17. Otto N. Larsen, *Milestones and Millstones: Social Science at the National Science Foundation, 1945–1991* (New Brunswick, N.J.: Transaction, 1992), p. 138.

18. William Sims Bainbridge, "The Scientific Research Potential of Virtual Worlds," *Science* 317 (2007): 472–476.

19. Edward Castronova, *Synthetic Worlds: The Business and Culture of Online Games* (Chicago: University of Chicago Press, 2005).

20. Edward Castronova, "On the Research Value of Large Games: Natural Experiments in Norrath and Camelot," CESifo Working Paper Series No. 1621, Indiana University, Bloomington, December 2005.

21. William Sims Bainbridge and Wilma Alice Bainbridge, "Electronic Game Research Methodologies: Studying Religious Implications," *Review of Religious Research* 49 (2007): 35–53.

22. Dmitri Williams, "Why Game Studies Now? Gamers Don't Bowl Alone," *Games and Culture* 1 (2006): 13–16.

23. Sara M. Grimes, "Online Multiplayer Games: A Virtual Space for Intellectual Property Debates?" *New Media & Society* 8 (2006): 969–990; Chek Yang Foo and Elina M. I. Koivisto, "Defining Grief Play in MMORPGs: Player and Developer Perceptions," in *Proceedings of ACE04* (New York: Association for Computing Machinery, 2004), pp. 245–250; K. K. Kimppa and A. Bissett, "Is Cheating in Network Computer Games a Question Worth Raising?" in *Ethics of New Information Technology*, edited by Philip Brey, Frances Grodzinsky, and Lucas Introna (University of Twente, Enschede, Netherlands, 2005), pp. 259–267; Steven Daniel Webb and Sieteng Soh, "Cheating in Networked Computer Games: A Review," in *Proceedings of DIMEA 2009*, Perth, Western Australia (New York: Association for Computing Machinery, 2007), pp. 105–111.

24. Nick Yee, Jeremy N. Bailenson, Mark Urbanek, Francis Chang, and Dan Merget, "The Unbearable Likeness of Being Digital: The Persistence of Nonverbal Social Norms in Online Virtual Environments," *CyberPsychology & Behavior* 10 (2007): 115–121.

25. Anders Tychsen, "Role Playing Games—Analysis across Two Media Platforms," in *Proceedings of the 3rd Australasian Conference on Interactive Entertainment* (New York: Association of Computing Machinery, 2006), pp. 75–82.

26. Georgia Leigh McGregor, " Architecture, Space and Gameplay in *World of Warcraft* and *Battle for Middle Earth 2*," in *Proceedings of the International Conference on Game Research* (New York: Association for Computing Machinery, 2006), pp. 75–82.

27. Bonnie Nardi and Justin Harris, "Strangers and Friends: Collaborative Play in World of Warcraft," in *Proceedings of CSCW 2006* (New York: Association for Computing Machinery, 2006), pp. 1–10.

28. A. Fleming Seay and Robert E. Kraut, "Project Massive: Self-Regulation and Problematic Use of Online Gaming," in *Proceedings of CHI2007* (New York: Association for Computing Machinery, 2007), pp. 829–838.

29. Lisbeth Klastrup, "Death Matters: Understanding Gameworld Experiences," in *Proceedings of the International Conference on Advances in Computer Entertainment Technology (ACE) 2006*, June 14–16, Hollywood, Calif. (New York: Association for Computing Machinery, 2006); "What Makes *World of Warcraft* a World? A Note on Death and Dying," in *Digital Culture, Play, and Identity: A World of Warcraft Reader*, edited by Hilde G. Corneliussen and Jill Walker Rettberg (Cambridge, Mass.: The MIT Press, 2008), pp. 143–166.

30. Yasmin B. Kafai, David Feldon, Deborah Fields, Michael Giang, and Maria Quintero, "Life in the Times of Whypox: A Virtual Epidemic as a Community Event," in *Communities and Technologies*, edited by C. Steinfield, B. Pentland, M. Ackerman, and N. Contractor (New York: Springer, 2007), pp. 171–190; Eric T. Lofgren and Nina H. Fefferman, "The Untapped Potential of Virtual Game Worlds to Shed Light on Real World Epidemics," *The Lancet Infections Diseases* 7, 2007: 625–629; Brian Vastag, "Virtual Worlds, Real Science: Epidemiologists, Social Scientists Flock to Online World," *Science News* 172 (October 27, 2007): 264–265; Carolyn Y. Johnson, "Online Gamers Become Guinea Pigs: Epidemics Uncorked in Virtual Worlds, *Boston Globe*, August 25, 2007, http://www.boston.com/news/local/articles/2007/08/25/online_gamers_become_guinea_pigs.

31. T. L. Taylor, *Play Between Worlds: Exploring Online Game Culture* (Cambridge, Mass.: The MIT Press, 2006).

32. Nicolas Ducheneaut, Nick Yee, Eric Nickell, and Robert J. Moore, "Building an MMO with Mass Appeal: A Look at Gameplay in World of Warcraft," *Games and Culture* 1 (2006): 281–317; Dmitri Williams, Nicolas Ducheneaut, Li Xiong, Yuanyuan Zhang, Nick Yee, and Eric Nickell, "From Tree House to Barracks: The Social Life of Guilds in World of Warcraft," *Games and Culture* 1 (2006): 338–361; Nicolas Ducheneaut, Nicholas Yee, Eric Nickell, and Robert J. Moore, "The Life and Death of Online Gaming Communities: A Look at Guilds in World of Warcraft," in *Proceedings of CHI2007* (New York: Association for Computing Machinery, 2007), pp. 839–848.

33. J. R. R. Tolkien, *The Hobbit* (London: G. Allen & Unwin, 1937); *The Lord of the Rings*, three volumes (London: Allen & Unwin, 1954–1955).

34. Jacob Grimm and Wilhelm Grimm, *Grimm's Fairy Tales*, http://www.gutenberg.org/etext/2591.

35. L. Frank Baum, *Ozma of Oz* (Chicago: The Reilly & Britton, 1907); Ruth Plumly Thompson, *The Gnome King of Oz* (Chicago: The Reilly & Lee, 1927).

36. Richard Matheson, *I Am Legend* (New York: Fawcett Publications, 1954).

37. Richard Wagner, *The Art-Work of the Future* (1849), http://users.belgacom.net/wagnerlibrary/prose/wagartfut.htm; Ernest Newman, *Wagner as Man and Artist* (New York: Random House, 1924).

38. Georg Simmel, *The Sociology of Georg Simmel* (Glencoe, Ill.: Free Press, 1950).

39. To check how long a character has been played, one need only enter "/played" into the command line of the chat interface; Maxrohn and Catullus were played the longest, 705 and 451 hours respectively.

40. Jennifer Sims, Kenny Sims, and Dexter Hall, *World of Warcraft: Wrath of the Lich King* (Indianapolis, Ind.: BradyGames, 2008), pp. 14–31.

41. William Sims Bainbridge, *Satan's Power: A Deviant Psychotherapy Cult* (Berkeley: University of California Press, 1978); "Science and Religion: The Case of Scientology," in *The Future of New Religious Movements*, edited by David G. Bromley and Phillip E. Hammond (Macon, Ga.: Mercer University Press, 1987), pp. 59–79; William Sims Bainbridge and Rodney Stark, "Scientology: To Be Perfectly Clear," *Sociological Analysis* 41 (1980): 128–136.

42. Markus Montola, "Designing Goals for Role-Players," *Proceedings of the International DiGRA Conference*: June 16–20, 2005; http://www.digra.org/dl.

43. http://www.worldofwarcraft.com/index.xml.

44. Daniel Sánchez-Crespo Dalmau, *Core Techniques and Algorithms in Game Programming* (Indianapolis, Ind.: New Riders, 2004).

45. Edward Castronova, *Synthetic Worlds: The Business and Culture of Online Games* (Chicago: University of Chicago Press, 2005), p. 96.

46. Kathryn Merrick and Mary Lou Maher, "Motivated Reinforcement Learning for Non-Player Characters in Persistent Computer Game Worlds," *Proceedings of ACE '06*, June 14–16, 2006, Hollywood, Calif.

47. Keith R. A. DeCandido, *Cycle of Hatred* (New York: Pocket Star Books, 2006).

48. Christie Golden, *Lord of the Clans* (New York: Pocket Books, 2001).

49. Daniel Vanderlip, "Ragefire Chasm," in *World of Warcraft Dungeon Companion*, edited by Christian Sumner, Ken Schmidt, Brian Shotton, and Michael Owen (Indianapolis, Ind.: BradyGames, 2006), pp. 218–225.

## Chapter 2

1. Tanya Krzywinska, "World Creation and Lore: *World of Warcraft* as Rich Text," in *Digital Culture, Play, and Identity: A World of Warcraft Reader*, edited by Hilde G. Corneliussen and Jill Walker Rettberg (Cambridge, Mass.: The MIT Press, 2008), pp. 123–141.

2. Jessica Langer, "The Familiar and the Foreign: Playing (Post)Colonialism in *World of Warcraft*," in *Digital Culture, Play, and Identity: A World of Warcraft Reader*, edited by Hilde G. Corneliussen and Jill Walker Rettberg (Cambridge, Mass.: The MIT Press, 2008), pp. 87–108.

3. Percival Lowell, *Mars as the Abode of Life* (New York: The Macmillan Company, 1908).

4. Richard A. Lupoff, *Edgar Rice Burroughs and the Martian Vision* (Westminster, Md.: Mirage Press, 1976); Irwin Porges, *Edgar Rice Burroughs: The Man Who Created Tarzan* (Provo, Utah: Brigham Young University Press, 1975).

5. Abraham Lincoln, address to the Wisconsin State Agricultural Society in Milwaukee, Wis., on September 30, 1859, *Complete Works* (New York: The Century Co., 1902), p. 584.

6. Edward Gibbon, *History of the Decline and Fall of the Roman Empire* (New York: E. P. Dutton, 1927–1936).

7. Oswald Spengler, *The Decline of the West* (New York: A. A. Knopf, 1926–1928).

8. William Sims Bainbridge, *The Spaceflight Revolution: A Sociological Study* (New York: Wiley, 1976).

9. James Burnham, *Suicide of the West: An Essay on the Meaning and Destiny of Liberalism* (New York: John Day, 1964); Patrick J. Buchanan, *The Death of the West: How Dying Populations and Immigrant Invasions Imperil Our Country and Civilization* (New York: St. Martin's Press, 2002).

10. Pitirim A. Sorokin, *Social and Cultural Dynamics* (New York: American Book Company, 1937).

11. Mansoor Moaddel, *Islamic Modernism, Nationalism, and Fundamentalism: Episode and Discourse* (Chicago: University of Chicago Press, 2005).

12. Samuel P. Huntington, *The Clash of Civilizations and the Remaking of World Order* (New York: Simon & Schuster, 1996).

13. Christie Golden, *Rise of the Horde* (New York: Pocket Star Books, 2007); on endogamy, see p. 89.

14. Claude Lévi-Strauss, *The Elementary Structures of Kinship* (London: Eyre & Spottiswoode, 1969).

15. Christie Golden, *Rise of the Horde* (New York: Pocket Star Books, 2007), p. 178.

16. Aaron Rosenberg, *Tides of Darkness* (New York: Pocket Star Books, 2007), p. 353.

17. Esther MacCallum-Stewart, "'Never Such Innocence Again:' War and Histories in World of Warcraft," in *Digital Culture, Play, and Identity: A World of Warcraft Reader*, edited by Hilde G. Corneliussen and Jill Walker Rettberg (Cambridge, Mass.: The MIT Press, 2008), pp. 39–62.

18. Ellen P. Kiley (editor), *World of Warcraft: The Roleplaying Game* (White Wolf Publishing, 2005), p. 10–11.

19. Bart G. Farkas, *Warcraft III: Reign of Chaos Official Battle Chest Guide* (Indianapolis, Ind.: BradyGames, 2004), p. 65.

20. William Sims Bainbridge, *Dimensions of Science Fiction* (Cambridge, Mass.: Harvard University Press, 1986).

21. Indiana Jones in *Raiders of the Lost Ark* (1981). Michael Crichton, *Jurassic Park* (New York: Knopf, 1990).

22. Douglas J. Preston, *Dinosaurs in the Attic: An Excursion into the American Museum of Natural History* (New York: St. Martin's Press, 1986).

23. Alfred Korzybski, *Science and Sanity: An Introduction to Non-Aristotelian Systems and General Semantics* (New York: The International Non-Aristotelian Library Publishing Company, 1941).

24. A. E. Van Vogt, *The World of Ā* (New York: Simon & Schuster, 1948).

25. William Seaman Bainbridge, *Life's Day: Guide-Posts and Danger-Signals in Health* (New York: F. A. Stokes, 1909).

26. Alfred Schütz, *The Phenomenology of the Social World* (Evanston, Ill.: Northwestern University Press, 1967).

27. Alfred Schütz, "On Multiple Realities," in *Philosophy and Phenomenological Research* 5 (1945): 533–576.

28. Daniel C. Dennett, *Consciousness Explained* (Boston: Little, Brown and Co., 1991); Paul Bloom, *Descartes' Baby: How the Science of Child Development Explains What Makes Us Human* (New York: Basic Books, 2004); Marvin Minsky, *The Emotion Machine: Commonsense Thinking, Artificial Intelligence, and the Future of the Human Mind* (New York: Simon and Schuster, 2006).

29. H. Porter Abbott, *The Cambridge Introduction to Narrative* (New York: Cambridge University Press, 2002).

30. H. G. Wells, *The Time Machine* (New York: H. Holt, 1895).

31. Claude E. Shannon, "A Mathematical Theory of Communication," in *Bell System Technical Journal* 27. (1948): 379–423, 623–656.

32. Tanya Krzywinska, "World Creation and Lore: World of Warcraft as Rich Text," in *Digital Culture, Play, and Identity: A World of Warcraft Reader*, edited by Hilde G. Corneliussen and Jill Walker Rettberg (Cambridge, Mass.: The MIT Press, 2008), p. 134.

33. http://www.wowwiki.com/Varian_Wrynn.

34. http://www.wowwiki.com/Gates_of_Ahn%27Qiraj.

35. Richard A. Knaak, *The Well of Eternity* (New York: Pocket Books, 2004); *The Demon Soul* (New York: Pocket Books, 2004); and *The Sundering* (New York: Pocket Books, 2005).

36. Alfred Wegener, *The Origin of Continents and Oceans* (New York: Dover, 1966).

37. http://sfwriter.com/styousee.htm.

38. Richard A. Knaak, *The Demon Soul* (New York: Pocket Books, 2004), p. 312.

## Chapter 3

1. Émile Durkheim, *The Elementary Forms of the Religious Life* (New York: Macmillan, 1965).

2. Rodney Stark and William Sims Bainbridge, *The Future of Religion* (Berkeley: University of California Press, 1985); *A Theory of Religion* (New York: Toronto/Lang, 1987); *Religion, Deviance and Social Control* (New York: Routledge, 1996).

3. William Sims Bainbridge, *Satan's Power: A Deviant Psychotherapy Cult* (Berkeley: University of California Press, 1978); *The Endtime Family: Children of God* (Albany, N.Y.: State University of New York Press, 2002); *The Sociology of Religious Movements* (New York: Routledge, 1997); *Across The Secular Abyss* (Lanham, Md.: Lexington, 2007); *God from the Machine* (Walnut Grove, Calif.: AltaMira, 2006).

4. Sigmund Freud, *The Future of an Illusion* (Garden City, N.Y.: Doubleday); *Civilization and Its Discontents* (New York: Norton, 1930); Geza Roheim, *Magic and Schizophrenia* (Bloomington: Indiana University Press, 1955).

5. Steven Pinker, *How the Mind Works* (New York: Norton, 1997).

6. Pascal Boyer, *Religion Explained: The Evolutionary Origins of Religious Thought* (New York: Basic Books, 2001), pp. 16–17.

7. Justin L. Barrett, *Why Would Anyone Believe in God?* (Walnut Creek, Calif.: AltaMira, 2004), p. 125.

8. S. Zeki, "The Disunity of Consciousness," *Trends in Cognitive Sciences* 7 (2003): 214–218.

9. Paul Bloom, *Descartes' Baby: How the Science of Child Development Explains What Makes Us Human* (New York: Basic Books, 2004).

10. http://www.sonsofthestorm.com/memorial_twincruiser.html.

11. Tanya Krzywinska, "Blood Sythes, Festivals, Quests, and Backstories: World Creation and Rhetorics of Myth in World of Warcraft," *Games and Culture* 1 (2006): 387.

12. Richard A. Knaak, *The Demon Soul* (New York: Pocket Star Books, 2004), p. 70.

13. Christie Golden, *Lord of the Clans* (New York: Pocket Books, 2001), p. 213.

14. http://wowwiki.com/Moon.

15. http://www.wowwiki.com/List_of_priests.

16. http://www.wowwiki.com/Druid_trainers.

17. Cicero, *On Divination*, book 1, 41, p. 90; http://penelope.uchicago.edu/Thayer/E/Roman/ Texts/Cicero/de_Divinatione/1*.html.

18. Cited with commentary by Harry Thurston Peck, *Harper's Dictionary of Classical Antiquities* (1898), http://www.perseus.tufts.edu/cgi-bin/ptext?doc=Perseus%3Atext%3A1999 .04.0062%3Aid%3Ddruidae.

19. Ellen P. Kiley (ed.), *World of Warcraft: The Roleplaying Game* (China: White Wolf Publishing, 2005), p. 251.

20. Richard A. Knaak, *The Sundering* (New York: Pocket Star Books, 2005), p. 246.

21. Richard A. Knaak, *Day of the Dragon* (New York: Pocket Books, 2001), p. 135.

22. Richard A. Knaak, *Day of the Dragon* (New York: Pocket Books, 2001), p. 344; *The Well of Eternity* (New York: Pocket Books, 2004), pp. 3, 7–8.

23. Richard A. Knaak, *The Well of Eternity* (New York: Pocket Books, 2004), pp. 52–58.

24. Ellen P. Kiley (ed.), *World of Warcraft: The Roleplaying Game* (China: White Wolf Publishing, 2005), p. 23.

25. Richard A. Knaak, *The Sundering* (New York: Pocket Star Books, 2005), p. 12.

26. Franz Boas, *Race, Language and Culture* (New York: Macmillan, 1940).

27. Ruth Benedict, *Patterns of Culture* (Boston: Houghton Mifflin, 1934).

28. Friedrich Nietzsche, *The Birth of Tragedy* (New York: Random House, 1967); Sigmund Freud, *A General Introduction to Psychoanalysis* (New York: Boni and Liveright, 1920); William James, *Pragmatism and Other Essays* (New York: Washington Square Press, 1963); Anthony F. C. Wallace, "The Institutionalization of Cathartic and Control Strategies in Iroquois Religious Psychotherapy," in *Culture and Mental Health*, edited by Marvin K. Opler (New York: Macmillan, 1959), pp. 63–96.

29. Carlos Castaneda, *The Teachings of Don Juan: A Yaqui Way of Knowledge* (Berkeley: University of California Press, 1968).

30. Christie Golden, *Rise of the Horde* (New York: Pocket Star Books, 2007), p. 206.

31. Christie Golden, *Rise of the Horde* (New York: Pocket Star Books, 2007), p. 272.

32. Christie Golden, *Rise of the Horde* (New York: Pocket Star Books, 2007), p. 229.

33. Christie Golden, *Rise of the Horde* (New York: Pocket Star Books, 2007), p. 324.

34. Christie Golden, *Lord of the Clans* (New York: Pocket Books, 2001), p. 141.

35. Christie Golden, *Lord of the Clans* (New York: Pocket Books, 2001), pp. 163–164.

36. George R. Stewart, *Earth Abides* (New York: Random House, 1949).

37. Anthony F. C. Wallace, *Religion: An Anthropological View* (New York: Random House, 1966).

38. Kevin J. Christiano, "Assessing Modernities: From 'Pre-' to 'Post-' to 'Ultra-,'" in *The Sage Handbook of Religion*, edited by James A. Beckford and N. J. Demerath (Los Angeles: Sage, 2007), pp. 39–56.

39. Aaron Rosenberg, *Tides of Darkness* (New York: Pocket Star Books, 2007), p. 183.

40. William Sims Bainbridge, "A Prophet's Reward: Dynamics of Religious Exchange," in *Sacred Canopies, Sacred Markets*, edited by T. G. Jellen (Lanham, Md.: Rowman-Littlefield).

41. Anonymous, "Work for the Downtown Poor," *New York Times*, November 9, 1895: 5.

42. Lucy Seaman Bainbridge, no title, *New York City Mission Society Monthly*, January 1892: 61.

43. Ellen P. Kiley (ed.), *World of Warcraft: The Roleplaying Game* (China: White Wolf Publishing, 2005), p. 71.

44. http://www.wowwiki.com/Church_of_Light.

45. Richard A. Knaak and Jae-Hwan Kim, *Ghostlands* (Tokyo: Tokyopop, 2007) unpaginated but about p. 5.

46. Bronislaw Malinowski, *Argonauts of the Western Pacific* (London: G. Routledge & Sons, 1922); *Magic, Science and Religion* (Boston: Beacon Press, 1948); E. E. Evans-Pritchard, *Witchcraft, Oracles and Magic among the Azande* (Oxford: The Clarendon Press, 1937); *Nuer Religion* (Oxford: Clarendon Press, 1956).

47. Richard A. Knaak, *Day of the Dragon* (New York: Pocket Books, 2001), p. 350.

48. P. Schuyler Miller, "Then and Now," *Analog* 71 (July 1963): 87.

49. P. Schuyler Miller, "Magic and Mechanism," *Analog* 73 (August 1964): 84.

50. Courtenay Grean Raia, "From Ether Theory to Ether Theology: Oliver Lodge and the Physics of Immortality," *Journal of the History of the Behavioral Sciences* 43 (2007): 19–43.

51. James George Frazer, *The Golden Bough: A Study in Comparative Religion* (New York and London: Macmillan, 1894); http://www.gutenberg.org/dirs/etext03/bough11h.htm.

52. Jeff Grubb, *The Last Guardian* anthologized in *The Warcraft Archive* (New York: Pocket Books, 2002), p. 398.

53. Jeff Grubb, *The Last Guardian* anthologized in *The Warcraft Archive* (New York: Pocket Books, 2002), p. 408.

54. Jeff Grubb, *The Last Guardian* anthologized in *The Warcraft Archive* (New York: Pocket Books, 2002), p. 430.

55. Ronald L. Johnstone, *Religion in Society: A Sociology of Religion* (Upper Saddle River, N.J.: Prentice-Hall, 2001), p. 15.

56. http://www.worldofwarcraft.com/info/basics/worlddungeons.html.

## Chapter 4

1. http://www.umm.maine.edu/faculty/necastro/chaucer/texts/ct/01gp07.txt line 308.

2. William Sims Bainbridge, *God from the Machine: Artificial Intelligence Models of Religious Cognition* (Walnut Grove, Calif.: AltaMira, 2006).

3. William Sims Bainbridge, *Experiments in Psychology* (Belmont, Calif.: Wadsworth, 1986).

4. Marc Prensky, *Digital Game-based Learning* (New York: McGraw-Hill, 2001).

5. Anthony Papargyris and Angeliki Poulymenakou, "Learning to Fly in Persistent Digital Worlds: The Case of Massively Multiplayer Online Role Playing Games," *SIGGROUP Bulletin* 25 (2004): 46.

6. Bonnie A. Nardi, Stella Ly, and Justin Harris, "Learning Conversations in World of Warcraft," *Proceedings of the 40th Annual Hawaii International Conference on System Sciences* (Washington, D.C.: IEEE Computer Society, 2007), p. 79.

7. http://www.wowhead.com/?quest=10516.

8. http://www.worldofwarcraft.com/info/basics/partyrules.html.

9. Espen Aarseth, "A Hollow World: *World of Warcraft* as Spatial Practice," in *Digital Culture, Play, and Identity: A World of Warcraft Reader*, edited by Hilde G. Corneliussen and Jill Walker Rettberg (Cambridge, Mass.: The MIT Press, 2008), pp. 111–122.

10. Albert Bandura, *Principles of Behavior Modification* (New York: Holt, Rinehart and Winston, 1969).

11. The location is 11,75 in Dun Morogh, inaccessible except by sea.

12. William Sims Bainbridge and Wilma Alice Bainbridge, "Electronic Game Research Methodologies: Studying Religious Implications," *Review of Religious Research* 49(1), 2007: 35–53.

13. Michael Lummis and Edwin Kern, *World of Warcraft Master Guide* (Indianapolis, Ind.: BradyGAMES/DK Publishing, 2006).

## Chapter 5

1. http://www.sacred-texts.com/cla/sappho/sappho1.htm#30.

2. Malcolm Brabant, "Lesbos Islanders Dispute Gay Name," BBC News, May 1, 2008, http://news.bbc.co.uk/2/hi/europe/7376919.stm.

3. Michael Kosfeld, Markus Heinrichs, Paul J. Zak, Urs Fischbacher, and Ernst Fehr, "Oxytocin Increases Trust in Humans," *Nature* 2, June 2005, 435: 673–676; Paul J. Zak, Angela A. Stanton, and Sheila Ahmadi, "Oxytocin Increases Generosity in Humans," *PLoS ONE* 2(11): e1128; doi:10.1371/journal.pone.0001128.

4. William Sims Bainbridge, "Values," in *The Encyclopedia of Language and Linguistics*, edited by R. E. Asher and J. M. Y. Simpson (Oxford: Pergamon, 1994), pp. 4888–4892; *The Secular Abyss* (Lanham, Md.: Lexington, 2007).

5. Robert Axelrod, *The Evolution of Cooperation* (New York: Basic Books, 1984).

6. Cliff Lampe and Paul Resnik, "Recommender and Reputation Systems," in *Berkshire Encyclopedia of Human-Computer Interaction*, edited by William Sims Bainbridge (Great Barrington, Mass.: Berkshire, 2004), pp. 595–598.

7. Peter Kollock, "The Emergence of Exchange Structures: An Experimental Study of Uncertainty, Commitment, and Trust," *American Journal of Sociology* 100 (1994): 313–345; Russell Hardin, "Trustworthiness," *Ethics* 107 (1996): 26–42.

8. George Caspar Homans, *The Human Group* (New York: Harcourt, Brace, 1950); *Social Behavior: Its Elementary Forms* (New York: Harcourt, Brace, Jovanovich, 1974).

9. Edward J. Lawler, Shane R. Thye, and Jeongkoo Yoon, "Emotion and Group Cohesion in Productive Exchange," *American Journal of Sociology* 106 (2000): 616–657, quoting pp. 616–617, 619, 621, and 625; cf. Edward J. Lawler and Jeongkoo Yoon, "Commitment in Exchange Relations: Test of a Theory of Relational Cohesion, *American Sociological Review* 61 (1996): 89–108; because the authors cite the first edition of *Social Behavior* in both papers, I assume that the senior author, at least, must have read *The Human Group*.

10. Toshio Yamagishi, Karen S. Cook, and Motoki Watabe, "Uncertainty, Trust, and Commitment Formation in the United States and Japan," *American Journal of Sociology* 104 (1998): 165–194; Karen Schweers Cook, "Networks, Norms, and Trust: The Social Psychology of Social Capital 2004 Cooley Mean Award Address," *Social Psychology Quarterly* 68 (2005): 4–14; Linda D. Molm, Nobuyuki Takahashi, and Gretchen Peterson, "Risk and Trust in Social Exchange: An Experimental Test of a Classical Theory," *American Journal of Sociology* 105 (2000): 1396–1427.

11. Émile Durkheim, *The Division of Labor in Society* (New York: Free Press, 1964).

12. Aaron Rosenberg, *Tides of Darkness* (New York: Pocket Star Books, 2007), p. 82.

13. http://www.wowhead.com/?quest=947 and http://thottbot.com/q947.

14. http://www.wowhead.com/?quest=253 and http://thottbot.com/q253.

**Chapter 6**

1. Scott Rettberg, "Corporate Ideology in *World of Warcraft*," in *Digital Culture, Play, and Identity: A World of Warcraft Reader*, edited by Hilde G. Corneliussen and Jill Walker Rettberg (Cambridge, Mass.: The MIT Press, 2008), p. 20.

2. Paul Graham, *Hackers & Painters: Big Ideas from the Computer Age* (Sebastopol, Calif.: O'Reilly, 2004), pp. 87–108.

3. Karl Polanyi, *The Great Transformation* (New York: Holt, Rinehart, 1944).

4. Mark Granovetter, "Economic Action and Social Structure: The Problem of Embeddedness," *American Journal of Sociology* 91 (1985): 481–510.

5. http://www.wowwiki.com/Twink.

6. http://www.wowwiki.com/Enchanting.

7. http://www.wowwiki.com/First_aid.

8. Peter Letkemann, *Crime as Work* (Englewood Cliffs, N.J.: Prentice-Hall, 1973).

9. http://www.wowwiki.com/Goblin.

10. http://www.wowwiki.com/Venture_Trading_Company.

11. http://www.wowwiki.com/Windshear_Crag.

12. *The Instance* 17, April 29, 2006; http://www.myextralife.com/wow.

13. Richard Scott, "The Business End of Playing Games," *BBC News* online, April 25, 2007, http://news.bbc.co.uk/2/hi/technology/6592335.stm; Torill Elvira Mortensen, "Humans Playing *World of Warcraft*: or Deviant Strategies?" in *Digital Culture, Play, and Identity: A World of Warcraft Reader*, edited by Hilde G. Corneliussen and Jill Walker Rettberg (Cambridge, Mass.: The MIT Press, 2008), pp. 203–223.

14. T. L. Taylor, *Play Between Worlds: Exploring Online Game Culture* (Cambridge, Mass.: The MIT Press, 2006), p. 130.

15. http://www.wowforever.com/faq.asp, March 25, 2007.

16. *The Instance* 91, January 5, 2008; http://www.myextralife.com/wow.

17. http://us.blizzard.com/support/article.xml?articleId=20572&categoryId=2693&parentCategoryId=2691&pageNumber=1.

**Chapter 7**

1. Erik Erickson, *Identity, Youth and Crisis* (New York: W. W. Norton, 1968).

2. Andreas Schneider and David R. Heise, "Simulating Symbolic Interactionism," *Journal of Mathematical Sociology* 20 (1995): 271–287.

3. Charles Horton Cooley, *Human Nature and the Social Order* (New York: Scribner's, 1922).

4. Erving Goffman, *The Presentation of Self in Everyday Life* (New York: Anchor, 1959).

5. Herbert Blumer, *Symbolic Interaction* (Englewood Cliffs, N.J.: Prentice-Hall, 1969).

6. Vivian Hsueh-hua Chen and Henry Been-Lirn Duh, "Understanding Social Interaction in World of Warcraft," *Proceedings of ACE'07*, June 13–15, 2007, Salzburg, Austria (New York: Association of Computing Machinery, 2007): 22.

7. Richard Matheson, *I Am Legend* (New York: Fawcett Publications, 1954).

8. http://en.wikipedia.org/wiki/The_Abominable_Dr._Phibes.

9. http://en.wikipedia.org/wiki/Vincent_price.

10. Nicolas Ducheneaut, Nick Yee, Eric Nickell, and Robert J. Moore, "Building an MMO with Mass Appeal: A Look at Gameplay in World of Warcraft," *Games and Culture* 1 (2006): 281–317; Dmitri Williams, Nicolas Ducheneaut, Li Xiong, Yuanyuan Zhang, Nick Yee, and Eric Nickell, "From Tree House to Barracks: The Social Life of Guilds in World of Warcraft, *Games and Culture* 1 (2006): 338–361.

11. Ragnhild Tronstad, "Character Identification in *World of Warcraft*: The Relationship between Capacity and Appearance," in *Digital Culture, Play, and Identity: A World of Warcraft Reader*, edited by Hilde G. Corneliussen and Jill Walker Rettberg (Cambridge, Mass.: The MIT Press, 2008), pp. 249–263.

12. Hilde G. Corneliussen, "*World of Warcraft* as a Playground for Feminism," in *Digital Culture, Play, and Identity: A World of Warcraft Reader*, edited by Hilde G. Corneliussen and Jill Walker Rettberg (Cambridge, Mass.: The MIT Press, 2008), pp. 63–86.

13. Richard A. Knaak and Jae-Hwan Kim, *Shadows of Ice* (Tokyo: TokyoPop, 2006).

14. Richard A. Knaak and Jae-Hwan Kim, *Dragon Hunt* (Tokyo: TokyoPop, 2005), unpaginated but about p. 128.

15. Richard A. Knaak, *Day of the Dragon* (New York: Pocket Books, 2001), p. 15.

16. Keith R. A. DeCandido, *Cycle of Hatred* (New York: Pocket Star Books, 2006), pp. 54, 117, 121, 196.

17. Keith R. A. DeCandido, *Cycle of Hatred* (New York: Pocket Star Books, 2006), p. 53.

18. Aaron Rosenberg, *Tides of Darkness* (New York: Pocket Star Books, 2007), p. 156.

19. Keith R. A. DeCandido, *Cycle of Hatred* (New York: Pocket Star Books, 2006), p. 35.

20. Mary R. Jackman, "Violence in Social Life," *Annual Review of Sociology* 28 (2002): 387–415; Shelley J. Correll, "Constraints into Preferences: Gender, Status, and Emerging Career Aspirations," *American Sociological Review* 69 (2004): 93–113.

21. Edward Castronova, *Synthetic Worlds: The Business and Culture of Online Games* (Chicago: University of Chicago Press, 2005), p. 119.

22. Edward Castronova, *Synthetic Worlds: The Business and Culture of Online Games* (Chicago: University of Chicago Press, 2005), p. 76.

23. Edward Castronova, *Synthetic Worlds: The Business and Culture of Online Games* (Chicago: University of Chicago Press, 2005), p. 45.

24. Charlotte Hagström, "Playing with Names: Gaming and Naming in *World of Warcraft*," in *Digital Culture, Play, and Identity: A World of Warcraft Reader*, edited by Hilde G. Corneliussen and Jill Walker Rettberg (Cambridge, Mass.: The MIT Press, 2008), pp. 265–285.

25. World of Warcraft Terms of Use Agreement, updated January 11, 2007; http://www .worldofwarcraft.com/legal/termsofuse.html.

26. *The Instance* 15, March 15, 2006, http://www.myextralife.com/wow.

27. http://www.aquarterof.co.uk/everton-mints-p-121.html.

28. Sherry Turkle, *The Second Self: Computers and the Human Spirit* (New York: Simon and Schuster, 1984); Edward Castronova, *Synthetic Worlds: The Business and Culture of Online Games* (Chicago: University of Chicago Press, 2005).

29. Tom Boellstorff, *Coming of Age in Second Life: An Anthropologist Explores the Virtually Human* (Princeton: Princeton University Press, 2008).

30. http://www.selene-institut.de/portrait.htm.

31. Edgar Rice Burroughs, *A Princess of Mars* (Chicago: A. C. McClurg, 1917).

32. http://en.wikipedia.org/wiki/Tars_Tarkas, April 28, 2007.

33. Edgar Rice Burroughs, *The Master Mind of Mars* (Chicago: A. C. McClurg, 1928).

34. The Mastermind of Mars, at Project Gutenberg, http://gutenberg.net.au/ebooks01/0100201 .txt.

35. Ernest Jones, *Hamlet and Oedipus* (New York: Norton, 1949).

36. Erving Goffman, *The Presentation of Self in Everyday Life* (Garden City, N.Y.: Doubleday, 1959); *Encounters* (Indianapolis: Bobbs-Merrill, 1961), pp. 83–152; Howard S. Becker, *Boys in White: Student Culture in Medical School* (Chicago: University of Chicago Press, 1961); Robert Cohen, "Role Distance: On Stage and On the Merry-Go-Round," *Journal of Dramatic Theory and Criticism* 2004 (Fall): 115–124.

## Chapter 8

1. Chris Metzen, "Of Blood and Honor," in *Warcraft Archive* (New York: Pocket Books, 2002), pp. 545–613.

2. Chris Metzen, "Of Blood and Honor," in *Warcraft Archive* (New York: Pocket Books, 2002), p. 575.

3. Edgar Rice Burroughs, *The Chessmen of Mars* (New York: Grosset & Dunlap, 1922); http://www .gutenberg.org/dirs/etext98/cmars13.txt; cf. http://en.wikipedia.org/wiki/Jetan.

4. http://www.worldofwarcraft.com/index.xml, March 5, 2008.

5. http://www.geocities.com/rgfdfaq/sources.html.

6. Richard A. Bartle, "MUDs," in *Encyclopedia of Human-Computer Interaction*, edited by William Sims Bainbridge (Great Barrington, Mass.: Berkshire, 2004), pp. 472–475.

7. Bruce Damer, *Avatars! Exploring and Building Virtual Worlds on the Internet* (Berkeley, Calif.: Peachpit Press, 1998).

8. http://www.activeworlds.com.

9. Mike Schramm, "More rumors of a mobile WoW," *WoW Insider*, June 5, 2008; http://www.wowinsider.com/2008/06/05/more-rumors-of-a-mobile-wow.

10. Edward Castronova, *Exodus to the Virtual World* (New York: Palgrave Macmillan, 2007).

11. Edward Castronova, *Synthetic Worlds: The Business and Culture of Online Games* (Chicago: University of Chicago Press, 2005), p. 207.

12. Edward C. Banfield, *The Moral Basis of a Backward Society* (Glencoe, Ill.: Free Press, 1958).

13. Keith R. A. DeCandido, *Cycle of Hatred* (New York: Pocket Books, 2006).

14. John Bohannon, "Slaying Monsters for Science," *Science* 320, June 2008, http://www.sciencemag.org/cgi/content/short/320/5883/1592c.

15. http://www.worldofwarcraft.com/legal/termsofuse.html.

16. Johan Huizinga, *Homo Ludens* (London: Routledge & K. Paul, 1949).

17. http://www.sonsofthestorm.com/memorial_twincruiser.html.

18. http://www.wowwiki.com/Lament_of_the_Highborne.

19. John Bohannon, "Scientists Invade Azeroth," *Science* 320, June 20, 2008: 1592.

20. John Bohannon, "Slaying Monsters for Science," *Science* 320, June 20, 2008, http://www.sciencemag.org/cgi/content/full/320/5883/1592c.

# Index